THE ULTIMATE
LOST
AND
PHILOSOPHY

The Blackwell Philosophy and Pop Culture Series

Series Editor: William Irwin

THE ULTIMATE
LOST
AND
PHILOSOPHY

THINK TOGETHER, DIE ALONE

Edited by
Sharon Kaye

WILEY

John Wiley & Sons, Inc.

Published by John Wiley & Sons, Inc., Hoboken, New Jersey
Published simultaneously in Canada

For general information about our other products and services, please contact our Customer Care Department within the United States at (800) 762–2974, outside the United States at (317) 572–3993 or fax (317) 572–4002.

Wiley also publishes its books in a variety of electronic formats. Some content that appears in print may not be available in electronic books. For more information about Wiley products, visit our web site at www.wiley.com.

Library of Congress Cataloging-in-Publication Data:

The ultimate Lost and philosophy : think together, die alone / edited by Sharon Kaye.
   p. cm.—(The Blackwell philosophy and pop culture series ; 35)
Includes index.
ISBN 978-0-470-63229-1 (paper : alk. paper); ISBN 978-0-470-93073-1 (ebk);
ISBN 978-0-470-93075-5 (ebk); ISBN 978-0-470-93078-6 (ebk)
  1. Lost (Television program) I. Kaye, Sharon M.
PN1992.77.L67U48 2010
791.45'72—dc22
                                                    2010028339

Printed in the United States of America

10 9 8 7 6 5 4 3 2 1

CONTENTS

INTRODUCTION
Lost and F.O.U.N.D.

As an avid fan of *Lost*, I've been trying to figure out what it is about this show that has such a hold on me. Other fans I've talked to feel the same way. It sinks its teeth into you and won't let go. After wondering about it for some time now, I think I finally figured out what it is. And so I have a question for you.

Have you ever been lost? Or rather, how did you feel when you were lost? Because you have been. We all have. Few of us have been stranded on a tropical island, but we have all had those moments when, far from home, we are suddenly struck by the horror that we will never find our way back.

[Fade to flashback.]

It's a meltingly hot, sunny day, June 1974, and we're at the annual summer carnival. The carnival comes to Madison, Wisconsin, for ten days every summer. It is the highlight of the year. Kids spend long, grueling hours babysitting, mowing lawns, and begging their parents for cash to buy the longest possible strip of tickets. One ticket will only get you on a baby ride; the best rides—the ones that gave you bat belly and bring you closest to mystical transcendence—cost four.

[Carnival music. Chillingly alluring. Then children's voices.]

"Are you going on the Zipper this year?"

"No way!"

"Wus!"

"Well, not if they have that same guy strapping people in."

"It's never the same guys."

"That's true. Okay, I get the outside seat . . ."

At the carnival there are dangers of every kind, and each child is called on to perform at least one truly outstanding feat of bravery. I didn't know any of this, though. I was only three years old, tagging along with the big kids for the first time.

True, I spent most of my time with my parents, observing my sisters and their friends, sampling the cuisine, and taking in the occasional baby ride. But my special challenge came at the end of the day.

There were seven of us, all sweaty and a bit dazed but still chattering away, as we trooped through the converted farmer's field back to our car. It was a 1967 Volvo. A midnight-blue two-door with a brick-red vinyl interior and no seatbelts. This was the age of innocence, when you packed as many people into cars as you could fit, the littlest ones perching on the biggest ones' laps.

Getting everyone in was a bit of a trick that day, with all of our carnival paraphernalia and the seats being hot enough to burn striped patterns on your butt right through your terrycloth short shorts. Everyone vied for the best positions, and there was some bickering. Yet soon enough the little Volvo was on its way. Windows were cranked all the way down, and a windy discussion of the plan for the rest of the evening commenced.

Then, halfway home, Marcy, our neighbor, suddenly said, "Where's Sherri?"

"She's in the front."

"No, she isn't. She's in the back."

"Come on, quit kidding around."

"We're not kidding. She isn't here.

"Oh, my gosh! We left her."

It never occurred to anyone, not even to my parents, that I may have been snatched up by a pervert. (Such was the age of innocence.) Their only theory was that I must have somehow been hit by a car. As they sped back to the fairgrounds, my mother scanned for emergency vehicles. Everyone was asking the same question: Why didn't she get in the car?

Why, indeed. It remains a mystery.

There were no emergency vehicles in the parking lot, and I was nowhere to be seen amid the cars. On reentering the carnival gates, however, my dad soon spotted me. I was sitting serenely on a bench between two old ladies. They had apparently found me wandering and bought me a soda. Although I was not crying, my face was red and streaked.

When I heard my name and caught sight of my family, a crushing wave of mixed emotions passed across my face. I welcomed their enthusiastic hugs and kisses, but I didn't answer anyone's questions, and I was quiet for the rest of the night. Once you have been lost, you are never quite the same.

The ABC hit drama *Lost* speaks to our deepest fear: the fear of being cut off from everything we know and love, left to fend for ourselves in a strange land. This fear is a philosophical fear, because it speaks to the human condition. It forces us to confront profound questions about ourselves and the world.

Why am I here?

Does my life matter?

Do I have a special purpose?

Can I make a difference?

[Fade to flash-sideways. More carnival music.]

How can it already be time to go home?

I am watching my feet as I shuffle along the fairgrounds. Bits of hay and interesting pieces of garbage are scattered about everywhere.

I stop to examine a paper boat containing a half-eaten hot dog. Though it looks just like many hot dogs I have eaten before, I strongly suspect I will not be allowed to taste it. I glance up to see if anyone is watching.

"Sherri, come on!" my sister shouts.

She does not see me pick up the hot dog. I grip it tighter and hurry along. I will bide my time and find the right moment for at least a taste.

My cheeks feel hot from a long afternoon in the sun, and the cotton candy sugar high that had me singing "Baa Baa, Black Sheep" at the top of my lungs not long ago has crashed hard, leaving me lethargic and irritable.

We reach the front gate of the carnival. My parents turn to see that everyone is in tow. My sister stops to take my hand. I shake her off, whining, "No!"

"Well, come on, then."

Everyone is heading for the Volvo. I know that once we reach it, my salty, greasy treat will be discovered. I look around desperately for cover.

A white van is parked not far ahead. The side door slides open. Just inside sits the clown who made me a kitty cat out of a long skinny pink balloon earlier today. He is eating a hot dog and looking right at me.

I slow to a stop, staring. He beckons me to come to him.

I cast a glance at my family, already loading the detritus of our day into the trunk, and begin to angle toward the van.

As I think about how tragic that day at the carnival might have turned out, I begin to wonder more about the two old ladies who saved me. Who were they? Was one of them me—time traveling from the future? What if they were two different future flash-sideways versions of me teaming up to make sure that I didn't come to an untimely end?

As I ask myself these questions, I begin to feel that my life may be important in ways I have not yet realized. Once you have been found, you are never quite the same.

The nineteen essays contained in this volume search for answers through the deepest philosophical labyrinth ever portrayed on television. We published the first version of this volume, *Lost and Philosophy*, in 2008, after the show's third season. The ultimate guide you now hold in your hand updates its best chapters in light of the second half of the series and adds six new chapters. I have organized them loosely into five main groups.

Part One: F Is for Fortune

The first set of essays probes the issue of time travel and alternate time lines, which became such an integral component of the show. Great thinkers throughout history have suggested that time travel is possible. What about the resulting metaphysical paradoxes, though? Metaphysics is the branch of philosophy that concerns phenomena that lie beyond the explanation of science—but not beyond our philosophers.

Part Two: O Is for Origin

The second set of essays explores crucial epistemological issues raised by the show. Epistemology is the branch of philosophy that concerns the nature and extent of human knowledge. What have our survivors learned about the capacities and limits of the human mind?

Part Three: U Is for Unity

The third set of essays looks at the most pressing social and political issues raised by the show. Social and political philosophy concerns all of the difficulties that arise when humans try to live together and form a unit larger than the individual. The island is a microcosm of the power dynamics we observe in our own communities.

Part Four: N Is for Necessity

The fourth set of essays examines the most heart-wrenching ethical issues raised by the show. Ethics is the branch of philosophy that concerns values, along with the nature of right and wrong. Being in such extreme circumstances, the characters on *Lost* face difficult decisions that reveal insights for the rest of us to consider in our own moral lives.

Part Five: D Is for Destiny

The fifth set of essays investigates the most intriguing religious issues raised by the show. Philosophy and religion are historically two sides of the same coin. By applying a rational analysis to some of the mystical moments portrayed on *Lost*, we can more fully appreciate their significance.

As a bonus, a handy appendix that gives you the lowdown on the philosophers' names that crop up on the show is included at the end of this volume. I hope you enjoy it as much as I did. On behalf of the authors, let me wish you the best of luck in your search for answers.

PART ONE

F IS FOR FORTUNE

LOST IN
LOST'S TIMES

Richard Davies

Lost and Losties have a pretty bad reputation: they seem to get too much fun out of telling and talking about stories that everyone else finds just irritating. Even the *Onion* treats us like a bunch of fanatics. Is this fair? I want to argue that it isn't. Even if there are serious problems with some of the plot devices that *Lost* makes use of, these needn't spoil the enjoyment of anyone who finds the series fascinating.

Losing the Plot

After airing only a few episodes of the third season of *Lost* in late 2007, the Italian TV channel Rai Due canceled the show. Apparently, ratings were falling because viewers were having difficulty following the plot. Rai Due eventually resumed broadcasting, but only after airing *The Lost Survivor Guide*, which recounts the key moments of the first two seasons and gives a bit of background on the making of the series.

Even though I was an enthusiastic Lostie from the start, I was grateful for the *Guide*, if only because it reassured me that I wasn't the only one having trouble keeping track of who was who and who had done what.

Just how complicated can a plot become before people get turned off? From the outset, *Lost* presented a challenge by splicing flashbacks into the action so that it was up to viewers to work out the narrative sequence. In the fourth and fifth seasons, things got much more complicated with the introduction of flash-forwards and time travel. These are two types of narrative twists that cause special problems for keeping track of a plot and that also open a can of philosophical worms about time itself.

Constants and Variables

To set the scene about plot complication, I want to call on some very influential thoughts first put forward by the ancient Greek philosopher Aristotle (384–322 B.C.E.).

In his *Poetics*, Aristotle discussed tragedy, a form of theater written for civic and religious celebrations, in which the best plays were awarded prizes. Because ancient Greek tragedy was designed to gain the approval of the judges and the public, it followed certain formulas (think the Oscars, rather than Cannes or Sundance). Aristotle's analysis of these formulas can provide us with pointers for assessing the difficulty with *Lost*.

Most tragedies are based on well-known historical or mythic events. For instance, *Ajax* by Euripides (480 B.C.E.–406 B.C.E.) concerns a great hero of the Trojan War who commits suicide in a fit of shame and self-disgust when he does not receive the reward he thinks he deserves.

Using this example, Aristotle argued for two principles. First, every tragedy should deal with a single episode in the life of its main character. The audience should follow a clear causal chain from start to finish. Let's call this "the principle of closure." In line with this principle, Euripides' play begins with Ajax's coveted reward being given to someone else and ends with his death.

Second, there should be some unity to the action, which is to say that merely accidental or unrelated events should be excluded. Let's call this "the principle of relevance." In line with this principle, Euripides' play does not recount Ajax's boyhood, regardless of how interesting this topic might be.

Does *Lost* follow Aristotle's principles of closure and of relevance? At the outset of the series, Oceanic flight 815 crashes, providing a clear starting point for the succeeding chain of events. We are introduced to the survivors, who all share the same predicament. Although the flashbacks begin right away, they are all carefully designed to shed light on the island narrative.

Complications, however, arrive with the Others. Although at first they function merely as antagonists for our survivors, they soon take on lives of their own. For example, through the character of Juliet, we follow a causal chain that begins before the crash of Oceanic flight 815 and ends before the resolution of the survivors' predicament. Aristotle would not give up on *Lost* so easily, though.

In addition to single tragedies, Aristotle discussed longer poetic compositions, known as epics, such as the *Iliad* and the *Odyssey* of Homer. These are big stories, the former dealing with the Trojan War and the latter with the ten-year journey home of one of its heroes. In epics, the narrative structure is much more complex than that of the standard tragedy. Yet Aristotle notes that even here, the story concentrates on a sequence of interconnected phases of action.

Thus, the *Odyssey* effectively begins, in Book One, not by focusing on its hero, Odysseus, who has not yet returned from the war, but on his son Telemachus, who is told to go and track down his father. The two don't actually meet until Book Fifteen (out of twenty-four). In the meantime, they are wandering around the Mediterranean and often find themselves recounting their travels to others, thus supplying the hearer/reader with backstories. For example, during his journey (and before the time of the events recounted in Book One), Odysseus outwitted the one-eyed monster known as Cyclops, but we find out about this only much later, in Book Nine, when Odysseus narrates his trick to the Phaeacian king. In this way, even though many events are presented out of their chronological order, we don't have too much trouble constructing a coherent time line.

It seems that *Lost* is not so much a tragedy as an epic. Any given episode of *Lost* features a single individual who stands at the center of attention and who is the primary subject of the flashbacks and the flash-forwards. Although many episodes finish with cliff-hangers, the principles of closure and relevance are still at work over the longer run.

So Juliet's causal chain can become part of the story as long as the audience cares about her connection to the survivors of Oceanic flight 815. If her mud fight with Kate wasn't enough to make us care, then her relationship with Sawyer was.

A blur of unrelated incidents that is spread out over too long a time and that involves too many characters will not hold our attention. The point seems obvious. On the other hand, a story that is too simple is just boring. The hard part is finding a balance between narratives that are challenging and those that are merely confusing.

We're All in This Together

Aristotle has a lot of other rules, and perhaps *Lost* does occasionally break them. But so did Shakespeare, and we can gain more pointers from what critics have said about him.

Taking a cue from a brief passage in Aristotle's *Poetics*, some critics have objected that many of Shakespeare's plays bring together an inappropriate array of characters. For example, in *A Midsummer Night's Dream*, nobles interact with "rude mechanicals." Although there may be more than a little elitism behind this concern, we can take a point about the importance of portraying plausible social relations.

The premise of *Lost* deliberately throws unlikely people together. For sure, there are differences between those who were previously mixed up in crime (Sawyer, Kate, and Jin) and those who had been "pillars of the community" (Jack, Marshal Mars, and, in a sense that might make Americans uncomfortable, perhaps Sayid). But we're on the Island of Second Chances, and such distinctions have been erased by the crash of Oceanic flight 815.

Aristotle made the further claim, however, that tragedy properly concerns noble persons (not merely those with noble titles), whereas persons of little worth are the suitable subjects of comedy. After all, why would an audience cry over someone they didn't care about? And how could they laugh at someone they did?

Clearly, *Lost* evokes both laughter and tears, but there is an easy out here. We can consider it a tragicomic epic that involves both noble and ignoble characters, or—better still—both noble and ignoble phases in its characters' lives. We do laugh at those we love in their lesser moments, and we cry for those we don't love in their best.

The same readers of Aristotle, however, have further objected that Shakespeare's plays do not observe the so-called unity of genre. What this means is that Shakespeare often alternated scenes of dramatic tension with knockabout farce and facetious wordplay.

And, of course, so does *Lost*. For example, scenes of Hurley building a golf course are interspersed with scenes of Sayid being taken prisoner ("Solitary").

Yet who says genre should be unified anyway? Would Aristotle really have approved of a play that was unrelentingly tragic? Unlikely. Surely, even Ajax could provoke a giggle or two, depending on exactly how the actor played the part.

Another Aristotelian rule concerns realism. Thus, someone might object to Shakespeare's *The Tempest* on the grounds that it demands that we believe in a magic island where witches and various types of monsters lurk. Likewise, the polar bear and the Smoke Monster of *Lost* might put viewers off.

But who's to say that what we're doing when we are watching these sorts of productions should be described as "believing" anything? For my part, I don't find Shakespeare's magic island any less believable than the Dharma Initiative. Yet I'd have to be very literal- (not to say narrow-) minded to let that get in the way of my enjoyment. Indeed, suspending disbelief is an important part of the fun. More on this to come.

The Aristotelian tradition has two things to say about the presentation of the characters in a play. One is that there should not be too many, and the other is that they should be consistent during the course of the action.

The first of these can be applied to Shakespeare's *King Lear*, a chaotic business in which lots of men with the names of English counties shout at one another. For sure, telling your Northumberland from your Westmoreland takes a bit of work to begin with, but it is a labor of love! Consider the average soap opera. Although soaps repeatedly introduce "your-mother-is-your-sister-but-your-uncle-doesn't-know" sorts of complications, they are followed by millions of uncomplaining viewers.

Of the forty-eight survivors of Oceanic flight 815, only relatively few—hardly a quarter of the total, when you think about it—come into any sort of focus. The rest have little more than walk-on parts. Likewise with the Others: most of them do little more than stroll about on the lawns. In this sense, *Lost* is hardly more abundant in characters than the average TV show.

As to the idea that the persons depicted should be consistent over time, Aristotle seemed to mean by this that each person should correspond to some virtue or vice or other stable character trait. Yet we have to be very careful not to interpret this in a way that contradicts Aristotle's rule about realism. After all, people don't stay the same; they change, as does Shakespeare's Henry V, when he goes from listless prince to brave king. Aristotle may simply have meant that the decisions a character makes at any given stage should be psychologically plausible. In any case, if, again, our point of reference is the epic (or the soap), lapse of time and variation in influences can make significant differences to temperament.

We may consider a couple of cases where the stability-of-character criticism might be applied to *Lost*. Perhaps the least problematic is that of Kate. Once we grasp why she led the tear-away life she did before being arrested, we can understand why, on the island, she behaves, as Jack testifies at her trial, as someone who cares for others ("Eggtown"). It's not Kate who's changed but her circumstances. Perhaps something of the same can be said about Sawyer.

Slightly more demanding is the case of Locke. In terms of psychology, his rugged individualism remains pretty constant. What does, of course, change is his physical state. He was in a wheelchair on boarding Oceanic flight 815 and gains the use of his legs once on the island. It's only when we first see him in flashback ("Walkabout") that we begin to have ominous thoughts about the healing powers of the island. If anything, this transformation—not to mention the later one when he returns to the island in a coffin ("There's No Place Like Home: Part 3")—is a challenge to what we are prepared to believe. But, as I said before and we shall see again, strict believability is not really the point: once we grant Locke's situation, his responses to it are what catch our interest.

The case of Ben is altogether more puzzling. As we try to find some principle or project that drives his various behaviors and attitudes, we suppose there must be *something* he's up to, but it is hard to tell what. At some level, much of his motivation derives from his vendetta against Charles Widmore. Yet the various positions and expedients he adopts seem to fall into the category of the predictably unpredictable. Ben makes me think of Shakespeare's character Iago: someone whose actions, for good or ill, seem underdetermined. As with Iago, what makes Ben interesting is that it is hard to guess what he'll say or do next.

Two other rules laid down by the Aristotelian tradition deal with limits on space and time. Concerning space, Aristotle suggested that the action of a play should take place in a single location. This follows from the physical configuration of theaters from Ancient Greece down to at least the time of Shakespeare: the substantial lack of props meant that it was hard to signal clearly that the action had moved from, say, the royal court to a tavern or a graveyard. But with the modern means to make obvious the difference between a scene set on the island and one set in an L.A. psychiatric institution (even when they are both actually filmed in Hawaii), this sort of criticism is a bit hollow if leveled at *Lost*.

A more aesthetic consideration in favor of the unity of place derives from the idea of the unity of plot. Yet also in this case, we may say that the island provides the spatial focus for everything else that goes on, and the backstories set elsewhere help us understand the problems of the individuals we find there. Even though they are spread out in space from Iraq to Australia, from Britain to the United States, these background episodes are funneled through the check-in at Sydney Airport. And on the island itself, we come to identify certain sites, such as the camp on the beach, the Dharma bunkers, and the Others' compound, as being places where the action is most decisive.

I submit that *Lost* is in the clear with regard to space and the other Aristotelian rules so far considered. Although *Lost* may sometimes push up against the limits of what viewers can handle by way of coordinated action and coherent character, it is not in flagrant breach of the Aristotelian standard of evaluation. Neither Aristotle himself nor Shakespeare and his admirers should object to the complexity of *Lost*, whatever some readers of Aristotle may say.

What about time, though? This question deserves careful attention.

"We Have to Go Back"

According to Aristotle, a tragedy should recount the action of not much more than a day. Although a television series of 120 episodes need not be this limited, a single episode that observes this rule helps the viewer keep track of things.

In its first three seasons, *Lost* uses flashbacks much more than most TV shows do. This doesn't cause real headaches, because the survivors come to life more if we know about Jack's "Daddy Issues," Kate's criminal deeds, and Hurley's lottery win. Yet the final scene of the last episode of season 3 ("Through the Looking Glass") introduces a very unusual sort of complication.

We've been watching scenes of Jack bearded and drink-and-drug-sodden but still capable of saving people from car wrecks. All the while, we've been assuming, perhaps somewhat uneasily, that they are flashbacks. What a shock, then, when this Jack meets Kate out near LAX and says, "We have to go back."

Up to this point, all of the off-island business we have seen is at least consistent with being earlier than 2004. Suddenly, just as things seem to be coming to a close (we know that this is the last episode in the season, and we're a bit afraid that there won't be a fourth), we are shown a meeting that, at the moment of first viewing, admits of two interpretations.

In one interpretation, Jack and Kate knew each other before boarding Oceanic flight 815—but this won't hold water. The sequence of their relationship—meeting after the crash, getting to know each other, and falling in love—couldn't have been a pretense. So we have to revise our assumption that what we are seeing is a flashback.

In the other interpretation, even if we have become accustomed to flashbacks as the narrative mode of *Lost*, we are pushed to understand "We have to go back" as a *return* to the island, meaning Jack and Kate have already left the island. Meaning we are at a date later than the narration of the preceding three seasons. After all, the on-island action into which this scene is inserted has a freighter arriving on the island. So we are ready to believe that the survivors are about to be saved.

As soon as I got over the shock, my first thought was, Well, at least we can look forward to a fourth season!

Then a second thought kicked in: Now that we have seen the "We have to go back" meeting, everything that happens on the island and whatever means Jack and Kate find to get off the island cannot *not* have their meeting as its outcome. The narrated time up to this point has counted as the past and the present. We know the past through flashbacks to off-island incidents, and we take the on-island narrative as the narrative present. Suddenly, though, just as Hurley and Desmond see Naomi parachute in before she actually does so, we can "see the future," and the future contains—already contains—Jack meeting Kate out near LAX.

I want to look a bit harder at what it can mean for the future relative to the freighter's approach to the island already to "contain" the meeting between Jack and Kate. There is a separate and very difficult question about what it might mean to "*see* the future." Yet I want to get clear why it might be puzzling to think that there is anything there to be seen.

The Course of the Future

To get a grip on why there's a problem here, it is a good idea to make a couple of distinctions. (This is a standard philosopher's trick to delay having to give an answer.)

First, we must distinguish a little bit more carefully between the narrative time of the characters' lives and the viewer's time in watching *Lost* on TV or DVD (assuming that the viewer respects the sequence of the seasons and the episodes). In one sense, the narrative time begins on September 22, 2004, and the events can be ordered as a sequence of presents from that point on. In another sense, the times of the flashbacks are earlier than that date and make up the past relative to what is happening in on-island time. In the sequence that the viewer sees, narrative times earlier than September 22 are spliced into times later than that date. This, if you like, is a description of what a flashback is: the past of the narration is shown as present to the viewer. In terms of this distinction, we can say that a flash-forward is showing the future of the narration as present to the viewer.

Second, we must distinguish two ways of understanding time itself. According to one way, the whole history of the world is, in some sense, already fixed or determined or written or scripted, and the relations of before and after, and of earlier and later, among events do not themselves change. In the other way of thinking, as time passes and the date of the present becomes successively later and later, events come into being as they are produced by what went before them. The English philosopher John McTaggart (1866–1925) first called attention to these two different ways of thinking about time. Philosophers have come to call the first position *eternalism* and the second *presentism*.

Because it is not immediately obvious what difference the distinction between eternalism and presentism might make, it may help to give a little bit more detail about these two views.

Eternalism is the view that a sentence such as "Oceanic flight 815 has crashed" is, in a certain sense, incomplete as it stands. To say what makes a sentence like this true, we have to separate two elements. The first is the element that describes a kind of event. Thus, in the eternal sentence "Oceanic flight 815 crashes," the verb "crashes" does not refer to a particular time, in just the way that the "is" in "two and two is four" does not refer to a particular time. So the second element is a relativization to a time or a date such as "on September 22, 2004." In this view, then, "Oceanic flight 815 crashes on September 22, 2004," can express the self-same truth whether someone says it in 1977 or in 2010. For eternalists, only sentences that spell out a date can express a genuine or complete truth about an event in time.

Presentism, on the other hand, takes it that there is nothing difficult about tense and no analysis is needed of "Oceanic flight 815 has crashed." According to presentists, eternalism puts the cart before the horse in thinking that we have to use a system of time or date coordinates when we talk about what is happening "now." Many presentists (including myself) think of the story of the world as becoming ever fuller and more complete as time passes: the future doesn't (yet) exist, but what is happening and has happened are genuine facts in their own right.

McTaggart himself thought that because eternalism cannot give an adequate account of change over time and because presentism cannot give a satisfactory analysis of when the present is, time is not really real but rather an all-pervasive illusion. Most of his readers, however, have not wanted to accept this conclusion. Eternalists bear the burden of showing that their account of change is, after all, adequate, while presentists have to explain why there is no need to say when the present is (other than by saying what the time is now).

What difference does the difference between eternalism and presentism make toward understanding what a flash-forward is? For eternalists, there is no problem. The arrival of the freighter occurs long before the "We have to go back" meeting. The fact that we initially thought that it was a flashback and knew nothing of what happened in between is irrelevant. The distance in time between the two events is a fixed quantity, just like the distance in space between Sydney and L.A.

For eternalists, then, TV can use props and locations to show first a scene in Sydney and then a scene in L.A., or vice versa. There is nothing puzzling about this as long as we have some markers of the difference, such as the Sydney Opera House. Likewise, TV can use props and locations to show first a scene in 2004 and then a scene in 2007, or vice versa. And there is nothing puzzling about this as long as we have some markers of the difference, such as the state of Jack's beard.

Most presentists, however, do see a problem. This can be expressed in terms of the viewer's entering into the narrative present of the on-island affairs at the moment when Jack is calling the freighter at the end of season 3. From that point of view, there are lots of things that Jack has to deal with—Locke, Rousseau, and Ben are all causing trouble, and he has to do something about each person. That is to say, what he decides and does will make a difference to the outcome. From his perspective, the future is not fixed, because the way things will turn out depends on his actions. So whether and how he is to get off the island is not "there" yet.

Of course, we're aware (perhaps somewhat distractedly) that *Lost* is scripted in advance, and there is nothing we, as viewers, can do to change the course of what has already been decided in building 23 of the ABC lot in Burbank. Yet when we are following Jack's actions, that fact of fixity has to be put on hold. If we don't put that fact on hold, we lose empathy and suspense: the sense that what is going on onscreen is present to us.

With the flash-forward, we have to adopt two sorts of attitudes at the same time. On the one hand, there is the attitude of seeing Jack call the freighter at the end of season 3, where his actions will make a difference to what happens next. And on the other, there is the attitude of seeing his actions in season 3 (that is, 2004) from the point of view of someone who knows about the meeting out near LAX, which occurs (or, if we prefer, recurs) in season 5 (that is, 2007), and so who knows Jack has already gotten off the island.

Eternalists will say that when all is said and done, Jack's making his call at the end of season 3 is just as much part of the plot as his meeting Kate out near LAX in season 5. In this sense, eternalists take the position of observers standing outside the narrative, which includes the two events on the same footing. Presentists, by contrast, think that only one of these times can, at any given time, be *the* present (at that time). In this sense, presentists privilege the position of agents within a plot and can adopt only one position at a time for the purposes of seeing the plot through.

What's more, presentists say that if—and presentists say that it is a very big "if"—there is, at the time of the call to the freighter, a fact about the meeting out near LAX, then there is nothing that Jack can do or fail to do between those two times that will make a difference to whether the meeting occurs. Eternalists are committed to saying that there is such a fact because if the sentence "Jack meets Kate in 2007" is ever true, it is always true. So it is also true in 2004. For this reason, presentists say that eternalism implies (or indeed is identical with) a view known as *fatalism*.

The Shape of Things to Come

In *Lost*, there is a great deal of talk about fate and destiny. A lot of it comes from Locke, who has a habit of appealing to fate when he is trying to get people to make up their minds in a certain way. For example, he convinces everyone to return to the island by appealing to what their destiny is ("The Life and Death of Jeremy Bentham").

This is a bit perplexing, because it seems to play on something like the double take of the flash-forward. On the one hand, if it really is Kate's destiny to return to the island, then she'll return there whatever she decides. And if it is not her destiny to return to the island, then she'll not return there whatever she decides. Appealing to what her destiny is can't really help her to decide. On the other hand, if there is no such thing as Kate's destiny and she is free to decide, she shouldn't be influenced by what anyone, including Locke, says is her destiny.

The most general sort of trouble with talk about fate or destiny is that it appears to be in conflict with what we take ourselves to be doing when we make a decision or perform an action. When we do these things, we generally assume that we are making something true that wasn't previously true and that wouldn't have been true if we hadn't done what we are doing. In a short-cut phrase, we believe that we have free and effective choice.

Yet fatalism denies that any choice is either free or effective, because fatalism is the view that everything that is ever true was always true. So either fatalism is false, or there is no such thing as what we generally understand ourselves to be doing when we exercise free and effective choice. What's more, if fatalism is implied by (or is identical with) eternalism, then, if eternalism is the fundamental truth about time, there is no such thing as what we generally suppose ourselves to be doing when we make a decision or perform an action.

For myself, it seems wildly implausible to think that nothing I have ever decided or done has ever made anything true that wasn't previously true and wouldn't have been true if I hadn't decided or done what I did. For instance, if I now decide to advise my gentle reader to reread the previous sentence, then that decision and my acting in accordance with it by typing these words is just what is making, at the time of typing, the present sentence the sentence it is, which it wouldn't have been if I hadn't so decided and typed in an exercise of free and effective choice. In this sense, I cannot bring myself to believe that fatalism is a true doctrine. That being so, and given the intimate relation between fatalism and eternalism, I cannot bring myself to believe that eternalism is the fundamental truth about time.

I admit that eternalism might be the fundamental truth about time, even though I cannot bring myself to believe it. And I think I can see why, whether it is true or not, eternalism might be attractive and believable to many people. One very strong attraction of eternalism lies in the effort to see the succession of the events that make up the whole history of the universe from a point of view outside that succession. Whatever else it is, the external point of view is more complete and objective than that of any of the partial and subjective positions from within the sequence of events.

The ideal of completeness and objectivity is not only noble, it is what scientific endeavor is all about. It is also the perspective that many philosophers and theologians have attributed to God, but we have to pass on that one for now. The trouble is that as of the time of my gentle reader's reading this sentence, the history of the universe is not yet complete. Unless you, gentle reader, are so radically unlucky as to spend the final moment of the Existence of Anything poring over this page of *The Ultimate Lost and Philosophy*, there is still some future to be filled in. Hence the external point of view is not yet there to be occupied, and no complete and objective story can yet be told.

In a certain sense, eternalism fixes us within a plot, whether it was scripted in building 23 of the ABC lot in Burbank or elsewhere, about whose later phases we just happen not to have enough flash-forwards. Presentism, on the other hand, will say that there isn't yet anything to have a flash-forward on. In either case, there is no question of whether we can "change" the future. For the eternalist, the future is just there waiting for us to experience it. For the presentist, we do what we can to make things happen that wouldn't otherwise have happened, by deciding and acting, by exercising free and effective choice.

Whatever Happened, Happened

If deciding and acting don't change the future, what about changing the past? Although the difference between eternalism and presentism divides philosophers into two heavily armed camps, the question of whether the past can be changed is, relatively speaking, a side issue. Almost all philosophers are in substantial agreement: No, sir, it cannot. Aristotle regarded the past as necessary, and St. Augustine (354–430 c.e.) thought that not even God can change the past. Surprisingly for philosophy, almost everyone who has thought about the matter has followed suit.

Only a few philosophers—plus the odd (both in the sense of "rare" and in that of "cranky") theoretical physicist—have tried to find some sense in the idea of bringing about what didn't happen. They are backed up by a grand tradition of science fiction tales, to which we now add *Lost*, beginning with the first episode of season 5 ("Because You Left"). The idea of changing the past exerts a great fascination, perhaps because it fulfills a pretty deep and widely felt wish. If it were possible to change the past, the pains of regret and remorse could sometimes be relieved. Almost everyone can think of a bit of the past he or she would like to be able to change, to do what was left undone (regret) or to undo what was done (remorse). So, nearly almost everyone would like time travel to be possible.

Interestingly, both eternalists and presentists deny that the past can be changed, and for very similar reasons. Eternalists will say that given a certain (complete and objective) history of the universe, which is made up of all of the truths there are, adding something else that is inconsistent with one of those truths will produce a contradiction. Presentists will say that given the history of the world so far, if we say of a certain past time that something both did and didn't happen, then we have a contradiction.

Why should contradictions bother us? After all, didn't Walt Whitman say in "Song of Myself," "Do I contradict myself? / Very well then I contradict myself / (I am large, I contain multitudes)"?

One thing about contradictions that bothers logicians—and most conscientious philosophers have a touch of the logician in them—is the fact that a contradiction is never true. Let's take, as an example of the basic form of a contradiction, the sentence "Hurley was in the Dharma Initiative in 1977, and Hurley was not in the Dharma Initiative in 1977." This sentence is made up of the affirmation that Hurley was in the Dharma Initiative in 1977 along with its negation. If the affirmation is true, then the negation is false, and if the affirmation is false, then the negation is true. Our sentence is made up of these two parts by way of an "and." A sentence in which "and" holds the parts together is true only if both of the parts are true, and if even one is not true, the sentence as a whole is false. Either the affirmation that Hurley was in the Dharma Initiative in 1977 or its negation must be false, granted that the other is true. That being so, the sentence as a whole is false.

Whether we take the eternalist view, from the complete and objective standpoint of the entire history of the universe, or the presentist view from a moment in, say, 2007, then either Hurley was in the Dharma Initiative in 1977 or he wasn't. Hence, there was nothing that Hurley could do in 2007 to make it true that he was in the Dharma Initiative in 1977 if he hadn't been in the Dharma Initiative in 1977, and there was nothing that he could do in 2007 to prevent his being in the Dharma Initiative in 1977 if he had been in it in 1977. If there is a past, then it cannot be changed.

The other thing that bothers logicians about contradictions is that they do indeed, as Whitman said, contain multitudes, but rather more multitudes than Whitman himself could contain. We're not and Whitman was not, after all, quite as large as Whitman thought he was.

The argument for this is swift, decisive, and absolutely general. It is swift in the sense that it can be presented in five easy steps. It is decisive in the sense that it depends only on the meanings of the really basic words *and*, *not*, and *or*. And it is absolutely general in the sense that any sentences whatever can be substituted for the example I offer of the situation in which Hurley finds himself in 2007, just before the moment at which his next experience will be that of being in the Dharma Initiative in 1977.[1]

Granted that a sentence in which *and* holds the parts together is true only if both of the parts are true (step 1), from "Hurley was in the Dharma Initiative in 1977, and Hurley was not in the Dharma Initiative in 1977" we can deduce (step 2) either of the parts, such as "Hurley was in the Dharma Initiative in 1977." Now, from any affirmation, we can deduce (step 3) a sentence in which the parts are held together by "or," because such a sentence will be true so long as at least one of its parts is true. Thus, from "Hurley was in the Dharma Initiative in 1977" we can deduce, with due respect to Douglas Adams, "Hurley was in the Dharma Initiative in 1977 or the Answer to the Question of the Meaning of Life, the Universe, and Everything is 42." Now, using same principle by which we deduced at step 2 "Hurley was in the Dharma Initiative in 1977" from our starting assumption of a contradiction "Hurley was in the Dharma Initiative in 1977, and Hurley was not in the Dharma Initiative in 1977," we can deduce (step 4) "Hurley was not in the Dharma Initiative in 1977." Now, if an *or* sentence is true and one of its parts is false, then it must be the other part that's true. So, taking the product of step 3, "Hurley was in the Dharma Initiative in 1977 or the Answer to the Question of the Meaning of Life, the Universe, and Everything is 42" along with the product of step 4 "Hurley was not in the Dharma Initiative in 1977," we can deduce (step 5) that the Answer to the Question of the Meaning of Life, the Universe, and Everything is 42. Some people find this last move a bit hard to follow, but if we think about a sentence like "My wallet is on the table, or my wallet is in my pocket," we can see that as soon as I know that my wallet is not in my pocket, I can deduce that it is on the table.

The point about the argument just outlined is that from a contradiction, anything and everything follows. So, to assert a contradiction is to assert anything and everything, including all of the possible Answers to the Question of the Meaning of Life, the Universe, and Everything and, among them, also the true one. The trouble is that given all of these multitudes contained in a contradiction, we still don't know which is the true Answer to the Question of the Meaning of Life, the Universe, and Everything (or, indeed, where my wallet is).

If time travel is possible, we can change the past—but changing the past leads to contradiction. A contradiction is never true and implies anything whatsoever. So time travel never happens. When we try to imagine time travel, we have to accept at least one contradiction and, consequently, all of the things that follow from it—namely, every possibility whatsoever.

The Total Experience

To return, in conclusion, to our "poetic" considerations about plots, we have already heard that Aristotle advised against introducing elements that run up against what is believable. If what we have said about changing the past is right, then we can see why the introduction of time travel as a key plot element is likely to have the effect of making the plot unbelievable.

Once time travel is introduced, it becomes harder to know *which* plot we are being asked to follow because it becomes uncertain what we are being asked to include and what we are being asked to exclude from the plot. This is because we don't know where we are being pointed by a contradictory plot element: Whitman's multitudes are too multitudinous for us to be sure how to slim them down to a single storyline.

Yet I have also admitted that the idea of time travel doesn't bother most people the way that it bothers the philosophers who sit around theorizing about time as eternalists or presentists and who object to time travel as a generator of contradictions. That is to say, it isn't time travel as such that causes problems for most people who watch science fiction or *Lost*. My guess is that most people—including logicians of either basic orientation in the philosophy of time—aren't too bothered by time travel as a plot element in science fiction or in *Lost*. And I guess that they aren't too bothered by it because, in one way or another, they shield it from its multitudinous consequences. What I mean by being "shielded" here is a cousin of the way that when we are following Jack's call to the freighter, we put on hold the fact of his later meeting Kate out near LAX.

One way we can think of shielding is this: We've been following Hurley from his lottery win through the downing of Oceanic flight 815 and the psychiatric institution back in L.A. to his return to the island on Ajira flight 316. So we've built up a sequence of how things have seemed to him at the various stages. Each of these experiences can be given a date. What is more important for Hurley, these experiences form a sequence for him. If, then, after an experience that can be dated to 2007 there comes an experience that can be dated to 1977, why should Hurley be bothered? The 1977 experience is just the one that, for him, comes after the 2007 experience. That is, if we put ourselves in the shoes of the time traveler, there is a sequence that doesn't too obviously lead to a contradiction because it is just one thing after another.

We generate the shield in order to be able to follow how things successively seem to Hurley, and we put on hold the idea that there would have to be two mutually contradictory 1977s for Hurley to "go to" from 2007, one in which he is in the Dharma Initiative and one in which he is not.

We privilege the sequence that starts on September 22, 2004, because that's the one we know about, and we put on hold the 1977 (in which Hurley perhaps wasn't even born) that led up to Hurley's boarding Oceanic flight 815. In privileging this sequence, we allow that there is a 1977 accessible from 2007 that has Hurley in the Dharma Initiative, even though that was not part of the past when he boarded Oceanic flight 815. We allow this because we are asked to by the people writing in building 23 of the ABC lot in Burbank. Given that they have done a good job in helping us shield the contradictions that arise from time travel, why not go with the flow?

What's more, even if we are not sure why we sometimes run into trouble when we try to follow a plot with time travel in it, the attempt is a challenge. We enjoy the challenge, just as we enjoy the other twists and turns of the plot.

Aristotle, in the only explicit reference he made to the so-called unity of time, was right to be a bit vague in saying that the action of a tragedy should correspond to "a single passage of the Sun, *or just a little more.*"[2] He was vague, because it is not clear exactly where the upper limit to plot complexity lies. And he specified only one day's events because he thought that was about as much as a viewer could take in at one sitting. Yet this leaves open the possibility—exploited by Shakespeare and others—that a longer span can be presented to and followed by an audience that is willing to take the right time-lapse cues and to interpret a change of props as a change of place, and so on.

Likewise, I want to suggest that even if I have philosophical worries about the genuine possibility of time travel, they don't bother me much when I am watching *Lost* and shielding a plot that has time travel as one of its elements. I want to leave it an open question where limits might lie in the massive use of time travel, as in *Lost*'s seasons 4 and 5, as a plot device that calls on viewers simultaneously to shield many different experienced time sequences so as to keep the multitudes at bay. I suppose it depends on how much help viewers get from building 23, how nimble they are at keeping the sequences distinct, and how willing they are to do the work. Although I may not always succeed, I'm willing to give it a try because it's all part of the fun.

NOTES

1. Even if readers don't like footnotes and don't like the symbols that logicians notoriously hide behind, this argument is so important and so general that I want to offer a schematic version of it, in which *p* stands for any proposition whatever and *q* stands for any proposition whatever:

1. p and not-p (assumption of a contradiction)
2. p (from 1, by the meaning of "and")
3. p or q (from 2, by the meaning of "or")
4. not-p (from 1, by the meaning of "and")
Therefore
5. q (from 3 and 4, by the meanings of "or" and "not")

2. Aristotle, *Poetics*, 1449b13.

IMAGINARY PEANUT BUTTER

The Puzzles of Time Travel in *Lost*

William J. Devlin

Perhaps the most intriguing idea presented in the latter half of *Lost* is the notion that once Ben turns the ancient wheel buried beneath the Orchid station, the island disappears and its inhabitants begin to travel through time—anywhere from the nineteenth century (or earlier) to 1954, to 1977, to 2001, and even to sometime in the future year of 2007 (or later).

Of course, such a notion can be just as confusing as intriguing. How can the same person exist in two places at the same time, such as when the adult Miles watches his father read to the younger Miles in 1977? Is it possible to change the past, as Jack attempts to do by using the hydrogen bomb to blow up the island in that same year, hoping to undo the event of Oceanic flight 815 crashing on the island in the first place? Could Sayid really be able to kill young Ben of 1977? If so, what would happen to the island and the castaways lost in time? Or must we resign ourselves to the fact that everything we do in the past has already happened, as Faraday initially maintains? Are there causal loops that arise when traveling in the past, such as Richard giving Locke a compass in 2007, only for Locke to give it back to Richard in 1954?

Through their time travels, the characters adopt different beliefs about the nature of time. Faraday and Miles, for instance, initially adopt the view that the past is fixed; it cannot be changed. So each person who has gone back in time is ultimately acting as he or she already has. Meanwhile, Sayid and Hurley adopt the belief that the past is alterable, so that one can make changes in the past, which will, in turn, alter the events of the future. This explains why Sayid tries to kill the young Ben and Hurley works on the screenplay of *The Empire Strikes Back*. Faraday ultimately becomes convinced of this view, as his dying hope is to save Charlotte from her future.

Building the Orchid Station: Basic Concepts of Time Travel

Time travel produces some delicious puzzles, and there is nothing philosophers love more than a puzzle sandwich. Before we dig in, however, it is important to discuss two questions:

- What do we mean by time travel?
- What do we mean by time?

Typically, when we think of traveling, we think of physically moving from one location to another. I may, for instance, take a train from Boston, Massachusetts, to Metuchen, New Jersey. Or I may catch a plane from Providence, Rhode Island, to Memphis, Tennessee. Such traveling is understood as moving from one physical location to another.

Yet what does it mean to travel from one time to another? To help us understand, we can turn to the philosopher David Lewis (1941–2001), who wrote about the philosophy of time travel. Lewis explained that in time travel, the difference between the traveler's departure and arrival times in the surrounding world does not equal the duration of the traveler's journey.

Take, for instance, the time-traveling event in which Sawyer, Juliet, Miles, and the rest of the group jump from 1954 (where they interact with a young Eloise and the ageless Richard) to 2004 (where Locke cries at the hatch and Claire gives birth to Aaron). Here, the traveling for the time travelers is only a few seconds. Nevertheless, the temporal locations, from departure to arrival, are separated by fifty years.

According to Lewis, there are two kinds of time for the time traveler. First, there is the *external time*, or objective measurement of time in reality. Second, there is the *personal time*, or the subjective measurement of time in the traveler's own personal journey through time. So, returning to our previous example, when Sawyer, Juliet, Miles, and the group time-leap from 1954 to 2004, they move fifty years through external time. Yet this time leap is only a matter of seconds in their individual, personal time. They themselves do not age fifty years in this traveling. So, travel through time is a movement from one temporal location to another when the personal time spent does not match the amount of external time that has gone by.

Can the time traveler go back to the past, however, and prevent past events from occurring the way in which they did? Or is time fixed in such a way that any action the time traveler performs in the past is an action that already happened, no matter what? The answer to this question depends on how we conceive of time. *Lost* leads the audience through two different conceptions of time: one in season 5, the other in season 6. Let's explore each in turn.

Whatever Happened, Happened

In the opening episode of season 5 ("Because You Left"), we glimpse a scene from 1977 on the island where Dr. Pierre Chang scolds the foreman working at the Orchid station for drilling too deeply. He explains that there is an "almost limitless energy" that the Dharma Initiative is trying to harness to "manipulate time." The foreman, ever skeptical, laughs and rhetorically asks, "Okay, so, what? We're gonna go back and kill Hitler?" Chang quickly responds, "Don't be absurd. There are rules, rules that can't be broken."

Chang's response suggests a specific conception of time that is echoed later by Faraday. As Faraday explains to Sawyer, "Time—it's like a street, all right? We can move forward on that street, we can move in reverse, but we cannot ever create a new street. If we try to do anything different, we will fail every time. Whatever happened, happened." ("Because You Left")

In other words, Faraday maintains that although one can travel through time, one cannot, in any way, make any changes in the past that would alter the future. Time is linear and so cannot branch off into any further possible direction. Although you may think you can do something "new," that action already happened exactly the way you perform it. In short, "whatever happened, happened," and there is nothing you can do to change that.

Philosophically, Chang and Faraday are both endorsing the theory of time known as *eternalism*. This theory, advanced by the mathematician Hermann Minkowski (1864–1909), holds that time is a fourth dimension added to the three dimensions of space (length, width, and depth). Together, these four dimensions embody the totality of reality. Furthermore, time itself consists of three distinct elements—past, present, and future—which are equally real, in terms of points on the space-time diagram. So, for example, Horace Goodspeed's drunken revelry at the outskirts of the Dharma Barracks in 1977, the Oceanic Six's return to the world in 2005, and Ajira Airways flight 316's crashing in 2007 are equally real, in the sense that each and every one of these events is fixed and unalterable. As such, every single point in time is exactly what it is and so cannot be changed.

This conception of time helps us understand many of the events that unfold throughout season 5. When Sawyer, Juliet, Miles, and the other time travelers journey near the hatch in 2001–2002, Sawyer plans to go through the hatch for supplies while he can. Faraday, however, stops him, explaining that he can't enter the hatch because Desmond is there, and Desmond never met Sawyer in the hatch in 1988. Because this encounter never occurred before, Sawyer cannot make it happen now. As Faraday explains, "You're wasting your time. . . . If it didn't happen, it can't happen. . . . You can't change the past, James!" ("Because You Left")

Likewise, the time travelers' entire encounter with the Dharma Initiative from 1974 to 1977 has already happened. Sawyer's and Juliet's rescue of Amy from the hostiles, for instance, was an event that had to occur the way it did, because it already happened. This explains why Faraday doesn't interfere with the rescue but instead remarks, "Doesn't matter what we do. Whatever happened, happened." ("LaFleur") Even Jack, Kate, and Hurley's 1977 entrance into the Dharma Initiative has to occur the way it unfolds for them. This also explains the presence of the 1977 Dharma Initiative recruiting photo on the wall in the Processing Center in the barracks in 2007, which Christian Shephard shows to Sun and Frank ("Namaste"). The reason that photo is there is not because Jack, Kate, and Sawyer changed the future; rather, they were always in that photo from 1977.

Even those who try to make changes to the past in order to change the future appear to fail. Consider two examples.

First, Sayid attempts to kill young Ben in 1977 ("He's Our You"), so that he can change the past (namely, stop Ben from growing into an adult) and so change the future (namely, prevent adult Ben from leading the Others and attacking the castaways). Not only does this effort fail, but the very attempt itself, along with Jack's subsequent refusal to save young Ben's life ("Whatever Happened, Happened"), has to happen the way it does, because it helps bring about the events in Ben's life where he becomes a member of the Others.

Second, as Charlotte is dying in Faraday's arms, she tells him that a crazy man once told her that she must leave the island and never return. She suggests that this man was Faraday ("This Place Is Death"). Heartbroken by Charlotte's death, Faraday initially hopes that he can save her life by never confronting her when she is a child. When realizing that the Incident is about to occur on the island in 1977, however, Faraday cannot help but fulfill the past ("The Variable"). Still hoping to change the past, Faraday faces his "timely" demise when he attempts to confront his young mother, Eloise, to learn the whereabouts of the hydrogen bomb. After Eloise shoots Faraday, and he lies there dying, Faraday comes to the horrific realization that he has to die in 1977 by the hands of his mother, and his mother, even in 2004, knows that this will happen and does nothing to try to prevent it.

We're the Variables

Although Faraday's fate seems to be sealed by the constraints of an eternalist conception of time, he does suggest an alternate account of time. As he explains to Jack and Kate in "The Variable,"

> I studied relativistic physics my entire life. One thing emerged over and over—can't change the past. Can't do it. Whatever happened, happened. . . . But then I finally realized I had been spending so much time focused on the constants, I forgot about the variables. Do you know what the variables in these equations are, Jack? . . . Us. We're the variables. People. We think. We reason. We make choices. We have free will. We can change our destiny. I think I can negate that energy under the Swan. I think I can destroy it. If I can, then

> that hatch will never be built, and your plane . . . will land, just like it's supposed to, in Los Angeles.

In other words, Faraday suggests here that the eternalist conception of time is incorrect.

Faraday's alternative account of time is best construed as a theory of time known as the *branching-universe model*. Under this model, time is depicted as a tree, where the trunk contains the temporal locations of the past, while the present is located at the fork where the branches begin. Future events are not fixed or complete; rather, they can be laid down in multiple ways, depending on the actions one chooses. As such, the future is open and marked by an unactualized set of possibilities, each of which is equally real.

The branching-universe model allows for the possibility that the past can be changed because there are possible branches along the past that link to alternative world time lines. The time traveler, then, can leave his or her present time, travel into the past, and make new changes that not only affect the future of the traveler's world, but also actualize other possible worlds.

Although Faraday himself doesn't live long enough to test his new hypothesis, Jack leads the charge to carry out Faraday's plan to detonate the hydrogen bomb at the Swan site ("The Incident: Parts 1 and 2"). As we learn from the opening episode of season 6 from a dying Juliet, the hydrogen bomb did go off ("LA X: Part 1"). The series allows the viewers to explore the other possible world it creates through each "flash-sideways," which shows what the characters would be doing under those circumstances.

Through season 6, we learn about this other possible world. First, and most important, Oceanic flight 815 does not crash on the island; instead, the plane safely lands in L.A. Second, the island is no longer above water. Rather, although once inhabited (the barracks remain, the foot of the statue remains, and so on), the island is now lying at the bottom of the ocean.

Third, we come to learn that many of the characters have different traits and experiences. Jack is still a surgeon, but he is also now a father ("Lighthouse"). Sawyer is no longer a con man but instead a cop, with Miles as his partner ("Recon"). Although Locke is still in a wheelchair, he is engaged to Helen ("The Substitute"). Desmond now works for Charles Widmore and doesn't meet Penny until 2004 ("Happily Ever After"). Hurley still wins the lottery but doesn't feel cursed and never enters the mental institution; instead, he believes himself to be the luckiest person alive ("Everybody Loves Hugo"). Ben never becomes the leader of the Others. Instead, he lives in the States, working as a European history teacher at a high school ("Dr. Linus").

Although the series finale reveals that the flash-sideways world is not an alternate time line, the show still uses the device of the flash-sideways to explore the possibility of Faraday's hypothesis. That is, we are initially led to believe that the different events that occur, along with the changes among the characters, can be explained by the branching-universe model of time. Following Faraday's prediction (and as Jack hoped), the detonation of the hydrogen bomb appears to create a new event in 1977 that hasn't occurred before. Yet rather than change the future of the original time line where Oceanic flight 815 crashes, let's call it 2004a, this new event made a nonactual possible branch time line actual. In other words, the flash-sideways world provides us with a view of 2004b, a time line that is caused by the detonation of the hydrogen bomb.

As Faraday further predicted, in this new time line, the hatch is not built to contain the energy, Desmond does not push the button (in fact, he winds up on flight 815), flight 815 does not crash, Faraday and Charlotte are not on the freighter to go to the island, and so on. Thus, given the branching-universe model of time, we are initially led to believe that the flash-sideways realm depicts a branching time line that stems from the detonation of the hydrogen bomb. Even though we learn later that this belief is false, the show is able to entertain a second account of time travel that, along with the eternalist account, sheds light on some of the common puzzles of time travel.

Loop, Dude

Let's begin with the simplest puzzle, a puzzle that is best personified through Hurley's confusion about time travel. When Hurley, Jack, and Kate are held inside the barracks by Miles (by order of Sawyer, for their safety), Hurley expresses his confusion to Miles in a humorous dialogue ("Whatever Happened, Happened"):

> Hurley: Let me get this straight. All this already happened.
> Miles: Yes.
> Hurley: So this conversation we're having right now . . . we already had it.
> Miles: Yes!
> Hurley: Then what am I gonna say next?
> Miles: I don't know.
> Hurley: Ha! Then your theory is wrong!
> Miles: For the thousandth time, you dingbat, the conversation already happened, but not for you and me. For you and me, it's happening right now.
> Hurley: Okay, answer me this. If all this already happened to me, then . . . why don't I remember any of it?
> Miles: Because once Ben turned that wheel, time isn't a straight line for us anymore. Our experiences in the past and the future occurred before these experiences right now.
> Hurley: Say that again.
> Miles: Shoot me. Please. Please!

Hurley: Aha! I can't shoot you. Because if you die in 1977, then you'll never come back to the island on the freighter thirty years from now.

Miles: I can die because I've already come to the island on the freighter. Any of us can die because this is our present.

Hurley: But you said Ben couldn't die because he still has to grow up and become the leader of the Others.

Miles: Because this is his past.

Although Miles can't help resolve Hurley's confusion, I think we could help Hurley understand the concept of time traveling by returning to David Lewis's analysis.

Recall that there are two versions of time implicit in time traveling: external time and personal time. In external time, it is true that Hurley and Miles already had the conversation they are having in 1977. Yet they have not had this conversation before in their personal time because they have yet to experience it. The continuation of their conversation is part of their future personal time. Thus, Miles cannot know what Hurley is about to say.

Likewise, it is possible that Miles can indeed die in 1977. The experience of being on the freighter in 2004 is part of his past, while the death Hurley proposes would be part of his future. The same cannot be said for young Ben, though. First, assuming the eternalist account of time, where the past cannot be altered in any way, young Ben must continue to become the adult Ben whom everyone has met earlier. Second, because Ben did not travel through time, his personal time is running parallel with external time. As such, young Ben's future in his personal time is identical to the future of external time. Young Ben has not yet experienced the future external time events of leading the Others, challenging the castaways, and so on. As such, it is not possible for him to die in 1977—he must still live out his future life for at least the next thirty years.

One Miles? Two Miles? How Many Versions of Miles Can There Be?

Yet there is another, more challenging puzzle. When Miles travels to 1977, he gets to know his father, Dr. Chang. Furthermore, he discovers that he was born on the island around this time. One night, when peering through his parents' window in the barracks, Miles sees his father holding a baby, which happens to be baby Miles ("Some Like it Hoth"). As such, in this moment in time, we have two versions of Miles only a few feet apart: "baby Miles" and "adult Miles."

This seems to lead us to a possible contradiction, because it runs counter to the *principle of indiscernibility of identicals*. This principle states that if what appear to be two or more objects are actually identical, there can be no property held by one and not the other.

Baby Miles and adult Miles appear to be two different people because they have different properties, or characteristics. For instance, baby Miles is young and small, while adult Miles is a young man and large. And yet they are both Miles. How can the same exact person have contradictory characteristics (young and not-young, small and not-small)? If they are indeed the same person, then we have a violation of the principle of indiscernibility of identicals. Otherwise, it seems we are forced to say that they are not the same person and so at least one of them cannot be Miles.

Lewis, however, once again comes to the rescue.

First, considered along his personal time line, Miles is still a single person. Until 2005, Miles's personal time coincides with external time. He is born in 1977 and lives normally for twenty-eight years. When he begins time traveling in 2005, his personal time separates from external time. Nevertheless, according to his personal time, he maintains a continuity of mental and physical states. Thus, the identity of Miles the time traveler is consistent along his personal time line.

Second, from the perspective of external time, Miles has two different bodies with different characteristics. That is, Miles is both baby Miles who is seen by adult Miles and adult Miles who sees baby Miles. They are two different people, in the sense that they are two different objects located in different spatial locations. Their personal connection does not matter from the external point of view. Miles is like a long worm whose head curls back to view its own tail. Baby Miles grows up into the adult Miles, who travels back to 1977 to see himself being held by his father.

There's No Place Like Home

Suppose that when Faraday seeks out his mother to find the whereabouts of the hydrogen bomb, instead of his mother killing him, he is able to shoot her first, thereby killing her. Is this scenario possible? Can Faraday kill his mother before he is born? If Faraday murders his mother in 1977, before she gives birth to him, he will have prevented his own birth. Yet if Faraday is never born, how can he exist through 2005 and travel back to 1977 to kill his mother in the first place? Will he, as Hurley worries about himself, begin to disappear? In the philosophy of time travel, this is known as *the grandfather paradox*.

The resolution of the paradox depends on which conception of time we adopt. The eternalist conception of time yields what may seem like a strange response: Faraday *can* and *cannot* kill his mother in 1977.

In one sense, we can clearly imagine Faraday, in a given moment, to have the ability to draw his gun toward his mother, pull the trigger, and kill her. That is, it is clearly *physically possible* for one person to kill another person. Faraday can have the ability, the intent, and the know-how to kill Eloise.

In another sense, however, this action, because it would occur in 1977, is not possible. Faraday needs to have been born so that he can live a life that leads him to travel to a time before he was born in order to do the killing. He therefore cannot kill the person who gives birth to him in the first place. In other words, it is a *logical impossibility* for Faraday to be able to kill his mother.

Although the eternalist conception of time entails that Faraday's act of killing his mother in 1977 is logically impossible, the branching-universe concept of time yields different results. This account agrees that Faraday is physically capable of the act, while rejecting the alleged logical impossibility. Given the notion that any moment in time has nonactual branching possibilities, ready to be actualized, it remains logically possible for Faraday to be born in a given external time line and travel back before his birth to change that moment in time so that he is not born in the first place. The logical contradiction will be resolved, because Faraday's act of killing his mother before he is born will move him into an alternative time line. In this other possible world, Eloise need not be his mother.

Well, What Goes Around, Comes Around

We have, thus far, examined and resolved several different puzzles of time travel through the assumption that we can make sense of continuity, even under different conceptions of time. Yet perhaps the most challenging time-travel puzzle from *Lost* comes about in a scenario that hinders the notion of continuity, whether it be personal time or external time. The scenario concerns Locke's sequence of time traveling. Specifically, we find that when Ben turns the ancient wheel, most of the time travelers travel together. Locke, however, traveling through the same sequence of time locations, travels alone.

On one occasion, Locke travels to a point where he witnesses the Beechcraft crash on the island. Here, Locke is shot in the leg by Ethan. Locke travels in time again to a 2007 where Richard takes the bullet out of his leg and gives him bizarre instructions. First, Locke is told that the next time he sees Richard, Richard will not know who he is. At that time, though, Locke must give Richard the compass Richard just gave him now. Second, Locke must die so that he can convince the Oceanic Six to return to the island ("Because You Left"). Later, Locke time travels to 1954, where he meets Richard (who doesn't know him), and gives him the compass that he had received from Richard in 2007 ("Jughead").

Where did the compass that was passed between Richard and Locke originate? From Locke's personal time line, Richard gives the compass to Locke in 2007, and Locke gives Richard the compass in 1954. From the external time line, Richard is given the compass from Locke in 1954, holds onto it for fifty-three years, and then returns it to Locke in 2007, only for Locke to then go back in time to give it to Richard in the first place.

The problem is that the possession of the compass has a circular causal sequence: (1) Locke enters 1954 with possession of the compass, (2) Locke gives the compass to Richard in 1954 so that he has possession of it, (3) Richard gives the compass to Locke in 2007 so that he once again has possession of it, (4) Locke enters 1954 with possession of the compass, and so on.

Although the events of the compass being exchanged between Locke and Richard have a causal sequence, this sequence, unlike normal causal sequences, has no beginning or end. It is an uncaused cause. This paradox is known among philosophers of time as a *causal loop*.

One response is to simply accept the possibility of uncaused causes. Someone could argue, for example, that the universe itself is best understood as not having an original cause, even if it causes other events in time. Not everything needs an independent point of origination. And so, the compass can be an uncaused cause in a causal loop.

Another response is to find an independent point of origination. Take, for example, another possible causal loop centered on the same events: the idea for Locke to try to die to convince the Oceanic Six to return to the island. Through most of season 5, it may appear as if this idea falls prey to a causal loop: (1) time traveler Locke receives this idea from Richard in 2007, but (2) Richard hears this idea only moments earlier from the other Locke, and, presumably (3) Locke has the idea in 2007 because he hears it from Richard when he is time traveling. So, initially, it looks like this idea travels in a circle as well, with no distinct point of origination. As we learn in season 6, however, the "other Locke" is not Locke, but the Man in Black. Thus, we find that it was the Man in Black who created this idea and passed it along to Richard, who, in turn, passed it along to Locke. In this way, then, we resolve the causal loop by marking an independent point of origination.

Of course, we are never given an independent point of origination for the compass. We don't know that the Man in Black gave Locke the compass, but we also don't know that he didn't.

None of It Matters Anyway, Then, Does It?

Throughout their adventures in time travel, the characters of *Lost* face famous, age-old puzzles concerning identity, freedom, causality, and time. As we've seen, the solutions to these puzzles depend on what we mean by time traveling and what we mean by time. Although the characters and the events that take place on the island suggest different conceptions of time, and hence different possible resolutions to the puzzles, the show as a whole makes time travel seem all that much more possible and tantalizingly real. When Charlie gave Claire a jar of imaginary peanut butter ("Confidence Man"), we learned that sometimes a good fantasy is all you need.

MEGA JACKPOT

MEGA NUMBER
3

Your numbers are:
4, 8, 15, 16, 23

IT DOESN'T MATTER
WHAT WE DO

From Metaphysics to Ethics in
Lost's Time Travel

Jeremy Pierce

Hurley: How long have you known he was your dad?

Miles: Third day we were here, I was in line at the cafeteria, and my mother got in line behind me. That was my first clue.

Hurley: But all those Dharma dudes end up dead. Don't you want to save him?

Miles: I can't save him! They're going to get killed no matter what I do, so why bother?

—"Some Like It Hoth"

In *Lost* season 5, several characters begin to jump through time, and questions immediately arise. Should they try to change what happened? Are they able to do things that conflict with what happened? The working theory of most of season 5 is that the past happened, and thus nothing can change what occurred. Everything the time-travelers do will be what had happened all along. Things do turn out to be a little more complicated than that but perhaps not as different as the writers have at times led us to believe.

The Metaphysics of Time Travel

According to Daniel Faraday, "It doesn't matter what we do. Whatever happened, happened." ("LaFleur") Philosophers sometimes call Daniel's view the *fixed* or *static* view of time. The alternative approach considers time open and the future not yet fixed. Only necessary truths about the future are true, things that have to happen no matter what, such as "1 + 1 = 2" and "Either I'll eat an Apollo bar tomorrow, or I won't."

In the open view, anything contingent (not necessary) is neither true nor false. This makes it difficult to see how time travel could be possible. If John Locke begins in 2004 and goes to 1954, and there's no truth about the contingent future at 1954, then there's no truth about Locke being in 2004 to have come back in time. To say that he'll be born and will end up on the island is to say something that is neither true nor false. What truths would explain why he's in 1954, then?

The only way to make sense of time travel with open time is to say that any events resulting from time travel are in a different past, not in the original past. For a while during season 6, the writers gave hints of misdirection along such lines. Maybe the flash-sideways reality that had Oceanic flight 815 landing safely in Los Angeles was caused by the final events of "The Incident" when the hydrogen bomb from 1954 exploded in the electromagnetic pocket under the Swan station. If so, then one reality contained an unsuccessful attempt to change the past, and another included the changed past.

No event would change the actual past. Yet events might generate something like a new time line, whose existence is caused by events in a previous time line. Perhaps, then, we should we call it a previous time line. It does seem as if there's something earlier about the original time line. It's what causes the later one, after all, and causes are supposed to precede their effects. We're talking about time travel, however, where causes don't always precede their effects. For example, Ben Linus turned the frozen donkey wheel in 2004 and caused events that brought Locke to 1954.

The original time line can't be earlier in time. The flash-sideways is 2004, a different 2004 from the original 2004—but is it later than the original? No, according to this theory, it's at the same time, but the same time on a different time line. So, how is one time line earlier? You have to postulate hyper-time. Within each time line, there's a temporal sequence, an ordering of events in a chronology, with earlier and later events. Yet one time line is later along a different axis, not on the axis of regular time but on the axis of hyper-time.

So, should we postulate a second dimension of time to make sense of time travel and changing the past, in which it's not really the past that you're changing but the creation of a new time line at a later point in hyper-time? Is this different from alternate realities? If Jack creates a new time line, it's a sort of alternate universe. It would be a different matter, though, to travel to an existing alternate universe and then do things differently from the past of the original universe you started in. The difference is whether the alt-reality is created by your actions in the past or already exists independently of your actions.

Lost executive producer Damon Lindelof cowrote an alt-reality time-travel story in the semi-reboot of *Star Trek* in 2009. It had no past-changing, because the people from the original time line traveled to the past of a different reality. The flash-sideways world of *Lost*, even well into the final episode, could have been that, but it turned out to be a sort of pre-afterlife, with no connection to the events of the Incident or any past-changing.

One reason to prefer fixed time is that it fits with physics. The open view requires a determinate fact about which events are now and which aren't yet (the ones not yet true or false). Physics, however, doesn't allow for determinate facts about which events are now, because facts about what's simultaneous with my current thought depend on the frame of reference. This means that according to the open view, (1) which statements are neither true nor false and (2) which statements are true or false depend on (3) what frame of reference you pay attention to. Yet how could whether something has any truth or falsity be based on which physical frame of reference you focus on?

A significant paradox can occur if you can change the actual past. It's a straightforward contradiction to say that Jack both did and didn't detonate a bomb at the Swan construction site. Except for parallel reality time travel or hyper-time, you get such a contradiction. Even with hyper-time, though, a paradox can occur. If Jack detonates the bomb and it leads to Oceanic flight 815 not crashing, then in the new time line Jack couldn't travel back in time to blow up the bomb. That means he wouldn't be there to prevent the Swan accident, and the plane would crash after all. Lindelof explains why they didn't want to do this on *Lost*: "Paradox creates issues. In *Heroes*, Masi Oka's character travels back from the future to say, "You *must* prevent New York from being destroyed." But if they prevent New York from being destroyed, Masi Oka can never travel back from the future to warn you, because Future Hiro no longer exists."[1]

The producers did not want to portray time travel that prevents its own occurrence, and that's what the flash-sideways would have been if it had involved past-changing. It had to be either an alternate reality or something altogether different, and it turned out to be the latter.

Given that the season finale didn't change the past, all time travel in season 5 assumes fixed time (with the possible exception of the never-explained outrigger following Sawyer and company when they flash to 2007 in "The Little Prince"). Some characters question the fixed view at the end of season 5, however, and we don't get resolution as to which approach is correct until the series finale.

When Daniel Faraday returns from Dharma Initiative headquarters in Ann Arbor, Michigan, to prevent the Oceanic flight 815 crash, he no longer believes "whatever happened, happened." Rather, he now sees free will as the variable that allows us to change the past. So he now thinks that he can prevent Charlotte's death by nuking the construction site of the Swan, right at the time when the Incident occurred at the Swan site when drills hit into the powerful electromagnetism of the golden light at the Heart of the Island. If the explosion could seal off the energy released by the Incident, Desmond wouldn't have been entering those numbers every 108 minutes, so he wouldn't have caused Oceanic flight 815 to crash by failing to get back to the Swan station in time to type them in.

Daniel had taken a different view earlier. In "Because You Left," Sawyer realizes that they're at a time after Oceanic flight 815 crashed, and he tells his companions they should try to stop the helicopter from leaving the island and (as far as they know) exploding. Daniel says it won't work. "Time is like a street. We can move forward on that street. We can move in reverse, but we cannot ever create a new street. If we try to do anything different, we will fail every time. Whatever happened, happened."

Later in the same episode, when Sawyer's group discovers that they're at a time between the creation of the Swan and the Oceanic flight 815 crash, Sawyer wants to get some food from the Swan. Daniel steers him away, though, "because Desmond didn't know you when he first came out of there. That means you never met, which means you can't meet." He adds, "You're wasting your time. If it didn't happen, it can't happen. You can't change the past, James."

Yet Daniel has strikingly different attitudes at other times. In "Jughead," he meets his mother, Eloise Hawking, in 1954, and he urgently pleads with her to bury the hydrogen bomb that was brought to the island by the U.S. military, saying that it won't blow up if they simply do what he says. In "LaFleur," however, they stumble on two Others attacking two Dharma Initiative members, and Daniel's response is, "It doesn't matter what we do. Whatever happened, happened." Why the urgency about the bomb, then?

Shooting Benjamin Linus

Sayid Jarrah, captured by the Dharma Initiative in 1977 ("Namaste"), finds that the boy who's been sneaking him food is Ben Linus ("He's Our You"), the future murderous leader of the Others. Sayid thinks he may be in 1977 to eliminate Ben before he can become evil. After Ben helps him escape, Sayid shoots him. When Jin finds young Ben ("Whatever Happened, Happened"), he brings him to Juliet, who can't save him. His only hope is with the Others. The ensuing debate gets to the heart of a crucial ethical question for time travel.

Kate wants to save Ben. He's only a boy. How could they allow him to die when they can save him? He'll become a murderer later, but he's not a murderer yet. Jack won't lift a finger, largely because of his attitude toward adult Ben. Kate thinks that maybe Jack is supposed to save Ben, and she believes they caused this by bringing Sayid back in time, so they ought to help. Meanwhile, Miles assures Hurley that Ben will survive, because they encountered him in the future. They may not know how, and they have no explanation of how Ben will forget that Sayid shot him when he meets Sayid in 2004, but they can be sure that he'll somehow survive, because he did survive.

Kate brings Ben to the Others, and Richard agrees to save him. He warns, though, that Ben will lose his innocence, and he'll forget what happened. So we see why Ben later doesn't remember Sayid, and we learn what turns Ben into the liar and murderer he ends up becoming. The very process of saving his life that Kate initiates leads Ben to become the kind of person Sayid wanted to prevent. Yet she wouldn't have taken Ben to the Others to have this happen if Sayid hadn't shot him. So, instead of preventing Ben's murderous ways, Sayid brings about the events that cause Ben to lose his innocence.

This is consistent with "whatever happened, happened." There's no past-changing, merely some characters thinking that they can, trying, and failing. There's even the ironic attempt to avert a bad result and indirectly bringing it about. If Sayid couldn't prevent "murderer Ben," should he have not bothered shooting him? If it's ever all right to shoot a child, it takes a great moral reason. Sayid thought that he had one, but what if it's impossible to change what happened? Should Sayid not have tried? Yet it also seems to follow that Sayid couldn't have refrained, because what actually happened was that he shot Ben. Does that mean none of our actions are our own choice?

The ancient Epicureans held that no one is free if any statements are true ahead of time, but Carneades the Skeptic (c. 214–129 B.C.) responded to the Epicurean view by distinguishing truth and necessity.[2] It might be true that I will do something even if it's not guaranteed by the very nature of the universe or even by things outside my control. What makes it true is that I'll do it. I choose to do it of my own volition. That's so for any future decision of mine. What makes it true hasn't happened yet, but it's true nonetheless. What anyone else does will either contribute to its happening or be irrelevant. We can't prevent what will happen, but at the same time, our reasons for what we do are our own. Truth about the future doesn't prevent freedom, in ordinary cases. So, returning to *Lost*, why should it prevent freedom with time travel?

The Man in Black: Manipulating Time Travel

The main antagonist of *Lost* is the Man in Black, the Smoke Monster, the twin brother of the island's protector, Jacob. For almost half of season 5, he was posing as John Locke. He manipulated Richard into telling a time-traveling real Locke that he needed to leave the island and then die to bring everyone back, knowing full well that Locke's corpse would arrive on Ajira flight 316 and that some of the Oceanic Six who had left the island were on that plane but had disappeared. The Man in Black got Richard to give Locke his compass so that Locke could give it to the younger Richard in 1954 to set Richard toward thinking that Locke was important. The Man in Black appeared to Locke as Christian Shephard at the frozen donkey wheel before Locke moved the island, explaining how important it was to bring everyone back who had left. It was important to his plan that all of Jacob's candidates die.

The Man in Black's manipulation of Ben required that Richard trust Locke to allow Ben to go with him into the chamber at the foot of the statue of Taweret, because the Man in Black was unable to kill Jacob himself. What the Man in Black set in motion was a causal loop, similar to Sayid bringing about the circumstances that cause Ben to lose his innocence, the very reason Sayid wanted him to die. The Man in Black learns what happens with Ajira flight 316, who was on it, and who died, and he sets in motion events that bring about the very arrival of that flight. Some of this he apparently discerns from Locke's memories as he adopts his form, but his chronologically earliest appearance to Locke was as Christian, right before Locke turned the frozen donkey wheel, at a time before the *Black Rock* destroyed the statue of Taweret in 1867. (Right before Locke turns the wheel, Sawyer and those with him see the full statue from behind, as shown in "LaFleur.")

This means that the Man in Black was able to anticipate much of his plan well ahead, perhaps from what he saw in Locke's mind as he spoke to him, although that couldn't give him all that he needed (say, to send him to Eloise). Perhaps he had limited foreknowledge (limited because he seemed unaware of his own death as it approached). This raises free will problems of its own, but Carneades' solution applies equally well to those. Someone can know what someone else will do, but what makes it true isn't the foreknowledge. It's the person's own action in the future. If he knows what's going to happen and what he needs to do to fulfill it, what should we say about his actions? The Man in Black kills indiscriminately and manipulates people to disastrous ends just so that he can get off the island. Is leaving so important to be worth it? Is it any excuse to say that whatever happens will happen? He's still responsible. Our ordinary moral views apply just as well to a being with such abilities, and the fatalistic argument that nothing we do matters seems to be a mistake here as much as it was with young Ben.

The Incident

The big time-travel quandary appears in the last few episodes of season 5, and the writers dragged out its implications all the way to the series finale. When Daniel returns from Ann Arbor ("The Variable"), he convinces Jack and Kate to go to the Others with him to find his mother, to convince her to detonate the bomb at the Swan site, with the hope of preventing the Incident that necessitated the pushing of the button every 108 minutes, which would prevent the Oceanic flight 815 crash. Lots of deaths and plenty of difficult circumstances could be prevented. Jack agrees.

Kate, on the other hand, doesn't see such results as good ("Follow the Leader"). Jack thinks he was sent to 1977 to fulfill this purpose. Kate accuses him of trying to kill them and everyone else on the island, because their current selves would die in a nuclear explosion, but then another time line would replace the current one without their having experienced the island. Sayid later asks her why she took Ben to the Others. Kate replies, "Since when did shooting kids and blowing up hydrogen bombs become okay?"

Sawyer has a similar view ("The Incident"). He tells Jack that he could have gone home and prevented his parents' deaths, but "what's done is done." When Jack says it doesn't have to be, Sawyer replies, "What did you screw up so bad the first time around you're willing to blow up a damn nuke just for a second chance?" Even self-interested Sawyer thinks it's too much to blow up a nuke for a redo, and Kate insists that you can't displace morality for a good outcome, when doing so will wipe out a whole reality. With past-changing, the consequences of any time travel could be astronomical. You could wipe out the entire world, only to replace everyone with near duplicates who have slightly different lives. Isn't that mass murder?

After Jack leaves, Miles comments, "Has it occurred to any of you that your buddy's actually going to cause the thing he says he's trying to prevent? Perhaps that little nuke is the Incident. So maybe the best thing to do is nothing. I'm glad you all thought this through." Miles assumes that Jack's goal is good. He turns out to be right that Jack causes what he tries to avoid. But was Jack's intended goal good? Kate and Sawyer think not. This is the same Miles who said he wasn't going to try to prevent his father's death ("Some Like It Hoth"), and his stated reason was that he couldn't prevent it if he tried (but given his animosity toward his father, perhaps he had other reasons). Is Miles right that it doesn't matter what you do, something Daniel had said (in "LaFleur") when he encountered the first people they saw in 1974? Or is Miles right that you should do nothing?

Kate uses ordinary moral considerations. We can't excuse inaction or refuse to do what we know is right. Even if it already happened that Sayid shot Ben, does that make it all right? It doesn't matter what he hopes to achieve. The action is wrong in itself, and Sayid did it knowingly and deliberately. It's not morally all right just because it was already true in 2007 that it had happened in 1977. He commits a well-intentioned moral wrong arising from his own beliefs, desires, and character. He's morally responsible.

Jack was also responsible for what he did. Rather than prevent the Incident, he caused it, as Miles had warned. That doesn't remove his responsibility for attempting to do something very bad, either in the case where he succeeds or in the actual outcome where he fails to change the past but succeeds in blowing up the bomb, thus creating the very thing he wanted to prevent, the Incident.

The Rules Don't Apply to You

Several instances show that Desmond is different. When he foresees Charlie's death but stops it from happening in season 3, he says that he's forestalling fate. Charlie will die, but Desmond keeps preventing it for Charlie's sake. This doesn't involve changing the past, because Desmond isn't time traveling, but there's some plan according to which things are supposed to happen, and Desmond modifies it by foreseeing things that he then prevents. Eventually, course correction kicks in, however, and Charlie does die.

In "Before You Left," Daniel attempts to save the time-jumpers by sending future Desmond to Eloise. He goes to the Swan and gives Desmond a message that somehow Desmond forgets for years but remembers suddenly in 2007, and by that time he knows who Daniel is and realizes that it was Daniel who'd asked this of him. Daniel tells Desmond that he's different, that the rules don't apply to him. What rules? Can Desmond change the past when no one else can? He doesn't change the past in this case. He has an encounter with a stranger, but he thinks little of it at the time and eventually forgets it, only to remember it suddenly years later.

We see other instances in which Desmond is special. Two involve time travel back and forth between the present and the past. In the season 2 finale, "Live Together, Die Alone," Desmond activates the Swan fail-safe. We learn in season 3's "Flashes Before Your Eyes" that the fail-safe sends his consciousness back to an earlier time in his life when he was about to propose to Penny but changed his mind. There he encounters Eloise and learns that he can change minor details about his past but not major things. The universe course corrects. This would be a flat-out violation of fixed time. Past-changing isn't possible with fixed time.

One way to avoid this is to interpret Desmond's consciousness-time-travel as a dream. He remembers things but differently, and whoever sends him the dream is sending him a message. That would make this more consistent with fixed time. Yet the next time he consciousness-time-travels (in season 4's "The Constant"), Desmond actually does something to change the past that then affects his present. He convinces Penny in 1996 to give him her phone number so that he can call her in 2004. He remembers her phone number in 2004, which he hadn't been remembering. Has he changed the past? It seems so.

The producers even indicate that they want to see Desmond's consciousness-time-travel as changing the past. The following exchange appears in the season 4 DVD commentary on "The Constant":

> [Damon Lindelof:] There it is. You can't change the future. Those are the rules on *Lost* which are very hard to adhere to. Because if you tell the audience that something that Desmond does in ninety-six can alter the present, you go back to the episode we did last year where Ms. Hawking comes to Desmond

and says no matter what you do the course of time will find a way to course-correct. So you can save somebody's life who's supposed to die but eventually the universe will find a way to kill them anyways.

[Mark Goldman:] So you can change the immediate future?

[Damon Lindelof:] Yeah, you can change the immediate future.

If this is how to think about Desmond's consciousness-time-travel, then it's not really fixed time. Time travel can change the past, in principle. It's just that something—perhaps we could say something-we-know-not-what, to use an expression from the real-life philosopher John Locke (1632–1704)—prevents it most of the time. Even in Desmond's case (presumably, his specialness allows him to do it), this something-we-know-not-what prevents major consequences beyond the immediate future of his later time-traveling self. He can influence an event that is about to happen by traveling back eight years.

What's going on metaphysically in these cases? It would make no sense if Desmond changed his actual past, because that would be contradictory. It can't be true that he didn't get Penny's number and also did get Penny's number. So it must be that he "first" didn't have it and "then" later did, where "first" and "later" don't mean moments in time but either (1) moments earlier and later in hyper-time or (2) events in one alternate reality causing events in another. Desmond must either create a new time line with different features from his original one, and then he will continue to experience the new one, rather than the original, or he's moving to an already-existing alternate reality whose past his consciousness was always in (and thus nothing actually changes).

The ethical questions depend on which theory is right. If Desmond causes things to happen differently in an alternate reality, where the original reality stays as he remembers it, then he's influencing another world, not changing anything. Any consequences are still important, because they affect real people, but he doesn't wipe anyone out of existence. Alternatively, if Desmond creates a new time line to replace the original, and it involves someone dying who otherwise might survive or someone surviving who otherwise might die, then the ethical issues come into play more immediately. It's good for our characters that the writers limited what could be changed to immediate-future events that would eventually be course corrected, and thus no big changes would occur. That rules out a nuclear explosion destroying much of the island and leading to Oceanic flight 815 not crashing. Otherwise, the potential ethical consequences could be enormous, as Kate and Jack's discussion about the bomb in "Follow the Leader" makes clear.

Time Travel Ethics in *Lost*

So, what should we conclude? *Lost* has designed time travel in a way that usually involves no changing of the past. It's almost as if the fixed view of time is correct. Yet small changes occur with Desmond, as long as they don't lead to major differences long term. The long-term consequences of any small changes aren't all that important, apparently, because course correction takes care of anything that is very different from what originally occurs or originally is supposed to occur (which is hard to imagine without some kind of intelligent Fate-like being, perhaps the island itself, guiding things along, but the show never gets close to speculating about such a being, aside from the characters' occasional comments about the island having purposes for people).

In a fixed-enough time line, how should we think about ethics? If you can't change the past, you obviously shouldn't bother trying, at least once you know that you can't. Yet is Daniel right when he says it doesn't matter what you do? Daniel convinces Pierre Chang to evacuate the women and children from the island, which saves a number of lives, including Miles and Charlotte and their mothers. Daniel already knew that they'd go, but he was willing to be the reason they did, because he had no idea what led to it. It turned out that it had been him. He similarly knew that the hydrogen bomb didn't explode in a way that would do any serious damage to the island. He still pleaded urgently with his mother to bury it. He knew she needed to, and he knew it would get done, but he also knew that he might be the only reason it would get done, so he embraced his role in bringing about the events he knew would occur. Why? Because he knew he should.

It turns out that the ethical issues during time travel aren't all that different from the moral choices that usually apply in our lives without time travel. It's wrong to shoot children, as Sayid did. It's dangerous to detonate a nuclear bomb in a huge electromagnetic field with very suspicious properties, because you have no idea what the consequences might be. Trying to do something that you know will kill lots of people is usually a bad idea, unless you're sure that the good effects are not only worth it but are so worth it as to count against the very strong resistance you should have to doing something like that. If you can prevent a horrible wrong, then do so. If you know you can't, try to do what you can to mitigate it.

These are basic ethical principles. Kate seems fully aware of them and perhaps offers the most balanced view on the ethics of time travel of all of the characters. Jack is too sure of a purpose that he has little evidence for, and he has no concept of what his actions might cause. Sawyer is largely acting out of self-interest. Sayid has good intentions but does wrong in carrying them out. Miles moves between anger at his father and a false cynicism that leads him to believe that interfering can't be good. Kate, however, recognizes the potential disaster that will occur if Jack's plan works, and she rightly resists it (not knowing that her worry is unwarranted, because the plan can't succeed). She condemns Sayid's action and insists that they help the boy. In the end, Kate rightly recognizes that morality in time travel is simply morality, period. The same principles apply.

NOTES

1. Jeff Jensen, "*Lost*: Mind-Blowing Scoop from Its Producers," *Entertainment Weekly* online, February 22, 2010, www.ew.com/ew/article/0,,20179125_3,00.html or http://tinyurl.com/lost-jensen.

2. Cicero (106–43 B.C.E.) reports Carneades' view, but it's hard to know where Carneades ends and Cicero begins. See Cicero, *On Fate* 18–48 (selections), in *Hellenistic Philosophy: Introductory Readings*, 2nd ed., ed. Brad Inwood and L. P. Gerson (Indianapolis: Hackett Publishing, 1997), pp. 46–49.

IF SAWYER WEREN'T A CON MAN, THEN HE WOULD HAVE BEEN A COP

Counterfactual Reasoning in the Last Season of *Lost*

Deborah R. Barnbaum

The first few seasons of *Lost* were filled with flash*backs*: glimpses of what happened before the crash of Oceanic flight 815, which informed the current responses of Jack, Sawyer, Kate, Hurley, and the rest of the principal characters. The last season of *Lost*, however, was filled with many scenes from the flash-*sideways* world: glimpses of what would have happened to the principal characters if the island had been destroyed and Oceanic 815 had landed safely in Los Angeles.

Debates still rage on: Did each flash-sideways take place in Jack's imagination as he tried to come to terms with having died, along with everyone else? Was the flash-sideways realm an actual alternative reality? Was it a depiction of heaven? And how plausible were these depictions of what would have been, had flight 815 landed safely in Los Angeles?

Philosophers, to put it mildly, are obsessed with understanding *what would have happened* if things had been different and spend huge amounts of time analyzing what it means for things to have been different. And they aren't obsessed with these questions merely because they realize, "If I hadn't become a philosopher, I would have been able to pay my mortgage."

Instead, they are obsessed with these thoughts because understanding *what would have happened* is metaphysically important: it tells us about the nature of reality. A flash-sideways shows us not what is actually true but what is possibly true, if things had been different. What does it mean, however, for something to be possibly true?

Counterfactual Reasoning

To understand the logic of possibility, we need to start with if-then statements and work from there. If-then statements are known as *conditionals*, such as: *If Hurley plays the lottery, then he will be a millionaire*. The "if" part of the conditional—"if Hurley plays the lottery"—is known as the antecedent of the conditional. The "then" part of the conditional—"then he will be a millionaire"—is known as the consequent of the conditional.

A straightforward conditional like this could have a true antecedent. After all, Hurley did play the lottery. Yet there are some conditionals with antecedents that are not actually true, ones that are merely possibly true. These conditionals are *counterfactual conditionals*, or simply *counterfactuals*, for short. They are conditionals that describe what would, could, should, or might have happened. For example: *If Sawyer weren't a con man, then he would have been a cop*. If the first five seasons of *Lost* portray what actually is true, then Sawyer actually is a con man. After his parents tragically die in the wake of the scheming con man "Tom Sawyer," the young James Ford vows vengeance.

James is then visited by Jacob. This series of events leads James to both adopt the alias "Sawyer" and pursue a life of petty crime and long cons, all in the service of repaying Tom Sawyer, who ruined him at a young age. It doesn't seem like a stretch, though, to imagine James becoming a cop instead of a con man, to accomplish the same goal.

The final season of *Lost* is filled with counterfactuals: If Sawyer weren't a con man, then he would have been a cop. If Sun and Jin hadn't married, then they still would have fallen in love. If Ben weren't an evil mastermind, then he would have gotten a Ph.D. in history and taught high school. If flight 815 had landed safely in Los Angeles, then Claire would have learned that the adoptive family didn't want Aaron. If Hurley hadn't suffered a mental breakdown, then he would have parlayed his lottery winnings into becoming a business mogul.

Many philosophers, for once resembling normal people, believe that other possible worlds are purely imaginary. The Princeton metaphysician David Lewis (1941–2001), however, famously held that possible worlds really exist. He thought that other possible worlds are just as real as our actual world is, except that from the standpoint of those other worlds, *our world* is one of the possible worlds, and *that world* is the actual world. In Lewis's view, we wouldn't be able to talk about other possibilities if they weren't real. And if they are real, then they must exist somewhere. Just because we can't gain access to them doesn't mean they aren't there.

Lewis suffered quite a bit of criticism, not to mention outright ridicule and more than one incredulous stare, for his belief in the existence of possible worlds. He would have been very grateful to Daniel Faraday for proving him right.

Counterfactuals Count

Counterfactual reasoning is not merely fun and games. Scientists use it to analyze what is meant by cause and effect; doctors do as well, to authorize treatment when a patient cannot give consent; and it's used by politicians to assess public policy.

We see the life-or-death implications of counterfactual reasoning illustrated again and again on *Lost*. When Oceanic 815 first crashed, before the hatch and the caves were found, resources were scarce. The survivors faced these questions: What counts as a fair distribution of food and water? Should Jack get more, because he's the only doctor, capable of saving others' lives? Or should Shannon get more, because she's suffering from asthma?

One answer to the question of what counts as a fair distribution was put forward by the eminent American political philosopher John Rawls (1921–2002), in his book *A Theory of Justice*.[1] Rawls argued for two principles as the basis for a just distribution of goods in society.

The first principle says that everyone should get an equal amount of goods, with that amount being as much as possible. The second principle says that inequalities are permissible, but only if they will help *everyone*, and no one is discriminated against when goods are distributed unequally.

Applied to our survivors, the first principle gives everyone an equal amount of water and the most water that can be equally shared. The second principle, however, gives Jack more because everyone will benefit from his life-saving services. Shannon is out of luck, because giving her more water doesn't help ensure that everyone else will be better off.

So the principles have surprising implications that some people might find objectionable. Rawls knew that not even a just society can make everyone happy all of the time. He defended his rules through an ingenious thought experiment.

Imagine yourself behind a veil of ignorance, which prevents you from knowing your social identity. You don't know whether you're rich, like Hurley, or on the verge of being fired from yet another dead-end job, like Locke. You don't know whether you're young, like Claire, or old, like Rose. You don't know whether you're an upstanding citizen, like Bernard and Juliet, or a career criminal, like Kate and Sawyer. You don't know whether you are male or female, black or white, gay or straight. You must decide how to distribute goods and services under this veil.

The veil prevents you from making a biased decision. You can't play favorites when you don't know who you are. For example, if you don't know whether you're rich or poor, you won't set up a system that allows the richest people to buy more water. Not knowing how to privilege yourself will make you fair. Rawls called the place behind this veil of ignorance the Original Position. He then asked this question as part of his thought experiment: What distribution of goods would people in the Original Position choose?

The crucial assumption underlying Rawls's thought experiment is rationality. As a human being, he argued, you are rational, even when you are working in conditions of ignorance. And rationality implies risk-aversion. (You would never agree to a distribution that was likely to leave you without water.) You want to ensure that you get as much as possible—this means choosing a distribution that will maximize the minimum. And your survival instinct is stronger than jealousy—this means that as long as you have enough water, you won't mind if someone else has even more, especially if that person may be able to help you in some other way.

Rawls concluded that his thought experiment vindicates his rules. "We shall want to say that certain principles of justice are justified because they would be agreed to in an initial situation of equality. I have emphasized that this original position is purely hypothetical."[2] Notice the counterfactual—"if people in an initial situation of equality were to agree to these principles of justice, then these principles would be justified." In other words, counterfactual reasoning determines the solution.

Yet Rawls's solution is controversial. Critics object to his assumptions about how human beings would respond in the

Original Position. Would you choose rationally under a veil of ignorance, and would your rationality take the form he suggested?

Much like Rawls's veil of ignorance, the use of the flash-sideways in the last season of *Lost* constitutes a provocative thought experiment—and they are equally controversial.

Closeness among Possible Worlds, or Why It Just Seems Wrong That Jack Fathered a Child with Juliet

One problem with counterfactuals is that it is hard to know their truth conditions. *Truth conditions* are the situations that make a particular statement true. Consider a counterfactual we discussed earlier: *if Sawyer weren't a con man, then he would have been a cop*. Recall that counterfactuals are conditions in which the antecedent—the "if" part of the conditional—isn't true. And in fact the antecedent *isn't* true: if we are to take the first seasons of *Lost* as what is actually true, then "Sawyer *isn't* a con man" is not a true statement. He *is* a con man—and a pretty good one. But why should we think that if Sawyer weren't a con man, then he would have been a cop, of all things? Maybe he would have been an armed mercenary, like Sayid, or a corrupt businessman, like Charles Widmore. To make matters more confusing, as David Lewis observes in his book *On the Plurality of Worlds*, possible worlds are divisible into parts: "There are ever so many ways that a part of a world could be; and so many and so varied are the other worlds that absolutely every way that a part of a world could possibly be is a way that some part of some world is."[3]

Yikes! So if Sawyer weren't a con man, he would have been a cop or an armed mercenary or a corrupt businessman or a spinal surgeon or a physicist who discovered a formula for moving backward in time? No—those last two just don't sound right. It's likely that were Sawyer not a con man, he would have been a cop or maybe even an armed mercenary. And it certainly isn't *impossible* that he could have been a spinal surgeon. But just because Sawyer *could* have been a spinal surgeon, that doesn't mean that the counterfactual—*if Sawyer weren't a con man, then he would have been a spinal surgeon*—is true. There needs to be some way to distinguish the counterfactuals about what *would* have been true from those that merely report what *could* have been true. Yet if using possible worlds is the primary way of interpreting counterfactuals, and all possible worlds are possible, then how do we distinguish what *would* be true from what *could* have been true?

In order to determine what *would* have been true and not merely what *could* have been true, philosophers look to the *closest* possible world. The closest possible world is the world that most resembles our own, except that in the closest possible world, the antecedent of the counterfactual is true, and the facts that make the antecedent true are also true.

For example, imagine a world in which James Ford's parents died after being conned by Tom Sawyer, a world in which James vows vengeance, but in which James doesn't become a con man. In that world everything else is the same—James is still the man from Tallahassee with the same thoughts, feelings, motive for vengeance, cynicism about human nature, and effortless charm. What better career than to be a cop, occasionally working undercover and using those skills and personality traits to trap aspiring con men? When we consider the closest possible world, we see that it makes sense to say: *if he weren't a con man, then he would have been a cop*. But when we examine another counterfactual—*if he weren't a con man, then he would have been a spinal surgeon*—this seems unlikely. To be a spinal surgeon, James would have spent decades in school, motivated by a deep desire to help people. It isn't clear that Sawyer even finished high school (he claims to have a high school transcript but is less forthcoming about his diploma). Sawyer has complex motivations, but no one ever accused him of having a deep desire to help others. This doesn't sound like the Sawyer most of us know (and many of us love).

The closest possible world to the actual world is the one in which the fewest facts are different from the actual world. Ideally, the only facts that are different are those facts that are sufficient to make the antecedent of the counterfactual true in that world. For this reason, understanding the "similarity relations" among possible worlds is paramount when using possible worlds semantics.

Lewis, in his essay "Counterfactual Dependence and Time's Arrow," says that similarities among possible worlds are governed by the following ordered priorities among natural laws (such as the law of gravity) and facts about the world:

(1) It is of the first importance to avoid big, widespread, diverse violations of the law.

(2) It is of the second importance to maximize the spatio-temporal region throughout which perfect match of particular fact prevails.

(3) It is of the third importance to avoid even small, localized, simple violations of the law.

(4) It is of little or no importance to secure approximate similarity of particular fact, even in matters that concern us greatly.[4]

In other words, if a single fact changed, even if that fact had significant consequences, then the world in which that one minor fact changed would be close to the actual world. For example, *if Locke had ducked when Anthony Cooper rushed at him, then he never would have been confined to a wheelchair*. In the closest possible world in which one small fact changed—Locke ducked, only a few feet—then everything would have been different for Locke. He would have had no impetus for signing up for a walkabout in Australia, and he wouldn't have been on flight 815. His whole life would have been different. Consider once again the counterfactual: *if Sawyer hadn't been a con man, then he would have been a cop.* In both worlds, James Ford's parents die at an early age because of a con man, while James vows vengeance and grows up cynical, yet charming. Along the way, though, one fact changes, and James, rather than becoming a con man, becomes a cop. (Given that the island had been destroyed in the closest possible world, that one fact may be James's childhood interaction with Jacob.) Some counterfactuals in the last season of *Lost*, such as this one, are entirely plausible.

Other counterfactuals in the last season of *Lost*, however, seem to violate Lewis's claims about what makes possible worlds more or less similar to the actual world. For example: *if the island had been destroyed, then Jack would have had a child with Juliet.* This counterfactual is problematic. The claim is that in the closest possible world, a world in which everything was the same except that the island was gone, Jack's life would have gone very differently from how it did in the actual world. Many facts about Jack's life would have been the same: his fraught relationship with his father, which led him to be emotionally distant from most people; his career; the fact that Claire was his long-lost half-sister; his being on flight 815.

Yet for the previously mentioned counterfactual about Jack to be true, we have to assume that Jack met someone more than ten years ago whom he otherwise wouldn't have (this isn't *too hard* to imagine). The woman he met would have been Juliet (a bit harder to imagine). She and Jack would have fallen in love, gotten married, and had a child (*much harder* to imagine, given that all of these other facts about his life remained the same). Having Jack and Juliet marry and giving them a son violates Lewis's requirement for similarity within the "spatio-temporal region throughout which perfect match of particular fact prevails." In other words, *too much* would change for viewers to reasonably assume that Jack and Juliet would have been married and had a son.

Counterfactuals give us a great a deal to think about in the last season of *Lost*. They help us understand that whereas a certain flash-sideways may have intuitive plausibility, another one may be implausible. They even help us make sense—along with a possible worlds semantics—of what would have happened if the island had been destroyed. It's enough to make you wonder: If you weren't a *Lost* fan, would you have found philosophy so much fun?

NOTES

1. John Rawls, *A Theory of Justice* (Cambridge, UK: Belknap Press, 1971).

2. Ibid., p. 21.

3. David Lewis, *On the Plurality of Worlds* (New York: Basil Blackwell, 1986), p. 2.

4. David Lewis, *Philosophical Papers: Volume II* (Oxford: Oxford University Press, 1986), p. 48.

PART TWO

O IS FOR ORIGIN

MEGA NUMBER

Your numbers are:
4, 8, 15, 16, 23

5

LOST IN DIFFERENT CIRCUMSTANCES

What Would You Do?

Charles Taliaferro and Dan Kastrul

Imagine that you were on Oceanic flight 815 and made it to the island. Life has abruptly become remarkably incongruous with life as you've known and understood it to be. Rather than interacting with people you are familiar with, you're now surrounded by a whole new group of people with differing, sometimes shifting, bizarre stories about their past. You are in shock but physically have survived relatively unscathed and possibly have been inexplicably healed from a previous injury. You can't help but notice that a lot of the people around you are better looking than average, which leads you to ponder the odds that your whole adventure is an accident, or perhaps it is somehow planned or controlled. All of this makes you further question whether you're truly alive. To be or not to be becomes a growing concern. I think, therefore I am, aren't I? Nevertheless, your mind continues to race forward with more questions than you can answer: Am I alive? If I am alive, will I be rescued? Until I'm rescued, how will I survive? Is the island real? Are my fellow castaways real? Am I imagining everything that's happening? If the people around me are real, are they truly the people they claim to be? Am *I* truly the person I claim to be? An even more troubling question: Am I the person I *believe* myself to be?

It's time for a reality check. Reflection on how you would act if you were in the world of *Lost* can shed light on your character. Would you let the numbers run down to zero and possibly endanger the whole world? If someone killed your loved one, would you seek revenge? If you encountered other inhabitants on the island, how would you treat them? How you *would* handle such different situations is important information about *who you are*.

Just Testing

Influenced by the ancient Greek philosopher Aristotle (384–322 B.C.E.), some contemporary philosophers argue that judging a person's character and action at any given time involves judging how the person would act under different conditions.

Imagine a neighbor, Fritz, who appears good-natured, but who would be a vicious scoundrel had he not married into a wealthy family. If we have reason to believe that working for a living would make him mean, don't we have reason to question the apparent niceness that easy money has afforded him?

Mr. Eko is another case in point. Whether he was heroically saving lives or brutally and heartlessly snuffing them out seems to have been very much driven by circumstance. He doesn't hesitate to kill an innocent elder villager when he believes that such drastic action is necessary to prevent ruthless guerrillas from killing his brother. He clearly is a loyal ally in certain situations, as well as a formidable adversary in others.

Another example is Benjamin Linus. When the castaways first find him, he explicitly and emphatically states he is one of the "good guys" and, in so doing, implies that there are bad guys lurking nearby. On the one hand, he frees Locke's leg from an entanglement with the hatch blast door, perhaps saving his life. On the other hand, he murders the very same man when it suits his purposes. Is Ben a good guy in some circumstances and a bad guy in others?

Aristotle's view is that many of the ways in which we describe ourselves ethically have distinctive implications for what would happen or what we would do under very different conditions. So, for example, the courageous person is not someone who is *always* performing brave acts under all conditions. Even brave people need to sleep once in a while. Yet being a courageous person means that the person would act bravely if faced with a dangerous situation. In this sense, the term *courage* is like other dispositional terms, such as *vain* or *irritable*, which imply future, probable behavior. Not necessarily all the time—but at least sometimes—the vain person boasts too much, and the irritable person frequently displays anger without much provocation. Likewise, the characters of Mr. Eko and Ben are not merely what they do, but what they *would* do.

Aristotle's teacher, Plato, conceived a famous thought experiment concerning hypothetical conditions. It asks you to imagine what you would do if you found a ring that would render you invisible. If you're honest, you'll admit that you would do all kinds of things you shouldn't, thereby proving that you are not innately good. Because of its historical importance and because we will have reason to discuss it again, we quote Plato's thought experiment, known as "The Myth of Gyges," at length:

> According to the tradition, Gyges was a shepherd [coincidence?] in the service of the king of Lydia; there was a great storm, and an earthquake made an opening in the earth even more incredible than the hatch [coincidence?] at the place where he was feeding his flock. Amazed at the sight, he descended into the opening,

where, among other marvels, he beheld a hollow brazen horse, having doors, at which he stooping and looking in saw a dead body of stature, as appeared to him, more than human, and having nothing on but a gold ring; this he took from the finger of the dead and reascended. Now the shepherds met together, according to custom, that they might send their monthly report about the flocks to the king; into their assembly he came having the ring on his finger, and as he was sitting among them he chanced to turn the collet of the ring inside his hand, when instantly he became invisible to the rest of the company and they began to speak of him as if he were no longer present. He was astonished at this, and again touching the ring he turned the collet outwards and reappeared; he made several trials of the ring, and always with the same result—when he turned the collet inwards he became invisible, when outwards he reappeared. Whereupon he contrived to be chosen one of the messengers who were sent to the court; where as soon as he arrived he seduced the queen, and with her help conspired against the king and slew him, and took the kingdom. Suppose now that there were two such magic rings, and the just put on one of them and the unjust the other; no man can be imagined to be of such an iron nature that he would stand fast in justice. No man would keep his hands off what was not his own when he could safely take what he liked out of the market, or go into houses and lie with any one at his pleasure, or kill or release from prison whom he would, and in all respects be like a God among men. Then the actions of the just would be as the actions of the unjust; they would both come at last to the same point. And this we may truly affirm to be a great proof that a man is just, not willingly or because he thinks that justice is any good to him individually, but of necessity, for wherever any one thinks that he can safely be unjust, there he is unjust.[1]

At least initially, the case for injustice seems quite forceful. If you had such a ring, wouldn't you do at least some things that are considered immoral? If the only reason we do "the right thing" is because we fear being caught, our ethical character is quite weak.

The Myth of Gyges thought experiment would probably expose the true character of more than one person on the island. Sun, prior to the crash of flight 815 and even during her early days on the island, comes to mind as one whose ethical character cries out for maturity and moral development. Sun tends to do what she pleases, unless or until she gets caught. Even as a little girl, after she accidentally breaks her father's glass ballerina, she does not own up to the truth and accuses the maid of breaking it, causing the maid to be fired. Sun, after learning that she is pregnant, does not tell her husband, Jin, about her affair. Jin is sterile, but up until Sun's pregnancy, he is led to believe that Sun is unable to conceive. Even though it turns out that the baby was conceived after the plane wreck and Jin is miraculously the father, one cannot help but imagine what Sun would do if she had the ring of Gyges.

Although the Gyges thought experiment would expose Sun's inner character, we disagree with the claim that it describes what most, let alone all, human beings would do.

What a Bunch of Characters!

In a sense, our question of what you would do if you were on the island could be asked of many different settings from television, film, theater, and literature. For example, would you have committed suicide if you were in the position of Leo Tolstoy's tragic heroine Anna Karenina? Island narratives, however, are especially effective in bringing to the fore a person's character because they invite us to entertain what we would do when separated from our cultural home. Consider two island narratives from the past that bear some relation to *Lost*: the Homeric epic poetry about Odysseus on Calypso's island, and Daniel Defoe's famous eighteenth-century story of a surviving shipwrecked sailor, *Robinson Crusoe*.

In Homer's poem the *Odyssey*, Odysseus is on a ten-year journey from the ruins of Troy back to his homeland, Ithaca, where his wife and son are waiting for him. Early on during his voyage home, Odysseus is washed up on the island of Ogygia, where Calypso, a beautiful divine nymph, takes him captive. He is placed under her spell as her lover and bondsman for a full seven years. He is tempted by her beauty and her promise of immortality (eternal youth) to forget his family, but eventually he pleads successfully with Calypso to release him and help him make his journey homeward.

This story illustrates a choice that some of us face: pursuit of the dream of endless youthful pleasure (with Eros) or commitment to a home and family and coming to terms with age. When Odysseus does come home, there is (after he rids the palace of rivals and enemies) a scene of enviable domestic joy. Odysseus and his wife, Penelope, spend their first night together doing three things: telling each other stories of their time apart, making love, and sleeping. Homer's epic effectively uses the narrative of life on an island so that its main character can discover whom he really loves (Penelope, not Calypso) and what he really stands for (loyalty, not self-gratification).

In *The Life and Strange Surprising Adventures of Robinson Crusoe of York, Mariner* (to give the full title of the book), a man of considerable wealth and ambition is completely cut off from his past life when he becomes shipwrecked on an island off the coast of South America. Rather than discover his commitment to true romantic and marital love, as Odysseus does, he comes to discover the need to understand his life in relationship with God. Crusoe moves from someone who earlier had designs to engage in the slave trade to someone who is moved by compassion and piety. Defoe suggested that without this radical break from "civilization," this transformation would not have taken place. After two years on the island, Crusoe records in his journal:

> It is now that I began sensibly to feel so much more happy this life I now led was, with all its miserable circumstances, than the wicked, cursed, abominable life I led all the past part of my days; and now I changed both my sorrows and my joys; my very desires altered, my affections changed their gusts, and my delights were perfectly new from what they were at my first coming.[2]

Being on the island provides a unique context for self-awareness and self-transformation.

Lost has some resonance with both of these classic works. As with the *Odyssey*, there is enchantment and good and bad magic and the opportunity to determine what one truly loves. And as with *Robinson Crusoe*, there are spiritual transformations with brooding hints of mystery and providence. There is also something of the existential feel to *Lost* that Defoe achieved in his book. Like Crusoe, there is a sense in which the characters are split, carrying some things from their home, but also encountering that which is strange and unpredictable. Consider the following exchange from "Tabula Rasa":

> Sawyer: You're just wasting your time, trying to save a guy who, last time I checked, had a piece of metal the size of my head sticking out of his bread basket. Let me ask you something. How many of those pills are you going to use to fix him up?
> Jack: As many as it takes.
> Sawyer: Yeah? How many you got? You're just not looking at the big picture, Doc. You're still back in civilization.

Jack: Yeah? And where are you?
Sawyer: Me? I'm in the wild.

This fascinating boundary between the wild and the "civilized" puts *Lost* squarely in the great tradition of island narratives that explore questions of character and identity.

There is a complex relationship between who the castaways were before the crash of flight 815 and who they've become since then. We learned, for example, that Michael's past was vexing. The mother of his son, Walt, had run off to Amsterdam to pursue her law career. Many years later, shortly after Walt's mother died in Sydney, Walt's adopted father asks Michael to assume custody of Walt. Michael is just getting to know Walt when, in the course of the father's and son's effort to escape the island, Walt is kidnapped by the Others. Michael serendipitously manages to find Walt, but in so doing, also becomes a captive of the Others. In order to escape, Michael cuts a deal: he gets Walt back, no strings attached, provided that he rescue Ben and ensure that Sawyer, Hurley, Kate, and Jack are captured. Michael is a man on a mission, and in passionately pursuing this quest to be reunited with his son, he executes two innocent women in cold blood (Ana Lucia and Libby).

Prior to that moment of extreme action, who would have thought that Michael was capable of murder? Yet the fact that he is means that his character is vulnerable and insecure. We find it revealing that Michael is not at Jack's father's funeral in the afterlife reunion, nor is he anywhere to be found during the entire afterlife segment.

Offering an interesting contrast to Michael's character is that of Charlie. Prior to the crash of flight 815, Charlie was a heroin addict. On the island, he overcomes his addiction (with a little help from his friend Locke), despite the fact that there is heroin on the island. Charlie continues to demonstrate his worthiness when he manages to turn off the switch in the underwater Looking Glass station, thereby preventing island communications from being blocked and opening the door to rescue. This brave deed costs him his life. Curiously, in the afterlife segment, once again Charlie is addicted to heroin. A deep flaw remains beneath his lovable personality.

James Ford, aka Sawyer, is quite the opposite. Underneath his hardened, sassy facade is a smart, sensitive, brave soul. Although he is always looking out for himself and has great survival instincts, he never hesitates to put himself in harm's way if such action results in saving his friends. For instance, he jumps out of a rescue helicopter into the ocean to save the lives of the other passengers. Sawyer clearly emerges to be one of the truest heroes of the entire cast of castaways. In these and other character surprises, *Lost* accurately reflects the unpredictable nature of human psychology.

Obviously, there have been and will continue to be layers upon layers of mystery in *Lost*. Many of our earlier questions have been answered, especially with regard to the origin of polar bears on the island; the identities of Jacob, the Others, and the French Woman; the contents of Jacob's list; and specifics of the Dharma Initiative. New questions have emerged, though. How does Jack get himself out of the hole and back to the spot where he dies? How does everyone manage to see Jacob? Whatever becomes of Richard Alpert? Does Jacob's brother have a first name? Does evil have a first name? What is the significance of Jack's dying at the very spot where he first awoke when landing on the island? What does it mean if in fact there is "no here, now," as Christian Shephard explains to his son, Jack? One of the qualities that has made and will continue to make *Lost* so special is the show's ability to stimulate our imaginations and present a story in such a way as to leave it open to multiple interpretations.

Lost takes a dramatic turn when the numbers are allowed to reach zero, as this threatens to bring about an apocalyptic end to the world. The word *apocalypse* comes from the words *apo* ("to remove") and *calypse* ("covering"). So the term *apocalypse* can be interpreted as meaning the removal of Calypso (removing the mere appearances of what you want, to get to what really matters). The fact that discovering the truth about the machine in the hatch might involve real destruction fits in with the long-standing warning in Greek tragedy that discovering your own identity can bring about disaster. (Recall that Calypso is also the name of the nymph goddess who kept Odysseus on her island so long.) Despite the driving force of the role of mystery in the *Lost* narratives and the threat that revelation and the uncovering of appearances may be destructive, there is a hunger in the main characters to uncover appearances and to get at what truly happened or is happening, come what may. Consider this briefly in connection with Kate and Jack.

We have a colorful glimpse of Kate's past, as she blows up her abusive father, runs away from the law, kills her boyfriend, robs a bank, and travels on flight 815 as a prisoner under federal marshal escort. Yet somehow, in light of this tumultuous history, we cannot help but be taken with Kate. She doesn't realize the abusive man she killed is her biological father until after the deed is executed. She doesn't mean for her boyfriend to die and is truly in love with him. She doesn't rob the bank for money but to recover a keepsake in a safety deposit box. How can we not be impressed by such heartbreak? This is a woman who tries to help out her mother by killing her mother's abuser, is genuinely in love and has that taken away from her, and goes to any extreme to "right" a wrong. Kate manages to fall in love again, with a policeman, but realizes she must tell him the truth, that she is a fugitive from the law. Kate is highly intelligent, compassionate, and committed to her beliefs, even when none of this is rewarded by society. In that sense, and based on her behavior while on the island, an argument can be made that she is brave and honorable, even in the face of conflicting evidence.

A key motivation in Kate's character is to know both herself and the others. It is as if she would love to have a *visibility* ring—a ring that would make clear what others are really thinking or wanting. In the afterlife segment, Kate is still a fugitive, but this time insists she is innocent. We believe her. If the eyes are truly the window to one's soul, all one needs to do is look into Kate's eyes to recognize that she's a remarkable soul.

On awakening from the crash, Jack is immediately thrust into a leadership role, tries desperately to save lives, heals the injured, and encourages everyone to work together for the common good. Jack is slow to trust but quick to try to do the right thing. He is a logical thinker thrust into an illogical environment. How does he make sense of his predicament? Can he reconcile the new, bizarre direction his life has taken? In order for Jack to truly understand his fate, he needs to first undergo a major paradigm shift regarding the circumstances he finds himself in.

One of the first steps in Jack's journey toward reconciliation of his castaway existence is when he believes the evidence that is presented to him, namely, that the Red Sox have finally won the World Series. Once he can fathom this, time travel, hydrogen bombs neutralizing electromagnetic radiation, and having a purpose to return to the island become child's play for him. Although Locke and Jack are often on opposite ends of different issues, both need to learn to "let go."

Kate and Jack are not mere Lotus Eaters, those creatures in Homer's *Odyssey* who placidly give themselves over to idle, drugged pleasures. They are energized by the quest for self-awareness and values, avoiding what Crusoe laments as the "stupidity of [his] soul, without desire for Good, or Conscience of Evil."[3] They want to come to terms with happiness, joy, and sorrow. And viewers are invited to participate in this quest, as we identify with the characters or resonate with their decisions and failures.

While endorsing this overridingly positive interpretation of the show, we think that *Lost* is a tad closer to Homer's world than to Defoe's. Amid all of his adventures, Defoe's Crusoe comes to believe in an all-good, all-powerful, provident God. *Lost*'s characters, in contrast, seem to live in something like Homer's strange cosmos of competing deities, only some of which are good.

The Ball's in Your Court!

Lost is bizarre on many fronts. The show offers profoundly improbable narratives in terms of persons and nature, but the one thing it does not offer is a complete reversal of values. Kidnapping children is still evil, even when the kidnappers think they have a really good reason for doing so. If, however, *Lost* involved a complete reversal of values, our thought experiments would collapse. Imagine that the show advanced the following premises: on the island cruel kidnapping is actually good, as is betraying friends, theft for personal gain, cowardice, and so on. Courage, compassion, fidelity, justice, fairness, care, and so on are all evil. Let's further imagine that the show asks us to accept these premises as not only about what is labeled "good" and "evil" but about the morality of the island itself. In this scenario, viewers are asked to imagine that cruel kidnapping is actually deserving of praise on the island; it is worthy of love and attention, while compassion truly is worthy of blame. Under this condition of complete reversal, let's go to our question: What would you do on that island?

With such a radical reversal of values, the question would lack sense, for it involves what might be called a moral impossibility. Although customs change across cultures (especially in matters of politeness and shame), if morality has *any* normative force, it cannot be regarded as *completely* relative to context. To take an extreme, particularly grotesque claim: if it is truly the case that skinning and salting a child is wrong, this cannot be wrong only in New Jersey. To bring this point home, consider the most good person you know. If you asked her or him the following question, "If you were on an island where skinning and salting babies is good, would you do it?" what do you think the person's response would be? His or her reaction would range from horror to an embarrassed, forced laugh—thinking that you were (unsuccessfully) making a joke. No person who is truly good would say that, oh yes, if it turned out that justice and compassion and so on were evil, and that skinning and salting babies good, they would get to work right away on such a cruel mission.

You can imagine worlds with radically different technology or laws of nature, but once you try to reverse all values, the world you are imagining will slip into what we can only find incoherent. So, in Homer's *Odyssey*, readers for at least the last twenty-five hundred years have enjoyed the story about the enchantress Circe who turns Odysseus's poor, unsuspecting men into swine, and they have cheered Odysseus on when he gets them changed back into human beings. We don't have to believe that there are such enchantresses in order to enjoy the story, but we do have to suppose that transforming humans into swine against their wishes is, well, at least not good, especially if the change is permanent and there is a lively market for pork.

Our thesis was stated quite well in a short story, "The Blue Cross," written in 1911 by G. K. Chesterton. In the story, the main character makes the following assertion about the permanency of overriding values.

> Reason and justice grip the remotest and the loneliest star. Look at those stars. Don't they look as if they were single diamonds and sapphires? Well, you can imagine any mad botany or geology you please. Think of forests of adamant with leaves of brilliance. Think the moon is a blue moon, a single elephantine sapphire. But don't fancy that all that frantic astronomy would make the smallest difference to the reason and justice of conduct. On plains of opal, under cliffs cut out of pearl, you would still find a notice-board, "Thou shalt not steal."[4]

We are not claiming that morality is as clear-cut as reading a notice board or that (except in our grotesque case involving salt) it is always obvious what acts are right and wrong. We are claiming, however, that if we ask our "What would you do if you were in that world?" question about a world in which values are completely overturned, the thought experiment cannot shed light on who you are now.

Hurley's pre-island history is certainly mystifying, especially his experiences of winning the lottery, suffering an unending streak of bad luck, and being locked up in a psych ward. In the episode "Dave," Hurley struggles with reality when his friend Dave appears to him. Is Dave imaginary, a ghost, or the creation of a manipulative Smoke Monster? He must be real in some sense, because when he hits Hurley on the head Hurley experiences pain. Yet how can Dave be real, since no one else perceives him? Hurley might wonder whether he genuinely is shipwrecked on a remote island, or whether the island is simply a metaphor representing the confines of a psych ward. Is Libby real? Hurley finds it difficult to believe that a woman so beautiful inside and out could be even remotely attracted to him. Apparently, two kisses from Libby are enough to convince Hurley that perhaps he really is on an island and Libby's affection for him is genuine. If he is correct, then he has much to look forward to. If not, why not end it all by jumping off a cliff, as Dave suggests, only to find himself waking up in a psych ward or, worse, assuring himself one doozy of a "cluckity-cluck-cluck day" by becoming a rotting mass of out-of-luck-beach-muck? At this juncture, Hurley opts to accept help from his friend Libby, heads back to camp, and moves forward with what appears to be his life.

While much was not evident to Hurley, what is clear is that in *Lost* there remains a core realization of basic goods and evils. If Libby lures Hurley to a premature violent death, this is bad. If she turns out to be a true friend and helps him recover, this is good. These value judgments remain stable, even when we are not clear about the conditions of our own reality.

Life Goes On

If you talk with ten different *Lost* fans, be prepared to receive ten unique perspectives about what has transpired on the show at any point in time. Although certain viewpoints can and will be debated for years, perhaps generations, to come, once the smoke clears *Lost* is about the journey of the soul and how important it is that we learn to "live together" so that we don't "die alone." As souls, we develop with the help of other souls, whom we are also helping to develop. We see a powerful example of such help in the afterlife segment, when Hurley reaches out once again to Sayid and convincingly explains to him that he can't let other people tell him who he is. He has to find that out for himself.

Lost has likely impacted us in more ways than we realize. How many devoted fans of *Lost* will think of Sawyer and Juliet the next time they use a vending machine? We certainly will. And just for the record, one of our favorite pearls of wisdom was offered by Miles when he mused, "I don't believe in a lot of things, but I do believe in duct tape."

For some characters—notably Locke—the island at times seems to be heaven. For others, such as Michael, the island appears to be hell. Yet for most, it is simply an exotic stopover on the journey of the soul.

So how about it, readers? How would *you* fare if faced with situations similar to those experienced by the survivors of flight 815 on *Lost*? Can you look yourself straight in the face and know in your heart of hearts that you'd survive with a little help from your fellow castaways, with your character and integrity fully intact?[5]

We leave you with a quote we first heard from Desmond: "See you in another life, yeah?" ("Man of Science, Man of Faith")

NOTES

1. Plato, *The Republic*, trans. Benjamin Jowett, numerous editions (including online), Book II.

2. Daniel Defoe, *Robinson Crusoe* (New York: Cosmopolitan Book Corp., 1920), chap. 9.

3. Ibid.

4. G. K. Chesterton, "The Blue Cross" in *The Innocence of Father Brown* (NuVision Publications, 2008) pp. 7–22.

5. We thank Sharon Kaye for her encouragement of this project and the opportunity to contribute to *The Ultimate Lost and Philosophy*. Thanks also to Tricia Little and Elisabeth Granquist for comments and assistance on earlier drafts.

"DON'T MISTAKE COINCIDENCE FOR FATE"

Lost Theories and Coincidence

Briony Addey

The flashback sequences of *Lost* were littered with apparently accidental connections between the characters' lives. In season 1, for example, we see Sawyer and Boone cross paths in an Australian police station, as Sawyer is arrested (in "Exodus") while Boone is making a complaint against Shannon's boyfriend ("Hearts and Minds"). By the end of the series we learned that many of the connections between the characters were no accident.

If you're like me, you were drawn to the show because you have experienced weird coincidences and wondered whether they had any significance. What exactly is a coincidence, though, and do coincidences ever really occur?

Take Your Chances

The *Oxford English Dictionary* defines *coincidence* as "a remarkable concurrence of events or circumstances without apparent causal connection."[1] Digging a little deeper, we can say that a concurrence of events or entities, say, A and B, must fulfill three criteria to qualify as a coincidence.

1. Those events or the entities, A and B, must have been previously connected in some way, X.
2. The events or the entities, A and B, now concur, not because of that previous connection X, but seemingly randomly.
3. The concurrence is improbable and therefore surprising or unexpected.

A good example from *Lost* is Jack meeting Desmond in the hatch. The two men had a previous connection, their conversation in the stadium in L.A.; their meeting in the hatch doesn't seem to be causally connected to that previous connection; and the meeting in the hatch seems highly improbable. Therefore, the meeting in the hatch appears to be a genuine coincidence.

Take Your Pick

Whether the various connections between characters were genuine coincidences made a huge difference to the type of answers that viewers of *Lost* gave to the question "What the hell is going on?" Of course, the viewers were not the only ones trying to figure this out. The castaways themselves had literally crashed into a situation that became more puzzling with each passing day. There have been many questions. What is the "sickness"? What was the Dharma Initiative up to? What is the black smoke? What was the monster/security system? The structure of the show for the first three seasons, alternating between thematically linked scenes of life on the island and flashbacks to life before the crash, suggested that there was some kind of real connection between the castaways and the island. Just think of Locke and his belief that it was his destiny to go on a walkabout.

While some viewers thought that all of the connections were purely accidental, others thought they were meant to be. Philosophically, the idea that someone is meant to be in a particular place at a particular time could be a description of one of three related but different theories: divine providence, fate, and determinism.

Divine providence is the idea that God has a plan for all of us. To say that the plane crash in *Lost* was providential is to say that it happened under the watchful eye of God, that what occurs does so because God wills it. Desmond would surely disagree. As he says, "Not even God can see this island!" ("Live Together, Die Alone")

We've all heard people make comments concerning someone's fate, such as "He was fated to die in a plane crash" (as we could perhaps say of the unfortunate Boone). There are also generally fatalistic comments like "It was inevitable that she would go insane" (as maybe some people say of Rousseau). Fatalism is the idea that no matter what choices a person makes, a certain thing will happen to him or her.

The most famous story concerning fate is *Oedipus Rex*. Oedipus is told that his fate is to kill his father and sleep with his mother. He desperately wants to avoid this and so leaves what he thinks is his family, not knowing that he was adopted. Even though he does everything he can to prevent these events from coming to pass, his rash nature makes him kill a stranger who has insulted him at a crossroad and marry a woman who turns out to be the stranger's widow. Unwittingly, he has fulfilled the prophecy, because the man at the crossroad was his father, the widow his mother.

Determinism is the idea that every event (including thoughts and actions) is necessitated by previous events and natural laws. According to fatalism, if one's doing X is fated, one will do X no matter what one decides or chooses. According to determinism, however, if one's doing X is determined, that's because one can only choose to do X, given previous events and the laws of nature. With fate, it seems that human choice is ineffective, whereas with determinism human choice is effective, within certain limits, as it forms links in causal chains. So we might say that Jack's being on Oceanic flight 815 was determined, not because he would have been on the flight no matter what decision he made, but because given certain facts about the kind of man he is, his choice to fly to Australia to find his father was itself inevitable.

All three theories seem to create problems for free will. If you believe in divine providence and that everything happens according to God's plan, which was formulated before your birth, how do you freely choose anything? If events in your life are fated, no matter what you do, how are you in control of anything in your life? If every event in the universe is determined, then that includes all of the choices you will ever make, in which case how are they really choices?

All three theories—divine providence, fatalism, and determinism—are linked to the idea of coincidence. Sometimes a belief in one of these theories will be sparked by an experience of an amazing and seemingly meaningful coincidence. If a man's plane crashes on an island where his brother's plane crashed years before, and he is a religious man, he might come to believe that it is part of God's plan. If a man who believes it is his destiny to go on a spiritual quest in a harsh, physically challenging environment crashes on an uninhabited island, he might believe it is fate. Sometimes the strange coincident events that happen to us seem so incredible that we suppose there must be some explanation other than chance or randomness. The explanation sometimes involves a divine force (providence) or a mysterious destiny (fate) or a kind of necessity (determinism).

In the third season, we discover Desmond's experience of going back in time, of revisiting past experiences with "memories" of the events on the island, which seems to have been a result of being blown up with the hatch. We discover that Desmond has flashes, apparent visions of the future, which resemble the memories of the future he had in that revisitation. He meets a woman (Eloise Hawking, in "Flashes Before Your Eyes") who tells Desmond that everyone has a path, and that the universe "has a way of course correcting." So when Desmond has a precognition of Charlie's death, he knows that no matter how many times he saves Charlie, the universe will "course correct" and Charlie will die. This idea seems to fit with fatalism, as Mrs. Hawking assures Desmond that choice isn't a factor: "It's your path to go to the island. You don't do it because you choose to, Desmond. You do it because you're supposed to." It appears that Locke's talk of what's "supposed to happen" (in "Through the Looking Glass") isn't far off the mark. For all of Jacob's talk of choice and free will, he brought the candidates to the island—at least that much appears to have been fated.

Jung and Locke

Carl Jung (1875–1961), the famous Swiss psychiatrist, was intrigued by the stories of meaningful and improbable coincidences that he came across in his investigations of what he termed the "collective unconscious." Through the theory of "synchronicity," Jung attempted to explain such coincidences. According to Jung, while some coincidences are simply meaningless, meaningful coincidences consist of the concurrence of (1) a person having a dream, an idea, an image, a premonition, or some other kind of unconscious mental state; and (2) some objective, external event that shares some significant feature with the mental state. For example, Jung had a patient who recounted to him a dream that she had the night before about a golden scarab. At that moment, a gentle tapping on the window drew Jung's attention to a scarab beetle (or its closest European equivalent) at the window.[2]

Jung saw synchronicity as a way of explaining certain kinds of acausal (uncaused) events that involve the psychic (or mental) and physical worlds. Such uncaused events require explanation (beyond saying that they are purely random or chance events) because they seem to be ordered. Acausal events that involve the mental and the physical worlds are governed by synchronicity in the same way that most events are governed by the principle of causation.

Locke seems to believe that at least some of the events, both on the island and leading up to the plane crash, are too improbable to be mere coincidences, but it is unclear whether he believes in fate or synchronicity.

In the episode "What Kate Did," Locke has a conversation with Mr. Eko about the pieces of the orientation film and says, "I mean, think about it. Somebody made this film. Someone else cut this piece out. We crash—two halves of the same plane fall in different parts of the island—you're over there, I'm over here. And now, here's the missing piece right back where it belongs. What are the odds?" Eko replies, "Don't mistake coincidence for fate."

In the episode "Man of Science, Man of Faith," Jack mocks Locke's belief by saying, "Is this what you were talking about, Locke? Is this your destiny? All roads lead here." So, it seems that the other characters think that Locke believes in fate.

Yet in the flashbacks of the episode "Walkabout," Locke has a strong feeling that he is meant to experience a situation with none of the comforts of Western lifestyles that will change him spiritually, and we see that his trip to Australia is an attempt to have that experience by being part of a walkabout (an ancient aboriginal spiritual journey in which the participant forms a special relationship with the land). When this ambition is thwarted Locke gets on Oceanic flight 815 to travel back home, which, of course, crashes on the island and starts a chain of events that leads to his having the exact experience that he believes he was meant to have. The belief, plus the coincidence of his experience on the island, could thus be seen as an example of synchronicity. Whatever the case, it seems clear that Locke has faith that the events and the coincidences are not merely accidental or random.

The Birthday Paradox

One central element of a coincidence is that it is improbable. If I walk out of my front door and bump into my neighbor, we would not call this a coincidence because it is pretty likely that this will happen on a somewhat regular basis. If, on the other hand, I walk out of my front door and bump into my long-lost cousin who has returned from the other side of the world with his new wife, who just so happens to live on my street, this highly improbable occurrence would be a coincidence. Still, as Locke observes, if something is *too* unlikely, this may suggest that it cannot be a coincidence, but rather must somehow be meant to happen. So we have a sliding scale of probabilities: too probable to be called a coincidence, just improbable enough to be called a coincidence, and too improbable to be called a coincidence.

Can we trust ourselves to judge how probable an event is, though? A famous philosophical puzzle called the birthday paradox indicates that the answer is no. Here is the puzzle (try it yourself before reading on to the answer): If there are twenty-three people in a room, how likely is it that two of them have the same birthday (excluding the year)?

Many people are surprised to learn that there is a 50 percent chance that two of those people will share a birthday. We're inclined to reason that if there are 367 people, 2 of them will definitely share a birthday, so for a 50 percent chance, we simply have to divide this figure in half. We therefore expect that for a 50 percent chance of 2 people sharing a birthday, there would have to be a group of roughly 183.

Ask your friends to try the birthday paradox and you will see just how terrible people are at guessing probabilities. Probability theorists use this puzzle to show that human beings are prone to judge situations to be less likely than they actually are. In fact, if you were at a party of about twenty-three people and found yourself talking to someone who shared your birthday, you would probably exclaim, "What an extraordinary coincidence!" And you might secretly begin to wonder whether there was some significance to your meeting this person, when in fact there was nothing extraordinary about the meeting at all.

Another way that our intuitions about probability lead us astray is in thinking about the probability of a particular hand in cards. Taken in itself, a bridge hand containing thirteen hearts is no less likely than any other bridge hand. There are a possible 635,013,559,600 different thirteen-card bridge hands, and any particular hand is equally improbable: 1 in 635,013,559,600. Of course, the odds of getting a hand specified in advance are much longer.

Consider also the law of truly large numbers. This law states that with an extremely large number of events, you would expect all kinds of events to occur, even occasionally very improbable events. For example, if you played enough poker, eventually you would expect to see a perfect hand of cards dealt to you. It would be highly improbable if no highly improbable events occurred! This also implies that given a large number of people, events that would be rare per person will be likely to occur to someone or other. After all, someone or other has to win the lottery, even though you would be amazed if it turned out to be you.

Consider the number of clients and employees Hurley deals with now that he is the CEO of a large company. That large number makes it more likely that he should bump into Locke, who works for a box company that Hurley owns, than if Hurley owned only a small business.

When we assess reasoning about apparent coincidences, we need to consider the possibility of *confirmation bias*: the tendency to ignore evidence that contradicts our theory or preconceptions or to search for information that supports them. In part to combat confirmation bias, the philosopher of science Karl Popper (1902–1994) emphasized the importance of falsifiability. Scientists must construct hypotheses that are in principle falsifiable and then seek to falsify them.

Confirmation bias connects with what is happening when people register "amazing" coincidences. We hear about and experience a great many events each day, but when one event coincides somehow with one of the great many dreams, thoughts, and images we have recently experienced, we take notice. We tend to ignore considerations that would falsify, or at least undermine to some extent, the remarkableness of the coincidence. In particular, we ignore two things:

1. All of the other different events that might have happened and would have been considered just as much of an amazing coincidence
2. The number of chances there are for us to experience something coincidental when we don't

There is also the problem of multiple endpoints. Whereas the odds of a particular event specified in advance (as an "endpoint") may be very low, the odds of a number of similar events could be pretty high. For example, while making a long trip on the highway, you are likely to see some vanity plates. When you see one that seems to be speaking directly to you (URCOOL), you may be struck by the coincidence. But, of course, any number of vanity plates may have "spoken to you."

Likewise, it seems really unlikely for Jack to meet Desmond on the island when he previously met him in L.A. Yet when we consider the number of people whom someone like Jack (a social, professional man in his thirties, who lives in a huge city) comes into contact with, along with the fact that if it were any of those people whom Jack met in the hatch it would seem to be an equally amazing coincidence, the coincidence doesn't seem quite as unlikely.

Noticing patterns and coincidences is a very important human skill. Much learning in children, such as language acquisition, depends on it, and many discoveries in the sciences also depend on it. When a scientist observes a coincidence or a regularity, he or she postulates that there is some kind of explanation for it, that it is not simply random, and proceeds on that basis, thinking about and inferring from the data what the best explanation for the phenomenon might be. This is called *inference to the best explanation*. The scientist then has a hypothesis or a theory that he or she can test by attempting to falsify it.

So maybe, if we were to approach *Lost* by theorizing scientifically, we, too, should make the assumption that the coincidences aren't merely random. We should make an inference to the best explanation and then test the hypothesis that we formulate.

It's a Small World, After All

Were the connections between the castaways really that unlikely or improbable? In the 1960s, the famous psychologist Stanley Milgram did a series of experiments called the "Small World Study." The experiment was set up so that randomly selected "starters" in one part of the United States were given a folder. The object was to get the folder to a specified person, the target, in another part of the country by sending the folder on to an acquaintance who might know the target. The experiment resulted in the famous phrase "six degrees of separation." Milgram thought that it proved that each person in the United States was connected to any other through an average of six people.[3]

A popular game based on this idea is Six Degrees of Kevin Bacon, in which players have to connect any actor to Kevin Bacon in as few connections as possible. For example, Matthew Fox, the actor who plays Jack, was in the TV show

Party of Five with the actress Neve Campbell, who was in the movie *Wild Things* with Kevin Bacon. Connections between people is a theme that fascinates *Lost's* cocreator J. J. Abrams. In fact, one of his other shows, which chronicles the lives of six New Yorkers and the ways their lives intersect in seemingly random ways, was titled *Six Degrees*.

Coincidence vs. Conspiracy

Most recent historical events have some conspiracy theories attached to them. There are conspiracy nuts who, for example, think that the moon landings were faked by the Americans in order to win the space race and get one up on the Russians in the cold war. Conspiracy theorists often cite strange, highly improbable coincidences surrounding events such as the moon landing as proof that there is more going on than meets the eye, because they find the coincidences too improbable to be truly coincidental. They call anyone who disagrees and believes they are simply weird coincidences *coincidence theorists*.

Theories about *Lost* while it was airing can be divided into two categories: those concocted by people who feel the need for an explanation of the connections between the characters (the conspiracy theorists) and those devised by people who don't (the coincidence theorists). It turns out, of course, that the conspiracy theorists were right about *Lost*. There was a hidden causal connection underlying the apparent coincidences between the castaways—their candidacy and Jacob's influence in bringing them to the island. Constructing a theory about a phenomenon involves knowing which aspects of the phenomenon are significant and need to be explained. In this case, it appears that the coincidences were significant, but in our theorizing about life, the universe, and everything, we can go drastically wrong (through confirmation bias, misunderstandings of probability, and so on) when we mistakenly think that a feature of a phenomenon is significant.

Jacob Have I Loved

It's a common complaint among *Lost* fans that the castaways display an almost unfathomable lack of curiosity. In season 6, the nature and the purpose of Jacob's experiment become more and more obvious: to test the candidates to see who's morally worthy to become his successor. Yet the fact that all of the candidates are (until very near the end of the experiment) ignorant of this is problematic.

First, let's consider a defense of Jacob's methodology. It's straightforwardly true that with some types of experiment, you get better results by deceiving participants about the nature of the experiment (these are known as deception experiments). When Jacob is asked by Richard Alpert in "Ab Aeterno" why he doesn't help the candidates he brings to the island, Jacob explains his reasoning to some extent: "Because I wanted them to help themselves. To know the difference between right and wrong without me having to tell them."

Consider Milgram's "Obedience Experiment." Participants were told that they were part of an experiment to study the effects of painful stimulus on learning. They were asked to administer electric shocks to "subjects" (actually, actors who were in on the deception) when they answered questions incorrectly in a memory test. The "voltage" (no one was actually shocked; all of the equipment was fake) ranged from mildly painful to extremely painful (and near fatal). If the participants knew that the real purpose of the experiment was to see how far they would go in administering the shocks, then their behavior would be changed by this knowledge.

Now let's consider two major criticisms of Jacob's (and the Others') approach to the experiment. First off, there's the issue of informed consent. If the experimenter hasn't informed the participant of the nature, the purpose, and the parameters of the experiment, then how can the participant's consent be characterized as "informed"? Informed consent is important because it is considered unethical to experiment on unwilling subjects—consent is supposed to guard against this. If the subject is in the dark about the nature of the experiment, however, consent can't be meaningful. The subject can't know what it actually is that he or she is consenting to. Conversely, if the stakes are high enough, then the lack of informed consent might be justified. So maybe the ends justify the means for Jacob.

Second, as Andreas Ortmann and Ralph Hertwig note, "Deception can strongly affect the reputation of individual labs and the profession, thus contaminating the participant pool."[4] Ortmann and Hertwig also observe that if the experimental subjects are suspicious of the researcher, they are unlikely to behave as they normally would, and the researcher's control of the experiment is compromised.[5] The point of deception experiments is to observe unreflective behavior that is ignorant of certain facts about the situation and therefore "natural." Yet if the participants are vaguely aware that they are being deceived, then the methodology might actually have the opposite effect and may cause participants to act in abnormal ways. So, deception can be a self-defeating methodology.

I think this applies directly to Jacob's experiment. How much of what happens to our candidates on the island is a direct result of the deceptions and the bizarre actions of the Others (who act in Jacob's name and whose intermediary—Richard—they include in their ranks)? Deception and evasion are part of the Others' modus operandi from beginning to end. Ethan is inserted into the castaways' camp when the plane has just crashed, and Juliet continues with evasions even after she has defected to the castaways' group. And the castaways are deeply suspicious. The results of the experiment are thus tainted—maybe to the extent that Jacob would have been better off explaining to the candidates the nature of the island, as well as the reason he had brought them there.

There is another reason to find Jacob's approach flawed. We know Jacob says that he considers free will to be important, insofar as a choice to act from the better, nobler parts of ourselves is meaningful only if it is a free choice. We also know that the selection of the candidates is set within the broader "experiment"—to prove to the Man in Black that sin is not unavoidable or an ineluctable part of human nature. Yet it's almost impossible to determine the right thing to do under conditions of ignorance.

To be able to understand, at least to a certain extent, the situation you're in is one of the "epistemic conditions"—a stipulation of the state of knowledge required—for freedom and moral responsibility. In contrast to such understanding, we need to consider *circumstantial ignorance* and *normative ignorance*. Circumstantial ignorance is to be ignorant of some matter of fact that is salient to a moral assessment of some action. Normative ignorance is to be ignorant of what the correct moral assessment of the action is or to be ignorant of the fact that there even is a correct assessment. Jacob seems to make the mistake of conflating these two in his conversation with Richard. The candidates could have a pretty good concept of right and wrong—they might not be acting under conditions of normative ignorance— but if they are unaware of morally significant facts about the nature of their situation, then their actions might not be truly free, and they might not be morally responsible for them.

There is a chance, though, that circumstantial ignorance might not mean that the candidates don't bear moral responsibility. It would depend on whether they bear responsibility for this ignorance. In philosophical terminology, it depends on whether the ignorance is culpable or nonculpable. Whether ignorance is culpable will depend on whether we've exercised due diligence in trying to understand the world in which we're acting. Gideon Rosen, in his article "Culpability and Ignorance," explains that it will depend on whether we've discharged our epistemic obligations: "We are under an array of standing obligations to inform ourselves about matters relevant to the moral permissibility of our conduct: to look around, to reflect, to seek advice, and so on."[6] If we do not fulfill these obligations or at least take the steps that any reasonable person in our situation could take to try to fulfill them, then our ignorance would be culpable, and we would bear at least some moral responsibility for both the ignorance and the action that resulted from it.

To make a moral judgment of the candidates, Jacob needs at least three stages of assessment:

1. An evaluation of the actions of the candidates, that is, their moral permissibility or impermissibility
2. A determination of whether any morally impermissible actions were performed in circumstantial ignorance (this might make up a high percentage!)
3. An appraisal of whether the morally impermissible actions were performed in culpable or nonculpable ignorance

If the candidates fulfilled their epistemic obligations and did their best (and did all that any reasonable person could be expected to do under the circumstances) to understand their situation, but their efforts were insufficient for knowledge because of Jacob's deception, then they would not be morally responsible for any wrongdoing that followed. If Jacob did not evaluate the candidates while bearing all of this in mind, we have a strong condemnation of his experiment.

Of course, it's not clear in the end that Jacob did evaluate or choose a candidate. Rather, he gave the candidates a choice. But if the mark of a good candidate is the castaway who has done the best job of trying to understand the island, its purpose, and the group's situation, while maintaining compassion, then I think we can agree that the right person got the job in the end. I'm talking, of course, about Hurley, rather than Jack. There's no question that "everybody loves Hugo," but what's interesting about his becoming the island protector is that Hurley always spoke for the fans. He often asked intelligent questions and provided a kind of meta-commentary on island events, displaying a curious and sharp mind. These qualities, along with his easy-going, kind, and compassionate nature, make him the best candidate by far.

It's Hurley

In the series finale, which for many fans constituted a betrayal of the effort they'd put into understanding the mysteries presented to them in the first five seasons, one of the best elements was the implication that although Jacob's methodology was flawed, Hurley could do things differently. Maybe Hurley will do as Ben suggests and "look after people"—telling people the truth and treating them like rational beings, as well as recruiting his eventual replacement with these values in mind.

While the writers were trying to hammer into fans the importance of faith, what I hope the fans will take away from their whole experience of the show, of researching and investigating the mysteries and the clues and critically engaging with the show on the level that many did, is the importance of intellectual curiosity. If they do, then *Lost* will have done something great—that is, to show that TV can be an active experience that expands the viewers' intellectual resources and changes the way they interact with pop culture for the better.

NOTES

1. *The Oxford English Reference Dictionary*, 2nd ed., edited by Judy Pearsall and Bill Trumble (Oxford and New York: Oxford University Press, 1996).

2. C. G. Jung and W. Pauli, *The Interpretation of Nature and the Psyche* (London: Routledge & Kegan Paul, 1955), p. 31.

3. In fact, Milgram's experiment was subsequently criticized for apparently targeting and looking for connections between the professional upper classes, making the "six degrees" results perhaps less surprising.

4. Andreas Ortmann and Ralph Hertwig, "The Question Remains: Is Deception Acceptable?" *American Psychologist* 53 (1998): 806–807.

5. Ibid., p. 807.

6. Gideon Rosen, "Culpability and Ignorance," *Proceedings of the Aristotelian Society* 103 (2003): 61–84.

LOST AND THE QUESTION OF LIFE AFTER BIRTH

Jeremy Barris

Unlike science, philosophy does not discover unknown things or give us new information about familiar things. Instead, strangely at first sight, it deals with things that we actually already know very well. It helps us understand the nature of these familiar things more deeply than we did before. This interest in a deeper understanding of familiar things is expressed in a sense of wonder about the things in the world around us, a feeling that we all sometimes experience. Plato (428–347 B.C.E.) wrote that "wonder . . . is characteristic of a philosopher . . . : this is where philosophy begins, and nowhere else."[1]

What each of us is *most* familiar with is his or her own life. In fact, our lives are so basic that we find other things meaningful only to the extent that they connect with something in our lives. As the great Spanish philosopher José Ortega y Gasset (1883–1955) argued, "Every other reality, different as it is from my life, is made known by some modality of my life. . . . God Himself, should He exist, will begin to be for me by existing somehow in my life." And so life is "the foundation of all other realities. . . . In the final analysis, every other reality will be a reality *in it*." My world "is only made up of whatever is lived by me."[2]

An understanding of life itself is necessary for us to understand the meaning of everything else that affects us. This is why the meaning of life is the most overwhelming question: it affects everything, including all other questions. And as we shall soon see, it also affects the meaning of, and the questions we ask about, *Lost*.

We often puzzle over whether there is a life after death and what that life might be. Yet even that question has meaning for us only in the context of our lives, in the context of the interests and the concerns that cause us to ask that question in the first place. So an even more important question is the question of life after birth.

As the German philosopher Martin Heidegger (1889–1976) pointed out, the clue to *all* questions about the nature of reality or being is the nature of the *asker* of the questions about reality or being—namely, *us*, here and now, as we ask these questions in our lives. Heidegger wrote, "Looking at something, understanding and conceiving it" are all part of the being of "those particular entities which we, the inquirers, are ourselves. Thus to work out the question of Being adequately, we must make an entity—the inquirer—transparent in his own Being."[3]

Our lives are what our understanding of the world most depends on and so what we most need to understand. Because our lives are what we most take for granted as obvious, they are also what we least understand and so most need help to understand.

TV shows, like anything else, have meaning for us only because they connect with our lives. When they are not only meaningful, but gripping and fascinating, it is because they connect with something important or basic to our lives.

Lost, in particular, connects with our lives in an especially full way, because the show expresses not merely a few common experiences in our lives, but aspects of the basic nature of each of our lives. In other words, *Lost* expresses what life itself basically *is*.

Why Are We Here?

Lost pays a lot of attention to why and how each person happened to arrive on the island. In many respects, the way the show presents and explores this issue echoes the way in which we, in our more reflective moments, are troubled by the question "Why are we here?" There are other senses of this life question that we'll discuss a little later, but one of its meanings is certainly this: "How did we happen to be put here; where did we come from?"

Like each of our births, the castaways' actual arrival, in the plane crash, is the result of a series of extraordinary chance events. The castaways' backstories show what unpredictable, coincidental, and intricately interwoven circumstances led to their being present on that particular plane at that particular time. The crash itself was caused entirely accidentally by a series of events having to do with Desmond Hume's own life and his own purely personal concerns. As we discover in the second season, he had, just once, neglected to reset the counter that had become his responsibility by sheer circumstance and whose purpose he didn't even know. As a result, a powerful electromagnetic field took effect at just the moment the castaways' plane happened to be flying overhead—something that itself happened only because instrument failures led the pilots to go wildly off-course—and brought the plane down.

It's true that unlike our births as we understand them in the most common perspectives these events can be and are explored in terms of the lives the castaways led before arriving on the island. Through these explorations, however, *Lost* highlights the mysterious circumstances that led to each of these people arriving in precisely this situation. For example, the simple explanation that Desmond let the counter lapse is kept hidden for most of two seasons. And the background information about the hatch that houses the counter, the counter itself, and the electromagnetic field is, in each case, revealed very gradually in enigmatic hints. As a result, the show is about the mystery. The backstories of each of the characters similarly emphasize the strange turns their lives take and the remarkable coincidences among their lives, which we'll consider shortly.

This mystery of the castaways' arrival on the island is at the heart of all of our lives, making us ask the life question "Why are we here?" In Heidegger's language, we, like the characters of *Lost*, find ourselves "thrown" into our life situations, as parts of an ultimately bewildering environment and history, neither of which we made, and both of which are in many ways indifferent to our concerns and to our existence itself.

Another sense of the question "Why are we here?" is whether there is a purpose to our being here, and if so, what that purpose is. *Lost* pays close attention to this sense of the question, too. Are the castaways there to carry out an important task, to serve some important although unknown goal, as Locke believes? Or are they perhaps there to be spiritually or morally redeemed? Mr. Eko believes so, and it's a possibility that former heroin-addict Charlie certainly has to consider. It's also a possibility that has potential significance for Kate, with her tortured criminal past, and for Sawyer, who has spent his life on a bitter quest for revenge.

Is the island a place for second chances of other kinds? Locke, Rose, and Jin are healed from incurable physical conditions (paralysis, cancer, and infertility, respectively). Shannon, Boone, Sayid, Sawyer, Jin, and Desmond each get the chance to change, or rework, their destructive dealings with others.

Or—a possibility that Hurley finds himself troubled by—is the entire experience only a delusion, a kind of dream, in which "all is vanity," and from which it would be better to wake up to reality?

Again, the fascination of these themes doesn't lie in the answers—*Lost* is notorious for delaying these answers and in fact for often providing new insights that actually complicate the original questions. Clearly, what keeps our interest is the mystery itself.

All of these experiences and concerns are, in one way or another, basic possibilities in all of our lives. At some point, we all want to feel that there is a purpose to our lives, to our being here. We want to feel that at least something we do is worth doing or that we are making a difference or contributing something. And we are always faced with the possibility of discovering that we have been living lives that don't work for us, lives that we feel have not been satisfactory or worthwhile or good, so that we might feel the need to find a way of starting over. What is more, as the existence of our many religions and philosophies shows, we are all liable to wonder, at times, whether this abundantly imperfect and painful reality can be the real deal, whether there isn't a very different reality that we simply can't see.

Lost, then, expresses themes that are basic, not to this or that area of life, but to life itself as a whole. These themes belong to the very nature of our lives, as an experience that begins, endures, and ends in circumstances mostly indifferent to us and our concerns, and that offers little idea of what we should do with ourselves now that we are here.

How Does It All Make Sense?

As the castaways' backstories and experiences unfold, all sorts of connections emerge among their stories and between their present challenges or opportunities and their histories, hinting at a meaning to the castaways' situation and to their being in it together. Yet the suggestions of meaningful patterns really organize and heighten the enigma of their situation. They raise the question of how it all makes sense, rather than answer that question. This quality of incomplete sense or of the mysterious nature even of what we already know is another of the basic structures of life.

Living a life naturally raises the question "How does it all make sense?" This question belongs to the nature of life because our lives are thoroughly limited; they are an experience with boundaries, in space and time and extension. As a result, although things do make some sense to us (otherwise, we wouldn't even know enough to be puzzled by them), they make sense only to an extent. The events of our lives always fit into a larger context that extends beyond our awareness, and so they are shot through with elements that do not make sense to us and that may or may not have a meaning we haven't been able to grasp. Because of this wider context, the things and the events of our lives, on the one hand, never make full and final sense but, on the other hand, don't even give us the security of knowing that we can dismiss them as making no sense at all so that we can move on.

Existentialism, a school of twentieth-century philosophy, explores themes of the nature of human existence (as we are doing now). Martin Heidegger, Jean-Paul Sartre (1905–1980), and Albert Camus (1913–1960) were perhaps the most famous existentialists. Some of them argued that life is simply absurd, without rhyme or reason, that we really are "lost" in the universe. We must therefore create our own meanings and purposes. Yet I think these existentialists didn't come to terms with just how lost we are. We really don't even have *that* much definite information about our situation—that we *are* definitely or completely lost.

Instead, it seems to me that life is only in part a jumble of arbitrary accidents and apparently inexplicable events. There is the "other hand": life is also shot through with strands and connections of sense. And this presence of both understanding and lack of understanding makes life neither reliably understandable nor reliably senseless, but more like a riddle or a mystery: deeply puzzling, but with enough things that we do understand to give us "clues" to wonder in particular directions for answers.

We definitely do understand some things to some extent. Otherwise, we couldn't even understand the possibility that we can't understand: this possibility is *itself* something we understand. And we couldn't have *that* understanding, in turn, without also understanding all sorts of other things.

The Austrian philosopher Ludwig Wittgenstein (1889–1951) made this clear. To understand that we might not understand, we need to understand the meanings of the words we use in expressing that thought. And to understand those, we need to understand a great deal about the things those words refer to and about the society in which we learned the words. Otherwise, we couldn't have learned to apply the words successfully in our environment (which is the same as learning them at all) or to work successfully with and so learn from the people who taught them to us. As Wittgenstein noted, "If you are not certain of any fact, you cannot be certain of the meaning of your words, either."[4] And, beyond the meanings of words, "If you tried to doubt everything you would not get as far as doubting anything. The game of doubting itself presupposes certainty." For, Wittgenstein asks, "Doesn't one need grounds for doubt?"[5] As a result, because even not understanding things or experiencing them as senseless depends on understanding or grasping the sense of some other things, we simply can't get to the point of finding everything senseless. We can only fool ourselves that we're doing that!

Because we do understand some things to some extent, we can never rule out the possibility that we might come to understand more. Yet because our lives are finite, the things we understand always have a wider context, and so we always only partly understand them. There are always things that we do understand, but there are always also important things that we don't understand.

Our understanding and lack of understanding interact with each other. The sense that things do make tells us that we don't yet have the whole story. The fact that we can never get the whole story, however, makes the sense we already have unsatisfactory. And so we're always aware that there is more to know even about the familiar things and events of our lives, and we're impelled to keep asking questions and find out more of the story.

As in life, the story on *Lost* unfolds in patterns and connections that hint at sense or meaningfulness. Connections abound among various characters, who often turn out to have been involved in some significant part of another character's life and even involved in the circumstances that directly led to that character's being on Oceanic flight 815 and therefore on the island. For example, before Jack and Sawyer meet for the first time on the island, Sawyer happens to encounter Jack's father in a bar and has a conversation with him about his troubled relationship with Jack. (Jack's father has just failed to get up the nerve to call Jack and reconcile with him, something he had apparently tried to do many times.) Shortly after that, Jack's father dies without yet having managed to tell Jack what he meant to him. Jack's father's death is the reason that Jack travels to Australia, the flight's place of departure, and also makes it necessary for Jack to take that particular flight to bring his father's body home. The plane's crash results in Jack's being on the island, where he meets Sawyer—who can then tell him about the love his father wasn't able to convey.

Another example is the connection between Hurley and Libby. They establish a love relationship on the island, but, apparently without either of them being aware of it, they turn out to have been patients at the same time in the same psychiatric ward. And it was in this ward that Hurley came across the numbers that later won him the lottery but also brought him terribly bad luck, which led him to Australia to try to undo that curse, which in turn brought him to flight 815, and so to the island.

Then there's the pre-island meeting between Jack and Desmond, in which Desmond offers the despairing Jack a perspective on possible miracles that leads to Jack's healing the patient he later marries. Within minutes of that conversation, Desmond is provoked to leave on the dangerous sailing trip that brings *him* to the island—where his unknowing negligence later causes the crash of flight 815.

Again, at the end of season 5, we find out that the mysterious Jacob, longtime inhabitant of the island and elusive authority behind leaders like Ben, has been present at crucial moments of each main character's life prior to his or her time on the island, moments in some way connected with the character's path to arriving there.

The use of the flash-sideways world in season 6 expresses in yet other ways the suggestion of meaning or of meaningful connections mixed with inexplicable mystery. For example, the surprising connection Kate feels with the pregnant Claire or that Libby feels with Hurley in the 2004 time line makes a kind of sense in light of the overwhelming, bigger-than-ourselves force of the bonds we sometimes experience with other people. *This* person becomes a part of who *we* are: as a result, it seems to make sense (and perhaps does make sense) that our connection with him or her would transcend the accidental circumstances and details of this time and place. The same is true of Claire's sense that the name of her baby, Aaron, which we already know from one of the other, unrelated time lines, is not an arbitrary choice but is somehow, strangely, the *right* name.

It's also interesting in this way that several of this small group have the names of great eighteenth-century philosophers: John Locke, (Desmond) Hume, and (Danielle) Rousseau. (What's more, the character Ben Linus is played by the actor Michael *Emerson*. Coincidence? Or has the island's electromagnetic field burst free of the writers' control and now started to draw our own world into its reality?)

A central feature of *Lost*, then, and one that rivets our interest is that everything seems to hint, but only to hint, at making sense. Tantalizingly, this is not enough sense to be quite understandable; it is a sense just beyond our grasp. In exploring this theme, *Lost* mirrors an important aspect of our lives: their quality of being a perpetual mystery, which we also can never rightly give up on. As Jack's father explains in the series finale, our goal is to remember *and* to let go and move on—and in fact to remember *so that* we can let go and move on.

Revealingly in this connection, the final episodes of the series *only* answer the question of life *after* death, a question that is never raised during the series, and the answer they give only explains the events of each flash-sideways, a phenomenon that occurs only in the sixth and final season. As a result, they leave us with all of the questions, untouched, that *are* raised during the previous five seasons and in much of the sixth season as well, questions about how to make more complete sense of all of the events the characters actually live through. We are left with a half-mysterious story about life after birth, full of tantalizing hints of incomplete sense, which it is up to us to remember and to resolve in whatever ways we can.

Because this half-present sense and meaningfulness of things is an aspect of the *nature* of our lives and not merely a particular experience *within* our lives, it is an aspect of what our lives, and so our selves, *are*. As a result, when *Lost* expresses this dimension of the nature of our lives, it is, like philosophy, expressing not only something *about* us, but what we are.

Expressing what we actually are (and not just something about what we are) is exactly the same as *being* what we are.

It *is* what we are, emerging, actively being itself, carrying itself out. Both philosophy and *Lost*, then, are not just "spectator sports." In expressing basic aspects of our nature, they are each an activation of what most makes us "us."

Is This Life the Whole of What There Is?

Lost also pays attention to a third very basic feature of human life, namely, that the castaways are mostly not content with being where they are. Whether they are on the island or off, most of them feel the urgent need to get to a home that is somewhere else. And although some of them want to huddle where they are and forget about the troublesome world beyond, this, too, is a way of shaping their lives by awareness of, and reference to, somewhere other than where they are.

In light of this need to be or to focus on somewhere else, along with not knowing why we're here and not knowing how it all makes sense, the theme of being "lost" wonderfully captures a basic part of our human situation. Part of being alive and conscious is to be driven by desire for what we do not have or have not achieved, to be partly dissatisfied with our situation in our lives. And, as we discussed, part of what it means to be alive and conscious is also to be unsure of the sense of the world that is our context. In other words, we're unsure, among other things, of whether and how we fit in or belong. One way of saying and experiencing both of these things is that we are not fully at home in life—and that our true home therefore lies somewhere beyond our always partly alien life circumstances.

The needs for sex and romance, for bonding or "fusing" with someone else, are two especially compelling expressions of this structure of our lives: of the general need to connect with what is beyond our finite selves and our finite situation, to be more complete and to belong. *Lost* actually demonstrates that sex and romantic love really are expressions of this deeper and more basic need. Although there are plenty of steamy scenes in the series, they almost always take a backseat to the ongoing, desperate search for "a real home."

Art and Entertainment

Enjoying *Lost* means having a deep, existential experience: in other words, one that connects with the themes basic to our human existence. *Lost* produces this kind of experience in an especially clear and direct way and so can also help us understand why certain other shows appeal to us so much, especially the many detective and other puzzle-solving shows that continue to keep our interest.

Cultural critics sometimes compare contemporary Western culture unfavorably with ancient Greek culture, whose story-telling art did not mainly provide a means of escape from life, but instead was a standard way of experiencing deep questions about it. I suggest, however, that one of the lessons of *Lost* is that our culture's standard, supposedly escapist entertainment is sometimes also that kind of deep art.

We may not be conscious of our depth, but that doesn't mean it goes away. Whether we know it or not, we never stop being entirely who we are and in one way or another experiencing and living out all of who we are. This is also true in our various forms of entertainment, whether we are their creators or their audience. It is true, as well, whether the entertainment is a famous public effort or simply our chatting with one another in our everyday lives.[6]

NOTES

1. Plato, *Theaetetus*, trans. M. J. Levitt, rev. Myles Burnyeat (Indianapolis: Hackett, 1992), pp. 155C–155D.

2. José Ortega y Gasset, *What Is Knowledge?* ed. and trans. Jorge García-Gómez (New York: State University of New York Press, 2002), pp. 66, 111.

3. Martin Heidegger, *Being and Time*, trans. John Macquarrie and Edward Robinson (New York: Harper & Row, 1962), pp. 26–27.

4. Ludwig Wittgenstein, *On Certainty*, ed. G. E. M. Anscombe and G. H. von Wright, trans. Denis Paul and G. E. M. Anscombe (New York: Harper & Row, 1969), p. 17e.

5. Ibid., p. 18e.

6. I would like to thank Sharon Kaye, Bill Irwin, Shai Biderman, and Bill Devlin for their helpful suggestions. Any remaining stylistic mistakes are due entirely to a mysterious contagion from that other book series on popular culture and philosophy.

SEE YOU IN ANOTHER LIFE, BROTHER

Bad Faith and Authenticity in Three *Lost* Souls

Sander Lee

Now that it's over, I feel confident in saying that *Lost* will go down in the annals of television history as one of the greatest series of all time. It profoundly changed our expectations about the topics and the level of complexity that may be achieved by a TV series on a commercial network. For me, the greatest single moment in the series, the point when I knew that the show was really something special, came in the opening moments of the first episode of season 2, "Man of Science, Man of Faith," when we were confronted with an unknown character using 1970s technology as he works on a computer and plays a record.

My initial reaction was to question whether I was watching the right show. Previously, the entire first season had taken place on a technology-less island, and the tools of civilization appeared only in flashbacks. The season had ended with the cliffhanger question "What's in the hatch?" Yet I had never considered the possibility that the hatch contained someone living in an entirely different reality from the one experienced by the survivors of Oceanic flight 815 (whom I will call the "castaways").

Indeed, one of the most interesting philosophical themes of the show is that people regularly construct paradigms or models of reality that are fundamentally different from those of the other people around them. While the castaways view themselves as survivors of a plane crash living on a desert island, only a few feet below them, Desmond thinks that he alone is saving the world every 108 minutes while hiding in a shelter that protects him from a "sickness." Evidence of Desmond's radically different view of reality is contained in the lyrics of the song to which he is listening in this scene, namely, Mama Cass's "Make Your Own Kind of Music."

When the two realities first meet, they clash violently, although eventually, through give and take, Desmond and the castaways are able to merge their disparate views of reality into a new view that encompasses the elements that conform best to their shared conditions.

This process repeats itself throughout the series. Again and again, characters are forced to confront the fact that their carefully constructed view of reality is radically at odds with that of "Others." In a trivial sense, we are always aware that elements of our worldview (Weltanschauung) are different from those of other people we know. My home is not your home, I was born in Texas while you come from Ohio, and so on. On *Lost*, however, these differences are often so radical as to be just about incomprehensible. For example, to Pierre Chang, Miles is simply a lower-level worker for the Dharma Initiative. From Miles's perspective, he is a visitor from thirty years into the future who knows for sure that Chang is his father. The trajectory of Ben Linus is another case in point. We first meet him in season 2 as the fake Henry Gale, and we move from initial distrust to hatred to understanding and, finally, for many of us, a form of pity and perhaps even sympathy in our assessment of his character.

Putting this point in philosophical terms, the important role of "seeing" (as symbolized by the close-up on Jack's eye in "Pilot: Part 1") becomes apparent. In *Being and Nothingness*, the French philosopher Jean-Paul Sartre (1905–1980), one of the founders of existentialism, described what he called "the Look." Those who watch create their own interpretation of those who are watched. The act of looking objectifies the world. Sartre famously gave the example of a man on his knees looking through a keyhole into a hotel room. While he is alone in the corridor, he is the subject of all he sees. Motivated perhaps by jealousy, he judges the meaning of the events he observes on the other side of the door. But suppose someone else (say, a woman) should turn down the corridor and see the man. Realizing that he is being "seen" by the other person, the man immediately becomes aware of how he must "look," down on his knees spying through the keyhole. Self-consciously, he leaps to his feet and hurries away, anxious to disappear before the other person has a chance to confront him. While he was alone, the man was in control of his identity, but once he became aware of the other's gaze, he realized that she may see him quite differently from how he sees himself. Although he may have thought that his actions were justified, he's very aware that the woman might see him instead as a voyeur, a Peeping Tom, or that most pathetic of creatures, a jealous husband.

Thus, in "Man of Science, Man of Faith," the opening minutes show us such a clash of perceived realities. What I find so remarkable here is that the writers of *Lost* chose initially to show us this clash by presenting us with the perspective of the "Other"—in this case, Desmond. Using the traditional approach to narrative, we would expect to first encounter the interior of the hatch from the perspective of the show's protagonists, the castaways. By starting instead from the point of view of Desmond, we are disoriented and forced to consider the possibility that the reality of *Lost* might be fundamentally at odds with the viewpoint that we have uncritically accepted up to this point. As in the famous 1950 Japanese film *Rashomon*, we are exposed to the notion that the "truth" of a situation may vary radically, depending on one's point of view. In fact, as these clashes of viewpoint occur again and again in *Lost*, we come to realize that there may be no absolute truth at all; each observer constructs his or her own meaning. Recognition of these changing perspectives and situations is captured in Desmond's unique phrase for saying good-bye, "See you in another life, brother." ("Man of Science, Man of Faith")

Furthermore, as a group of people share a common set of experiences, they may move from viewing themselves as separate individuals to a realization that they are part of a group with a common understanding of reality and even a common set of interests to protect. As an example of the first situation, Sartre discussed people waiting for a bus. These people don't know one another and simply happen to be waiting for the same thing at the same time. Such people are in what he calls a *series*.

The plane crash in *Lost* immediately puts the castaways in such a series. In the pilot episode, we watch as Jack begins to assign tasks to each of them, tasks they fulfill as they come to realize that they are now part of a group in a common situation, sharing common goals. First, they must help the injured and move safely from the crash site; later, they must find a way to survive and eventually escape from the island. Sartre called this new situation in which each individual chooses to work with others the *group in fusion*. Yet despite Jack's motto "Live together, die alone," within this new group there are still conflicts between those with different interpretations of reality and different plans for achieving their goals. The most famous such conflict in *Lost* is the one between Jack and Locke, each of whom struggles to find meaning in the face of the bizarre happenings on the island.

For most existentialists, including Sartre, the world is a meaningless and terrifying place without rational purpose, in which the individual is free to choose how to live. The individual is completely responsible for those choices, and there exists no objective external moral authority by which those choices may be accurately gauged. Realization of this condition usually results in an emotion described as despair or anguish. Anguish is the apprehension that comes from the realization that one is continually faced with situations in which a choice must be made—not to choose is a choice in itself—and there is nothing to guarantee the validity of one's choices.

Out of this anguish there arises what Sartre called *bad faith*. This occurs when a person tries to lie to himself and thereby disown his or her freedom and the responsibility that goes with it. No one can successfully lie to himself or herself, however, because it is impossible to deceive one's own consciousness completely. Such a person is necessarily aware of his or her own inconsistency and failure. Dilemmas of this sort pervade the lives of many of the characters in *Lost*, although they most obviously pertain to the characters of Jack, Locke, and Desmond.

The Man of Science

All *Lost* fans know that Jack and Locke fundamentally disagree on the proper roles of reason and faith. While Locke is the "man of faith," Jack is the "man of science." As a doctor, Jack initially trusts only the experiences of his senses. In this way, Jack has as much in common with the British philosopher David Hume (1711–1776) as does the character who bears his name, Desmond David Hume. Like Jack, David Hume was very skeptical of any claims not based on empirical data. For example, Hume argued that our common belief that every event has a cause is based more on the human desire to explain everything rationally than on the evidence of our senses. The same may be said for our belief in God or miracles.

Thus, when Jack first encounters Locke's claim that the island has brought them there for a purpose, he rejects it vehemently, even telling Kate in the first season finale ("Exodus: Part 2") that they have a "Locke problem." The conflicts between Jack and Locke manifest themselves in their differing attitudes toward the button in season 2. Although Locke is quick to believe Desmond's assertion that the button must be pushed every 108 minutes, Jack would probably never push the button at all if it were left only to him.

Jack's vehement opposition to Locke's mysticism is not based solely on his agreement with Hume. A central issue for Jack lies in the philosophical dichotomy between free will and determinism. Believers in free will, such as Sartre, claim that each of us has the power to choose our values and our actions. Through these choices, I create myself and construct the meaning of my world. In doing this, I am completely responsible for my own actions. For Jack, an acceptance of individual freedom and responsibility is the cornerstone of one's moral integrity. As we discussed, anyone who denies his or her freedom is engaging in a form of self-deception, what Sartre calls bad faith.

In Jack's view, his father's greatest flaw is his abdication of personal responsibility. The very first time we see him, Christian Shephard is lecturing a young Jack on the liabilities of caring. He tells Jack that he watched a boy die on the operating table that day and asks rhetorically how, after this, he can stand to come home in the evening and enjoy himself with his family. His answer is to detach himself emotionally from the events he witnessed and any concern for his own potential responsibility in the death. For Christian, only by not caring can Jack grow up to be a "real man," one who "has what it takes." ("White Rabbit") Although Christian suggests that his attitude makes him "strong," as opposed to Jack (whose caring for others makes him "weak"), we can see that Christian is an alcoholic, and his "strength" comes out of a bottle.

In his bad faith, Jack's father refuses to acknowledge his capacity for free choice and his own moral responsibility for his mistakes. Jack identifies his father's moral failure with a belief in determinism, the claim that our actions are the result of destiny. Such a belief in fate can be used as an excuse to escape accountability for the results of one's acts. Symbolic of these views is the phrase "That's why the Red Sox will never win the World Series." ("Outlaws") In saying this, Christian is claiming that events in life are beyond our control. It doesn't matter what the Red Sox do or which players they put on the field, it's their fate to be eternal losers. They might come one strike away from winning the World Series (as they did in 1986), but fate will inevitably intervene to destroy their hopes. Those who superficially appear to be the causes of these failures are not really responsible. So Red Sox fans must forgive Bill Buckner, and there's no reason to hate Aaron Boone or even Bucky Dent.

Ironically, given the fact that Oceanic flight 815 crashed on September 22, 2004, these references to the Red Sox's fate take place only a few weeks before the team reversed the curse and won its first World Series in eighty-six years. In "The Glass Ballerina," when Ben tries to convince Jack that he is in contact with the outside world, Jack believes Ben only after he watches a video of the Red Sox celebrating their victory, a victory that seems to nullify all of Christian's excuses for his personal failures.

Because of Jack's extreme commitment to existential notions of freedom and responsibility, he is contemptuous of Locke, whose belief in destiny can only remind him of his father. For philosophers such as Sartre and especially the German philosopher Martin Heidegger (1889–1976), whose methods greatly influenced Sartre, the person who fully accepts his or her freedom and corresponding responsibility is on the road to "authenticity." The opposite of bad faith is not good faith, because all forms of faith entail self-deception. Rather, authenticity means complete honesty, even when such honesty reveals unpleasant truths.

This explains why Jack is so intolerant of those who lie to him. Jack blames Locke for Boone's death in season 1 because Locke not only lied about the circumstances of the accident, but also ran away. In disappearing immediately after delivering Boone, Locke not only deprived Jack of the medical information he needed to treat Boone's injuries correctly, Locke also, like Jack's father, abdicated personal responsibility.

As someone committed to moral integrity in a world seemingly without divine purpose, Jack takes it upon himself to become a savior. As his father tells him, Jack's tragic flaw is that he cares too much. Like the doctor in the Albert Camus novel *The Plague*, Jack can't let go even when the circumstances seem to demand it. When Jack succeeds, his persistence makes him appear to be a miracle worker. Against all odds, he cures his future wife of her injuries, and later, during season 2, he revives Charlie, despite Kate's belief that it is too late. When he fails, however, as he does with Boone, Jack must attribute blame. His father must be held accountable for killing a patient, just as Locke must pay for Boone's death.

Throughout Jack's ordeal in season 3, first as a prisoner of the Others, then as Ben's doctor, and, finally, as the leader in the war against the Others, Jack continues to judge himself and everyone else by these rigid standards. In the season 3 finale, we see a flash-forward into a future where Jack has become a suicidal, pill-popping drunk who bitterly regrets his decision to leave the island. This suggests that despite everything, Ben wasn't lying when he told Jack that leaving the island was a mistake. Clearly, Jack now believes that he failed as a leader and he is punishing himself by becoming what he hates the most, a man just like his father.

In season 4, Jack struggles to return everyone to the island, believing that he does have a destiny after all. Yet his return to the island in season 5 disappoints him, because he finds himself stuck in 1977 working at a menial job for the Dharma Initiative. He deals with his disappointment by refusing to act, even when he is asked to save the injured young Ben. While the old Jack had to "fix" everyone, the Jack of season 5 has given up. Yet according to Sartre, choosing not to act is still a choice with consequences; had Jack been willing to operate on Ben, then Sawyer and Kate would not have needed to bring Ben to the Temple and Ben might not have joined the Others and planned "the Purge."

Eventually, however, Jack reverses his beliefs yet again, allowing himself to accept Daniel Faraday's theory that the crash of Oceanic flight 815 may be avoided altogether if only the atomic bomb, Jughead, is exploded at the precise moment of the "Incident." To accomplish this, Jack reverts to the role of leader, overcoming all obstacles to fix time itself. This decision effectively kills Juliet, while bringing everyone else back to the present time line in 2007.

With its initial split between the events on the island and those in the sideways world, season 6 presents us with bifurcated characters. Island Jack slowly starts to lead again as he comes to grips with the realization that Jacob has been manipulating his whole life. Sideways Jack, in contrast, still thinks he can fix anyone, including Locke, while he comes to grips with his own "Daddy Issues" through his relationship with his son.

In "The Lighthouse," Island Jack responds angrily as he realizes that Jacob has been watching him and manipulating him throughout his entire life. Yet as season 6 progresses, Jack becomes increasingly comfortable with his status as a candidate, until he finally decides that he is meant to become Jacob's replacement, even if it means sacrificing his life.

In "The End," Jack has reversed himself and become Locke's "man of faith," eager to fulfill his destiny and fix a problem worthy of his attention. As the new Jacob, Jack saves his friends, the island, and possibly the world. What could be more heroic? The writers of *Lost* have always enjoyed inserting references to *Star Wars* into the script, and they do so twice in the finale, first when Hurley says, "I have a bad feeling about this," and again when he compares Jacob to Yoda. In "The End," Jack resembles Luke Skywalker, a character who fulfilled his destiny by becoming a Jedi knight and destroying the evil emperor, while redeeming his flawed father.

Does this mean that *Lost* ultimately rejects the belief in existential freedom we have been discussing? Was Jack destined from the beginning to play this role? Although Jack himself might believe this, I would argue that the writers of *Lost* do not. During seasons 5 and 6, they make it quite clear that Jacob has intervened repeatedly in the lives of the candidates to manipulate them into acting the way he wanted them to act. We see him visiting each of them at pivotal moments in their lives, literally "touching" them and turning their lives in the directions he wanted them to take.

Returning to *Lost's* obsession with showing us the same events from a variety of different viewpoints, what appears to Jack as his destiny may in fact be the result of another *Lost* institution, "the long con." Repeatedly during the series, we have seen characters such as James Ford (Sawyer), Anthony Cooper (the original Sawyer), and Ben engage in lengthy confidence tricks to convince others to act as they wish. I would contend that Jacob was the greatest con man on the show. For thousands of years, he has schemed to bring people to the island in order to trick one of them into taking his job so that he could finally "let go" and die in peace. In this, he is acting just like his so-called Mother from the episode "Across the Sea." Like Jacob, Mother was willing to do anything, even kill, to manipulate Jacob into taking over her job and to trick his brother into killing her.

Although Jacob may have some supernatural powers, he was once an ordinary human being, not the divine source of goodness that some believed him to be. For instance, he commits many immoral acts in his battle against his nameless brother, the Man in Black. As the show repeatedly reminds us, everyone, including Jack, has choices. He did not have to volunteer to replace Jacob; he chose to.

The Man of Faith

In presenting Locke's story, the creators of *Lost* explore the moral dimensions of situations in which an apparently good man is confronted with the realization that life can be randomly incomprehensible and morally indifferent. Locke desperately seeks meaning and purpose for his life, yet again and again, he ends up disappointed and filled with anguish.

Through flashbacks, we discover how Locke's desire for a genuine relationship with his father (whom he never knew as a child) led him to give up one of his kidneys. Only after the operation does Locke discover that his father has conned him. Once Locke's father has received the kidney transplant, he has no interest whatsoever in maintaining a relationship with his son. Unable to move on with his life, Locke obsesses over his father, sitting every night in his car outside his father's estate and lying to his girlfriend, Helen, when she demands that he focus on her and forget the past.

Locke's initial optimism (some might call it gullibility) resembles some of the beliefs of the philosopher after whom he is apparently named. John Locke (1632–1704) is perhaps best known for his political views and their influence on the founding politicians of the United States, such as Thomas Jefferson and James Madison. Locke viewed human nature as basically good. For him, the social contract protects the rights of all against the small minority of people who miscalculate their self-interest, mistakenly believing that it is to their advantage to criminally deprive others of their rights. Thus, Locke had faith in a democratic form of government in which the majority could be trusted to decide issues in ways that were best for all. Although the philosopher Locke argued that a belief in God and divine purpose was rational, he did not privilege religious claims or scripture. The study of religion should be approached in the same way as science: all claims must be supported by empirical evidence and the use of reason.

During his initial days on the island, *Lost*'s Locke shares his namesake's optimism and faith in the basic goodness of others. The miraculous recovery of the use of his legs provides empirical evidence for his belief that he and the other survivors have been brought to the island for a reason. Locke is certain that he has a destiny to fulfill and he need only wait for the island to reveal this purpose to him. The discovery of the hatch and his vision of the location of the crashed drug plane in season 1 seem only to confirm this sense of destiny. When his faith is challenged by Boone's tragic death, Locke returns to the hatch door to pray for a sign. Kneeling with his forehead pressed against the cover in a posture of prayer, he is rewarded by a sudden appearance of light streaming through the hatch door's window. This leads him to believe that the obstacles he encounters (including Boone's death) occurred because the island is testing his faith. If he can meet these challenges with his faith intact, then the island will tell him what to do in order to fulfill his destiny.

Once Locke makes it into the hatch, meets Desmond, and views the orientation film, everything he has endured finally seems to have been worthwhile. Clearly, it is Locke's fate to make sure that the button is pushed every 108 minutes. In his devotion to the button, he moves beyond the rational faith of the philosopher John Locke and into the realm of the Danish thinker Søren Kierkegaard (1813–1855).

Indeed, Locke's role in Boone's death recalls the biblical tale of Abraham and Isaac, the story of a man who decides, against both his desires and his reason, blindly to follow God's command to sacrifice his son. Kierkegaard used this story to illustrate his belief that the only life worth living and capable of delivering us from despair is one that results from a "leap of faith." One must rely on an intuitive belief in God. A leap of faith requires us to do what we know in our heart is right, despite the fact that society will ridicule us, and despite the fact that no empirical evidence exists to prove that such a choice is justified. Locke takes just such a leap into the belief that he has been chosen to play a special role on the island and invites the ridicule and scorn of his fellow survivors because of his devotion to the button.

Kierkegaard contrasted the leap of faith with two unsuccessful ways of living: the aesthetic and the ethical. Those leading the aesthetic lifestyle, such as Sawyer and Charlie in season 1, seek fulfillment solely through the gratification of their senses. The aesthetic way of life ultimately leads to despair, because the empty pursuit of pleasure alone always leaves one hungry for more. Kierkegaard saw the ethical life as equally unsatisfactory. Building on a foundation of hypocrisy, the ethicist (Jack in the early seasons) pontificates about life's eternal truths, while simultaneously realizing that such unfounded claims are dependent on one's subjective perceptions.

Thus, Locke feels an obligation to reveal the true nature of the island's collective ethical dilemmas, despite his passionate desire to believe that the most profound metaphysical questions have answers. This is why Locke is so angry and self-critical in the final episodes of season 2. By this point, the fake Henry Gale (Ben) has claimed that he didn't input the numbers during the crisis in "Lockdown" and that the button is "just a joke." Later, Locke visits a new hatch with Mr. Eko and absorbs all of its evidence, evidence that suggests that the button pushing was never any more than a psychological experiment. From all of this, Locke concludes that he allowed his burning desire for a spiritual purpose (and the apparent miracle of his legs) to overcome an honest realization of his bleak situation.

Always one to swing to extremes, Locke becomes as dogmatic in his nihilism—a belief in nothing—as he once was in his faith. Determined to brook no opposition in his quest to prove that the button is a hoax, he uses Desmond to lock out Eko. As the countdown progresses, Locke refuses to hear Desmond's rational explanation of the button's true purpose and his compelling evidence that it was his own failure to push the button on September 22, 2004, that caused the crash of Oceanic flight 815. In his anger and despair, Locke destroys the computer monitor, leaving Desmond only one option once it becomes clear that their failure to push the button has triggered a catastrophe.

Locke's error lies not in his rejection of the button, but rather in his unwillingness to trust that a path exists by which he can find meaning and fulfill his sense of moral duty. Too late, he realizes that he has failed the most important test of his faith. When he finally encounters Mr. Eko at the end of "Live Together, Die Alone," all that he can say is, "I was wrong."

In season 3, Locke's faith in the mystic power of the island has returned, and this leads him to try to destroy all possible means of escape from the island. Locke's renewed spiritualism and overconfidence allow Ben to manipulate him onto the road that leads to his being shot. Like so many others on the island, Ben's relationship with his father was ghastly. Blamed during his childhood for his mother's death in childbirth, Ben patiently waits, planning his father's murder and the deaths of everyone in the Dharma community in the great Purge. Viewing Locke as a rival who threatens his leadership, Ben tests Locke by demanding that he kill his kidnapped father just as Ben himself killed his own father.

Although Locke's father has recently used the name Anthony Cooper, he is also the original Sawyer, the man responsible for the deaths of James Ford's parents. Locke, using this information, is able to manipulate Sawyer into killing Cooper, thus allowing Locke to fulfill Ben's demand. When Locke deposits his father's body at Ben's feet, Ben at last agrees to take Locke to meet Jacob, whom Locke sarcastically calls "the man behind the curtain." In *The Wizard of Oz*, the man behind the curtain turns out to be a powerless charlatan, and when Ben seems to be talking to an empty chair, Locke concludes that Ben is equally powerless and probably insane. Unfortunately, as usual, Locke has gotten it completely wrong. Jacob is very real, and when Ben realizes that Locke has the power to hear Jacob's pleas for help, he shoots Locke at the mass grave of his earlier Dharma victims. Locke should have paid more attention when Alex gave him a gun and warned him that he would need it if Ben was taking him to meet Jacob. As at the end of season 2, Locke again arrogantly refuses to believe until it is too late.

As with Jack's journey, Locke's path has taken many twists and turns. Bouncing back and forth between faith and despair, Locke is manipulated again and again by Ben, Charles Widmore, and the Man in Black. In season 5, Widmore gives Locke the name of another British philosopher (Jeremy Bentham) and sends him out to convince the castaways to return. This quest ends tragically when Ben stops Locke's suicide attempt only in order to murder him (after pumping him for information).

The use of Locke's body, now inhabited by the Man in Black, gives us a very different character in season 6, one who appears to be the opposite of the original Locke. Sawyer realizes immediately that Locke is no longer Locke because he now has no fear, and the audience experiences the odd pleasure of seeing Terry O'Quinn play a character more manipulative and powerful than Locke could ever have been. Yet Locke's original faith is reborn in Jack, who tells the Man in Black that "You're not John Locke. You disrespect his memory by wearing his face but you're nothing like him. Turns out he was right about most everything." ("The End")

The Failsafe

To complete our picture of bad faith and authenticity on *Lost*, we now turn to Desmond. When we see Desmond released from military prison at the end of season 2, we learn that his full name is Desmond David Hume. So, like Locke and Rousseau, Desmond shares his name with a famous philosopher. As we discussed earlier, David Hume, a Scot like Desmond, was a skeptic. Given this, we might expect Desmond to be somewhat skeptical of the claims of others and certainly less gullible than Locke. Indeed, this expectation is borne out in key moments of his story.

Although Desmond initially believes Kelvin's claims about the sickness on the island, Desmond eventually uncovers Kelvin's lies, noticing that his hazmat suit is torn and following him out of the hatch. Hume is also skeptical of Locke's claims to be an innocent survivor of a plane crash when he first encounters him in the hatch at the beginning of season 2. And when Desmond reappears at the end of the season 2, his skeptical nature leads him to challenge Locke's assertions that the button has no real function. Despite Locke's violent certainty, Desmond uses the readout from the other hatch to prove empirically that his failure to push the button on September 22, 2004, was responsible for the crash of Oceanic flight 815.

Yet unlike the philosopher David Hume, Desmond is open to the possibility of omens and miracles. We learn that Desmond at one point contemplated suicide but was deterred by the sounds of Locke banging on the hatch cover and his discovery of Penelope's letter. Ironically, Locke and Desmond's conversation about this incident has opposite effects on them.

Locke initially interpreted the light streaming through the hatch window to be a miraculous omen. By the time he talks about this with Desmond at the end of season 2, however, he is so bitter and disillusioned that he dismisses the significance of the light, suggesting that Desmond was probably just going to the bathroom. Hearing Locke's story has exactly the opposite impact on Desmond. When he learns that Locke caused the banging that prevented him from committing suicide and led him to turn on the light, he sees it as an amazing confluence of events in which two people received exactly what they needed at exactly the right time through a process of events that overtly appears to have been coincidental. Although the philosopher Hume would no doubt see this as purely accidental, Desmond is willing to see it as fate. It is this openness that leads Desmond eventually to conclude that it was his failure to push the button that caused Oceanic flight 815 to crash.

Thus, by the end of season 2, Locke and Desmond are moving in opposite directions, Locke toward nihilism and Desmond toward faith. Desmond's renewed faith and sense of moral duty eventually lead him to use the key, at the risk of his own life, in an attempt to save lives and stop the effects of Locke's destruction of the computer.

While one might assume that Hume's skepticism would entail the rejection of morality, in fact, he argued that all of us have a natural sympathy for others and that we should act morally for the sake of the overall public good, what he called *utility*. Thus, Hume would see Desmond's act of self-sacrifice as moral and commendable. In season 3, Desmond's sacrifice results in his seeming rebirth. Unlike the other survivors of the hatch explosion, Desmond has a mystical experience in which he travels through time and reemerges on the island naked as the day he was born. Desmond is now the one who must struggle, specifically with the dichotomy between free will and determinism.

In "Flashes Before Your Eyes," Desmond encounters Eloise Hawking, who tries to convince him that he must act in accordance with a predetermined path. Like her apparent namesake, the physicist Steven Hawking, she is a master of the intricacies of the space-time continuum. She claims that any attempts to change the time line will ultimately fail because the universe has a way of "course correcting." Interestingly, she also tells Desmond that if he doesn't go along with his destiny, then "every single one of us is dead."

This seems to be a contradiction. If everything is predetermined and the universe will correct any attempts to alter fate, then how could it be possible for Desmond to derail destiny sufficiently to kill us all? Perhaps because of his awareness of this paradox, once Desmond returns to the beach, he ignores Ms. Hawking's warnings and devotes himself repeatedly to saving Charlie from the death he has foreseen, even when, in "Catch-22," he believes that doing so changes the identity of the parachutist from his beloved Penny to Naomi.

In this episode, Desmond and Brother Campbell discuss the biblical tale of Abraham and Isaac mentioned earlier. Desmond tells Brother Campbell that he thinks it's interesting that the monastery chose the name Moriah, the name of the place where God asked Abraham to sacrifice his son ("Not exactly the most festive locale, is it?"). When Brother Campbell reminds Desmond that God ultimately spared Isaac, Desmond argues that God "need not have asked Abraham to sacrifice his son in the first place," leading Brother Campbell to respond, "Then it wouldn't have been much of a test, would it, brother? Perhaps you underestimate the value of sacrifice."

Brother Campbell seems to be urging Desmond to accept the need to abandon the ethical and make the Kierkegaardian leap of faith. Yet Desmond is not ready to do this. His conscience won't let him abandon Charlie, despite his overwhelming desire to see Penny. Like the philosopher Hume, Desmond skeptically rejects the possibility of miracles. He is unwilling to believe that if only he chooses to allow events to unfold without intervention, then his faith might be rewarded. Interestingly, Brother Campbell has a photo on his desk of himself with Ms. Hawking, suggesting that they may be colleagues. This makes sense, because they both preach the same message of stoical acceptance of one's fate.

In the final episodes of season 3, Desmond convinces Charlie that he must sacrifice himself so that Claire and Aaron may be rescued. Yet when the time comes to make the swim down to the Looking Glass station, Desmond once again changes his mind, demanding that Charlie stay safely in the boat. Ultimately, though, despite Desmond's best efforts, Charlie dies exactly as Desmond predicted.

Season 4 finally reunites Desmond with Penny in one of the most moving scenes of the entire series. Desmond and Penny go on to have a child, and Desmond succeeds in protecting Penny from Ben's threat to kill her. While Desmond initially participates in the events that bring the castaways face-to-face with Eloise Hawking, ultimately he has no reason to return to the island, so he walks away. Although we see him briefly on Oceanic flight 815 in the season 6 sideways opening, he doesn't reappear until "The Package," when it is revealed that Charles Widmore has kidnapped him and brought him back to the island because of his special powers.

In this episode, Desmond becomes the first of the castaways in the sideways world to remember the island; his faith and sense of purpose are thus restored. Yet again, Desmond encounters an Eloise Hawking who knows that they are in a divergent reality. She tries to convince Desmond not to rock the boat, but Desmond ignores her warning that he is not yet "ready," as he pursues his own version of Jacob's tour of the candidates. Unlike Jacob, however, Desmond does not manipulate people without their knowledge. While showing respect for their individual autonomy, Desmond places each of the castaways in situations where they will "wake up" and remember their real lives. Hurley soon joins Desmond in this reunion tour, until everyone but Jack has remembered his or her real life.

Returning to the island, Desmond now displays a calm fearlessness that baffles both Widmore and the Man in Black, each of whom plans to use Desmond for his own purposes. In "What They Died For," Widmore tells the Man in Black that Desmond is a "failsafe," a weapon of last resort capable of destroying the Man in Black, as well as the island, if all else fails. The Man in Black, in contrast, believes that he can use Desmond to gain his freedom.

In the end, both are proved partially right, because Desmond's removal of the stone in the Heart of the Island begins the destruction of the island, while simultaneously rendering the Man in Black mortal. Once Kate kills the Man in Black, Jack is then able to replace the "cork" and repair the light. While Jack dies, Desmond survives, and we are left certain that Hurley, the new Jacob, and Ben, his number two, will find a way to return Desmond to his wife and child so that he may live a full life now that the island is finally done with him.

It Worked

In "The End," the sideways world is revealed to be a kind of purgatory, a place between life and death where people may resolve their final inner conflicts until they are ready to let go and proceed together with those closest to them into the afterlife. Philosophically, this moves *Lost* firmly away from the secular existentialism of Sartre toward the existential religious beliefs of a Kierkegaard or a Martin Buber.

According to the Jewish theologian Martin Buber (1878–1965), God only enters the lives of those who wish it. If one chooses to live one's life without God, then rational explanations will be available for every experience. Many people choose to live self-obsessed lives in which others are seen as mere pawns to manipulate in order to fulfill one's desires. Such people relate to others in what Buber called an "I-It" relationship. For most of *Lost*, characters such as Ben, Widmore, the Man in Black, and even Jacob use other people to get what they want. They engage in "pseudo-listening," only interested in the thoughts and feelings of others to the extent that they can use these to reach their own ends.

Yet Buber contended that a true "Ich-Du" ("I-Thou") relationship is possible. Using the pronoun *du* (the intimate form of the second person singular in German, like *tu* in French), Buber described how one may construct an authentic and loving relationship with another person. For example, for the first few seasons, Sawyer, James Ford, was always working a con, using others to get what he thought he wanted (money, sex, revenge, and so on), while maintaining an attitude of arrogant superiority in which he mocked others and amused himself with his use of insulting nicknames.

James begins to genuinely care for others only after he exorcises his personal demon, the original Sawyer, Anthony Cooper. Indeed, James ultimately chooses to create an unexpected I-Thou relationship with Juliet that transforms him into an authentic person, capable of joining a loving community. For Buber, the disclosure to others of one's deepest feelings and hidden parts allows each of us to open up to the possibility of God by initiating a genuine dialogue with him.

The reunion of James and Juliet in the finale is one of its most moving scenes. In addition to the romance, the scene also contains a wonderful example of the writers' humor. After Juliet dies, Miles tells us that her last thought was "It worked." Most viewers interpreted this to mean that Jack's plan worked, and the sideways world was a real time line in which Oceanic flight 815 never crashed. When we finally hear Juliet say the line in the sideways world, however, we realize that she was referring not to Jack's plan to change the time line but instead to her own scheme for rescuing James's Apollo candy bar from the vending machine.

With its emphasis on the meaning of faith, *Lost* always had a spiritual dimension. From the second season on, the writers purposely misdirected the characters and the audience into believing that Jacob or possibly the Man in Black represented the divine. Yet as we have already discussed, Jacob was no perfect god. Although his intentions may have been more moral than the Man in Black's, Jacob was only a man who used dubious means to get people to do what he wanted.

Throughout the series, repeated references were made to "the rules," seemingly supernatural guidelines that must be followed by Jacob and the Man in Black (or Ben and Widmore) in the pursuit of their aims. But *Lost* itself undermined the importance of those very rules. For example, in "Across the Sea," a young Man in Black tells Jacob that if he devises his own game, he can make up the rules. Indeed, again and again, it is suggested that the person with the most power makes the rules and deceives everyone else into believing those rules are absolute. In "The End," we discover that there is spiritual meaning beyond the petty struggles of life (even beyond the struggle over control of the light on the island) and beyond the so-called rules for achieving salvation.

Once Jack "wakes up" and speaks to his father in the finale's closing moments, we see that they are in a building that, while resembling a church, is unlike any usual house of worship. This "church" displays the symbols of all religions, both Western (Christianity, Islam, Judaism, and so forth) and Eastern (Buddhism, Hinduism, Taoism, and so on). It is thus reminiscent of the claim of the great Indian spiritual leader Mohandas Gandhi (1869–1948) that all religions are paths to the same place. Gandhi believed that the different rules of the world's religions are irrelevant as long as one reaches enlightenment.

The prominent role of the Dharma Initiative in *Lost* indicates the writers' interest in Buddhism. Many Buddhists consider the Dharma (the teachings or rules of the religion) to be a mere vehicle to reach nirvana (the extinction of desire and suffering). Just as you leave your car behind when you reach your destination, you should abandon the need for absolute rules once you are ready to "move on" in loving community to the afterlife.

I started this chapter by praising *Lost*'s ability to show us that people regularly construct models of reality that are fundamentally different from those of the people around them. I end now by praising the show's ability to demonstrate that those carefully constructed models are ultimately irrelevant and unnecessary. It is only the Smoke Monster of intolerance, hatred, and greed that makes those differences seem important. Namaste.

PART THREE

U IS FOR UNITY

LOST'S STATE OF NATURE

Richard Davies

The phrase *state of nature* crops up frequently in comments on *Lost* for two main reasons. The first is that two of the leading characters in the program (John Locke and Danielle Rousseau) bear the surnames of two philosophers who are famous for having used the phrase *state of nature* as a key term in their writings on political philosophy. These are the Englishman John Locke (1632–1704) and the Swiss Frenchman Jean-Jacques Rousseau (1712–1788). The second, much better, reason the phrase crops up so much in discussions of *Lost* is that the situation the survivors of Oceanic flight 815 find themselves in after the crash can indeed be usefully described as a state of nature.

Before coming to some differences among the ways that Locke, Rousseau, and other philosophers have thought about the state of nature, let's consider a negative, and rather abstract, characterization of it that would be recognized by everyone working in the tradition of political philosophy that Locke and Rousseau consolidated: In a pure state of nature, none of the codes and expectations, none of the rules and hierarchies, none of the roles and presumptions that make up the fabric of our social lives is operative, can be relied on, or can be enforced. Presented in this abstract way, a situation like this is very difficult to imagine. After all, very few of us have any experience of anything remotely similar.

The very difficulty of imagining something that fits the (negative) bill can help explain why Locke, Rousseau, and other philosophers have taken differing approaches to giving a more positive and concrete account of the dynamics of a supposed state of nature. Indeed, many philosophers, including another who gives his name to a character on *Lost*, the Scotsman David Hume (1711–1776), have thought that the difficulty of imagining a state of nature is a reason for not taking it as a key concept in theorizing about politics. If it is a hardly imaginable situation, it won't be of much help in our understanding of the societies we actually live in.

In what sense, then, can the situation of the survivors of flight 815 be described as a state of nature? Well, at the outset, most of the people (except the pairs Jin-Sun, Shannon-Boone, Michael-Walt, and, to a small extent, Jack-Rose) are strangers to one another. They are individuals each with his or her own interests and aims, above all to survive in the face of the unfamiliar challenges of the island. They cannot be sure what the other castaways will be prepared to do to ensure their own survival, and they have no authority to turn to, either to tell them what to do or to protect them from harm. This, again, is a negative account of their situation, but I want to use some tools that have been developed within the tradition of the state-of-nature theory to help us understand some more positive factors in evidence in the early episodes of *Lost*'s season 1 that the survivors can use to patch together at least part of the social structure that has gone missing as a result of the crash.

Lining Up for Peace

In one sense (which Hume, the philosopher, was right about), a pure state of nature is just a philosopher's thought experiment, whose interest—if any—is only theoretical, but there is also a sense (where Hume missed a trick) in which we do encounter partial, or as I shall say "framed," states of nature all the time. Every time, in fact, that the interests of various individuals are in potential conflict for some limited good.

Although philosophers have been thinking about scenarios of how conflicts evolve ever since Plato, one of the most influential modern theorists of the state of nature was Thomas Hobbes (1588–1679). Hobbes's *Leviathan* (1651) takes its title from the monster in Job 41:24 and refers to the monarchical absolutist state that seemed to Hobbes the only viable alternative to the anarchy that he describes in chapter 13 of the book. In describing the state of nature, Hobbes takes aim at the idea that man is by nature a social animal by stressing the conventional nature of any way of resolving conflict.

Let's take a day-to-day example of a framed conflict. When I have filled my cart at the supermarket, my aim is to get out as quickly as I can. The same goes for all of the other stressed-out cart pushers. Each of us wants the immediate attention of the cashier, but there are only three registers open and fifteen loads of shopping to be paid for. In Hobbes's words, the fifteen shoppers are in a condition of "war, where every man is enemy to every man."[1] The surprising thing, then, is that, given Hobbes's drastic way of putting the matter, massacres at the supermarket checkout are fairly rare. What each of the fifteen shoppers normally relies on is the expectation that the other fourteen will follow the usual practice and form lines. This is a purely conventional practice that creates what I'm calling a frame.

When we form lines, the conflict between me and the other shoppers isn't exactly resolved but is at least kept under control. I still want to get out as quickly as I can and so do the others, but we all recognize a procedure for reducing the likelihood of violence. Each of us takes a step back from our own interests in the hope that the others will do likewise. Slightly less rare than supermarket massacres are those people who don't merely wish the others weren't there but act as if they weren't (or ignore the item limit in the express lane). If anything, it is these people who might deserve just a splash of bloodshed. They deserve it because they don't act within the frame established by line forming.

With this trivial example, we can get a measure of the purity or severity of a state of nature. Because getting out of the supermarket in two minutes, rather than ten, doesn't make a great deal of difference to my life, the other shoppers are my "enemies" only to the value of eight minutes of mortality (which I'd set aside in the first place when I decided to go shopping). Hence, the principle: *the more vital or scarce the good that is the object of conflict, the purer and more severe the state of nature.* Because I can be pretty confident that others will abide by the norms for forming lines, even the shoppers in front of me are, in a sense, also my allies because, by doing what's expected of them, they make shopping that much less stressful (and risky) for everyone. Hence, the principle: *the fewer or weaker (that is, the less likely to be observed) the frames, the purer and more severe the state of nature.*

In these terms, we can see that the survivors on *Lost* do find themselves in a pretty severe state of nature, because they are no longer guaranteed the means of basic survival that had been secured by the society from which they are now isolated. What's more to the point, it is hard for them to tell in advance what frames, if any, will apply to the distribution of those goods. Even if they know the conventions that apply in the supermarket, each is unprepared for the conditions of the island, and so each has reason to suppose that the others will be equally in the dark about how to act.

The question, then, is: What can they do to reduce the severity of the state of nature? This is a question about the procurement of the means of survival. More crucially, however, it has to do with the way each of the survivors can come to trust the others not to make things worse. How do conventions get set up?

Human Nature and Natural Man

One major question on which state-of-nature theorists have disagreed is whether, to understand the emergence of a society, we have to take a position on the very nature of mankind. Any effort to answer the question of "human nature" can easily lead to arguing in circles ("Man is by nature such-and-such because that's what he's like in a state of nature; so in a state of nature he acts in such-and-such a way"). Nevertheless, two sorts of stands have emerged about how to think of humanity in the raw.

Jean-Jacques Rousseau, for instance, is credited with thinking that by nature, man is a compassionate and altruistic creature. According to his *Discourse on the Origin of Inequality* (1755), the state of nature offers an ideal against which the corruptions of society can be measured. In this direction, Rousseau—and with him others such as David Hume—would say that humans are fundamentally governed by benevolent passions. In a similar vein, other philosophers, such as John Locke in his second *Treatise on Government* (1690), would say that as long as reason guides our behavior, we do not infringe on the rights of others. For short, we can call this sort of attitude "Innocence"—not least because it is a key term in Rousseau's writings.

In contrast, Hobbes is generally interpreted as regarding man as wholly egoistical and suspicious of his fellows. This, as we'll see, is not a necessary part of his theory. Instead of referring to the historical Hobbes, we can say that the view opposed to Innocence would be one according to which people always operate on the motto adopted by Special Agent Fox Mulder: "Trust no one" or, rather, "Trust No 1," which phrase we may use as a summary of the attitude in question. According to this more bitter view, human beings are fundamentally antisocial and aggressive in their self-defense, even when their behavior appears to respect conventional frames.

Innocence and Trust No 1 are labels for what are claimed to be the basic orientations of human beings, which would be given free rein in a situation where the norms of communal living have come unstuck. It may be that one or the other is a true description of what *would* happen in those circumstances. As I've said, though, we have little direct knowledge of what does happen in such an extreme situation.

Perhaps Innocence is not a wildly inaccurate description of how Hurley and Jack behave. And Trust No 1 is not a wildly inaccurate description of how Sawyer (at least in season 1) and Locke (the outdoorsman, not the philosopher) behave. But I, at least, don't claim to know that either Innocence or Trust No 1 accounts for the actions of all human beings. And I think we can get on perfectly well without them if we want to understand the interactions among the survivors on the island. Indeed, I think that we can understand the state of nature *better* if we are not distracted by speculative theories about the "nature" of the people in it, beyond recognizing that as animals they need such things as food, drink, and protection.

Amid the Wreckage

Immediately after the crash, the plane is the survivors' source of food and drink. As long as they believe that they will be rescued soon, they can consume these supplies without second thoughts.

After about a week, though, Hurley discovers that someone has taken some bottles of fresh water, leaving only eighteen for the rest of the group. Hurley's intuitive—and accurate—analysis is that the others would "freak out" if they knew ("White Rabbit"). They would freak out because each individual wants for himself as much of the limited good (water) as he can get, while knowing that the more he takes, the less there will be in the long run for everybody, himself included.

Unlike the supermarket, where my access to a limited good (the attention of the cashier) doesn't reduce the total amount of that good available to all (at least, until closing time), water is a good precisely when it's consumed: every drop I drink is a drop less for others who have some claim on it. Situations of this sort are a special case of the state of nature and are known as "tragedies of the commons." A tragedy of the commons is a situation in which it looks unreasonable for each individual to give up his or her access to a certain good, even though the cumulative effect of many individuals' access spells destruction of the good itself.

Charlie suggests rationing as a resolution to the water tragedy. That is, each survivor must reduce his or her own consumption to allow all to have at least a minimum. Yet this requires everyone to subordinate his or her own interests to those of a group that is only just forming. Each person can ask, "Why should I give up my water to people I don't know or care about?" The tragedy here is that it's very hard to answer that question. It's a question that would only be put by someone who doesn't recognize group survival as a good, over and above his or her own.

Jack refuses to decide anything about how to distribute the water, because he, too, is in the same situation as the others and—quite apart from his "Daddy Issues"—has no authority to impose rationing. In a fit of optimism to minimize the importance of the theft from the group's common property, Sawyer tells Kate, "Water has no value, Freckles; it's gonna rain sooner or later." ("White Rabbit") He's surely right that when there's enough water to go around, no one needs to privatize it. Yet it's the possibility of a "later" that comes after the castaways have all died of thirst that makes the tragedy urgent.

When Jack is led to discover a stream of fresh water later in the same episode, and the survivors pick up skills of hunting and fishing, they are no longer in tragic conflict with one another for vital goods. Because none of the other survivors is a threat to the survival of each of them, there's no reason not to group together. Because his immediate needs can be met, even Locke (the outdoorsman) can socialize with the others, although this is a matter of preference or temperament; if Sawyer shuns the company of the others on the beach, that does no one any harm. And because each person can look after himself or herself, there's no need to plan for more than the time being and no need for any of them to make any sacrifice for a common purpose—for instance, in making an effort to get off the island. There is no real urgency about Michael's raft, although we can understand that he does want to get home sooner or later.

The condition of minimal bodily security corresponds to the core of what Locke (the philosopher) had in mind when he talked about a state of nature. Prior to the formulation of a social contract, there's no government and no particular need for one. All humans are, as Locke said, equal and independent, and everyone has the right not only not to be harmed "in his life, health, liberty or possessions" but also to take and use the things he or she finds in the environment, so long as there's "enough and as good" left for the others.[2]

The Longer Haul

Although the survivors of flight 815 have been lucky in the climate and the availability of food and drink, there are several kinds of goods that they don't have the means or the skills to make for themselves. For instance, even though they cannot make new clothing, there's plenty on the plane, and, in any case, they don't need much more than beachwear. Other goods, unlike clothing, are in short supply. One case here would be Sawyer's cigarettes. If he's the only smoker, then the fact that he cannot renew his supply is a problem only for him (apart from Charlie, who also has a problem getting his drugs).

Likewise with Shannon's toenail polish: no one else wants a pedicure, so her using it causes no one else any upset (apart from the irritation factor for Boone ["Pilot: Part 1"]).

Things are a bit different when it comes to medicines. We have here the making of a tragedy of the commons that the survivors are not in a position to resolve.

In the first days on the beach, Jack takes it for granted that he's authorized to use all of the antibiotics he can find on the plane to treat Marshal Mars. Here, he must be supposing that their stay on the island will be short-lived and that the immediate use of the drugs is the only reasonable course of action to try to save a life.

If, however, he had thought that they were going to be stranded for a long time, it isn't clear that using up what there is in trying (and failing) to heal one severely injured man would be the best line to take. After all, the drugs could be of more benefit to more people if spread over more, and more curable, cases. As Sawyer says, Jack may not be "looking at the Big Picture, Doc." ("Tabula Rasa")

We can keep that problem of medical ethics on hold, while allowing that Jack did well to go through the luggage of the other passengers and take all of the stuff ending in "-myacin" and "-cillin" ("Pilot: Part 2"). That is, even if the antibiotics count as the common property of all of the survivors, Jack should be given control of them for the benefit of people who need them because only he knows how to use them.

Shannon, unlike her claim to her nail polish, isn't the only one who lays a claim to her antiasthma inhalers. Nonetheless, she has a double claim to them. First, consider that she (or, rather, Boone on her behalf) brought the refills with her; presumably, she paid for them and thus has what we might call a legal property right to them. Second, consider that her health depends on them; she's the only asthmatic on the island and thus has what we might call a moral priority in their proper use.

The trouble arises from Sawyer's having taken some of the contents of Boone's suitcase, such as his copy of *Watership Down* ("The Moth"). If the luggage of those who died in the crash can be rifled for clothes and antibiotics without injustice (when Kate takes the walking shoes off the corpse to make the expedition to find the plane's cockpit in "Pilot: Part 1," she isn't *stealing*), why not also that of the survivors? Isn't it all just luggage and, so, fair game?

When Jack confronts Sawyer in "Confidence Man," Sawyer brazens it out, saying that on the beach, "possession is nine-tenths," meaning "of the law," where the law is "finders keepers." This explains why he brushes off Jack's accusation of looting the fuselage in "Tabula Rasa." Although he doesn't say what the other tenth of the law is, Sawyer is standing up for the idea that in a state of nature, it's every man for himself, a clear instance of his Trust No 1 attitude.

As Hobbes put it, "If any two men desire the same thing, which nevertheless they cannot both enjoy, they become enemies." (*Leviathan*, p. 87) This means that the past property relation that Shannon enjoyed toward the inhalers is scrubbed by the new circumstances. Her legal right no longer counts, because there's no constituted authority (such as the police or law courts) to enforce it. And Sawyer is no more obliged to recognize her moral claim than, in "Pilot: Part 1," Hurley is *obliged* to give an extra portion of food to Claire because she's eating for two (although he does so out of Innocence).

Faced with Sawyer's refusal to "do the right thing" (and assuming, rightly or wrongly, that he has the inhalers), Sayid and Jack take it upon themselves to defend Shannon's cause by capturing and torturing Sawyer ("Confidence Man"). In so doing, they are beginning to move away from the Lockean state of nature toward a position in which legal and moral claims can be enforced and the use of violence (an infringement of the right not to be harmed in one's health) can be justified. Jack and Sayid are not acting in *self*-defense but are rather seeking to defend the rights of others, which is a different concept altogether: that of punishment. In doing so, they are on the way to constituting what Locke calls "a civil society"—of sorts.

Over or Under the Language Barrier

Neither Sayid nor Jack is stronger than Sawyer, but working together and using stealth (they attack him while he's napping), they can get the better of him. This is what Hobbes calls the "equality of ability": "the weakest has strength enough to kill the strongest, either by secret machination, or by confederacy with others." (*Leviathan*, p. 87) The association between Sayid and Jack requires them to trust each other for the purposes of getting information out of Sawyer about where the inhalers are hidden.

There are two obvious conditions for their being able to reach such an agreement. One is that they already agree on Shannon's claim—legal or moral or both—to the inhalers. The other is that they understand each other, that they share a language. This is also a condition for their being able to get information out of Sawyer: Sayid would be a useless torturer if he couldn't put the questions and get the answers. The fact that the overwhelming majority of the passengers on flight 815 are speakers of English, as a first or second language, means that they can share information and signal their intentions to one another. It also means they can lie to one another.

Jin is the exception; he can communicate only with Sun. As soon as they arrive on the island, Jin reaffirms their previous asymmetrical relationship (marriage), with him giving the orders and her taking them, because, at that point, he believes that she's not in a position to talk to the others ("Pilot: Part 1"). The pair keeps a distance from the wreckage, so Jin is the first to seek food from the sea. There are two possible interpretations of what he does after filleting the strange orange creature he has fished out of the water ("Pilot: Part 2").

According to one interpretation, rather than try the food himself, Jin is looking for guinea pigs to test its edibility. In this account, he doesn't care what happens to them because they are not a part of any group that he recognizes as binding on him. Jin would thus be applying Trust No 1. Even though Hurley tends toward the accepting attitude of Innocence, he declines the offer, not only because he prefers airline snacks—or even hunger—to natural food, but also perhaps because he's not sure of Jin's motives.

In the other interpretation—taking into account the fishing community Jin comes from—Jin can be understood as trying to overcome the language barrier by making a move that's widely recognized as a peace overture. Indeed, the offer of food convinces Claire of Jin's inclination toward Innocence.

Confidence and the Con Men

Even if a shared language is *necessary* for generating the higher grades of trust and cooperation, it's not *sufficient*.

On the one hand, we might think about the suspicions aroused by Walt's discovery, in "Pilot: Part 2," of the handcuffs in the jungle. The cuffs mean there's at least one person on the island who was regarded as a criminal and who therefore might still be dangerous. When, later in the same episode, Sawyer accuses Sayid of being a terrorist, he backs it up with the allegation that Sayid was sitting with his arms covered at the back of business class and never moved out of his seat. The others present at the scene can't tell whether Sawyer really saw what he says he did, but they are given some reason for thinking that it was Sayid who was wearing the handcuffs. What they don't know—but we do—is that Sawyer is a professional liar and, as we have already seen, inclined to Trust No 1.

On the other hand, there's Marshal Mars's warning to Jack that he should not trust Kate ("Tabula Rasa"). Jack can be pretty sure that a man—and a U.S. marshal at that—on his deathbed will be speaking the truth, but Jack still does not heed his words. We can distinguish two aspects of this.

One is that Jack trusts his own feelings more than Mars's information. For sure, Jack recognizes that he doesn't know whatever it is that the marshal knows about Kate's past, but he doesn't want to think the worst of a person who has so far behaved with fortitude and in the interests of everyone. After all, he has himself benefited from Kate's help in sewing up his wound on their first meeting ("Pilot: Part 1"), and, by dismantling and distributing the parts of the pistol, she made it impossible for any one individual to have a monopoly on its use ("Pilot: Part 2").

The other point—and this is a crucial feature of a situation in which people don't have background knowledge of one another—is that it's the "Island of Second Chances." As far as Jack is concerned, Kate is free to wipe the slate clean: there's a presumption of Innocence. In "Tabula Rasa," he repeatedly says things like "It doesn't matter who we were" and "It's none of our business."

We might pick up a hint of uncertainty here about the relations between "before" and "after" the crash. Although, in addition to Shannon's moral claim in virtue of being the only asthmatic, Jack defends her property right as a leftover from the society from which the survivors have been isolated, he seems not to think that Kate's criminal record means anything without the criminal system that keeps the paperwork.

Roles and Rules

What Jack undoubtedly carries over from his life before the downing of flight 815 is the fact of being a medical doctor. Equally obviously, he doesn't carry with him his degree certificates, and there's no authority on the island to license his practice of the Hippocratic art. By contrast, Arzt asks the others to address him as "Doctor," although he is in reality a schoolteacher. (The apparent title may be regarded as no more than a nickname understandable to someone who knows a bit of German.) It's the fact that Jack has acquired skills that makes him a doctor and, so, as Sawyer ironically puts it, "a hero" ("Pilot: Part 2") or, in Boone's challenge, "our savior" ("White Rabbit").

As we saw with the antibiotics, Jack's expertise confers rights, but it also carries with it the duties of a doctor, and it's up to him, more than to anyone else, to do what he can for the injured. When Sawyer fails to put Mars out of his misery with his one bullet ("Tabula Rasa"), Jack must act, as he had refused to act before, and put an end to his patient. In this case, his role as doctor means that he must break the rules that apply off the island and save Mars from an agonizing death that could not otherwise be avoided with the resources available. Another nice dilemma for the medical ethicists, but a clear case of the special responsibility of skilled practitioners to decide.

Although the previous occupations of most of those on the island have little bearing on how they interact, the crash itself produces a category to which they all belong: that of survivor. As Hurley says in "Pilot: Part 2," "We're all in this together." To get a bit clearer on who "we" are, he sets himself to compile his census, trying to find out from each of them where they come from and what they were doing on the flight.

When Hurley and Boone compare the resulting list with the flight manifest, they discover that the man who calls himself Ethan Rom was not on flight 815. This is clear confirmation that the island is not as deserted as it at first seemed, and means that the forty-six who have been trying to get to know one another now face a potential external threat: there's an "us" and a "them," the Others.

The immediate effect of this discovery is to bind the survivors together, and Locke (the outdoorsman), who had previously stuck to his motto, "You can't tell me what I can't do" (first announced in "Walkabout"), now becomes a defender of the group's integrity, organizing a search party to rescue Claire from the man who has abducted her and who is now definitely not one of "us." Here, his knowledge of the jungle gives him the right to give orders to his comrades.

As Locke (the philosopher) put it, the survivors determine to "act as one body." (*Second Treatise*, sect. 96) This is the moment at which we witness the birth of what can properly be called a commonwealth, in which, by the consent of its members, roles can be established and rules can be laid down for the good of all of those included. (*Second Treatise*, sect. 126)

Tit for Tat

So far, I've been running a counterpoint between the causes of conflict in a state of nature and the means of its resolution. I want to conclude by briefly illustrating a general ground for thinking that it's the condition of initial conflict that really matters to how a state of nature turns out.

Take any situation in which two people can either cooperate with each other or not in some enterprise, and suppose (1) that if they each cooperate with the other, then they will both get the optimum result; (2) that if they both refuse to cooperate, they will go without the full benefit but are not much worse off; and (3) that if one cooperates and the other doesn't, the non-cooperator gets a less-than-optimum result but still better than if they had both refused, while the cooperator gets the worst outcome.

This sort of situation is easily illustrated by the case of two suspects in a crime, in which, say, one held the bank staff hostage, while the other emptied the vault. The police don't have evidence enough to convict either man unless at least one suspect sings. The suspects are kept in separate rooms, and the police offer a deal to each: as long as he's the only one to accuse the other, he will get a reduced sentence to, say, a year and the other will go to jail for ten years. If each accuses the other, then they both go to jail for five years each. Because of the kind of case that can be used to illustrate the basic structure, the sort of choice involved is called a prisoners' dilemma. It's worth stressing that when we talk about "cooperating" here, we mean the suspects not squealing on each other. We're not talking about helping the police.

Even though the prisoners' dilemma can be illustrated with this sort of instance, two variables in the situation can be adjusted. One is the number of times the players have to make their choices. The other is the number of players involved. As the number of repetitions or the number of people involved increase, there start to emerge strategies for dealing with these sorts of situations.

What makes the prisoners' dilemma a dilemma is that the suspects don't know for sure what the other one has done or is going to do. In a prisoners' dilemma, the attitude we have been calling "Trust No 1" would indicate noncooperation to avoid the worst case for me. Even though I risk five years in jail, at least I can be sure not to go down for ten. Making the opposite choice, Innocence would offer cooperation out of fellow-feeling, even at the risk of coming off worst. I do not accuse my accomplice, in the hope that he, too, has faith in me.

Yet neither option is particularly convincing as it stands, and it would be crazy to rely on some theory of "human nature" to decide what to do if you might go to jail for ten years, rather than walk free. The craziness is most obvious when the dilemma is repeated more than once and involves the same people over again. In that case, the thing to do is consider what the other person did the last time and act accordingly.

What does *accordingly* mean here? Well, there is a strategy that has been shown to do better than any other over the long run, and that has been called "tit for tat." As its name suggests, tit for tat says that you begin by offering cooperation, and after that, you should do whatever the other person did last time around: if she didn't cooperate, you shouldn't; if she did, you should, too. If she, too, is running tit for tat, then, given that you both begin by cooperating, you should both continue to get optimum results.

Gaining Trust from the Past

The reason that I didn't want to attribute Trust No 1 to Hobbes is that I think that chapter 13 of *Leviathan*—the one I've been quoting from—envisages a situation in which a previous society has fallen apart by violence (for instance, a civil war—which was a particularly traumatic experience for Thomas Hobbes himself). When that happens, the first move everyone makes is to withdraw cooperation. In this sense, a Hobbesian state of nature begins at the second round of a repeated prisoners' dilemma in which the first round was noncooperative. Given what we've said about "acting accordingly," it's not a winning strategy for people to start cooperating when the others are being uncooperative. As Hobbes recognized, to begin cooperating—and, in particular, to be the first to begin—is to put yourself at your enemy's mercy.

For this reason, I suggest that pretty much everything in *Leviathan* that comes after chapter 13—with all of the famous stuff about natural laws, social contracts, sovereign "leviathans," and the rest—is wildly misleading: once you're in a pure Hobbesian state of nature, you're a goner. Hobbes himself might have half-seen the problem, which is why, at the end of chapter 14, he put in the idea of an "oath," sworn before God to reinforce the contract. Yet this is no solution at all; among other things, why should God be so bothered about having His name taken in vain, when there's so much other mayhem in the state of nature and all of the other Commandments (except perhaps the one about graven images) have been broken? Although I know that this is not a popular interpretation of the book, it might justify the fact that virtually no one can be bothered to read all of the remaining four hundred pages of text.

With the same people in it and with the same tendencies to diffidence or to trust as in a Hobbesian state of nature (second round), a Lockean state of nature has to begin with a first round of tit for tat and can only explain a breakdown of cooperation by the unreasonableness of some of the people some of the time. If the difference between Hobbes and Locke on the state of nature can be seen in light of the point reached in a repeated prisoners' dilemma, then the relations among the survivors in *Lost* can be understood in terms of how closely their behavior is modeled on tit for tat.

We've been looking only at the very early episodes of season 1 to see how, from being strangers to one another, the survivors come to adopt reasonable approaches on how to interact with one another so as to promote longer-term interests—their own and those of the group as a whole. What is pretty clear is that arbitrary theories of human nature, such as Innocence and Trust No 1, wouldn't really stand up over the long run.

Rather, the survivors used their shared language to signal their intentions to one another. By so doing, they overcame tendencies to uncooperativeness and thus got a community off the ground. Sometimes, as when the split occurred between the group on the beach and the group in the caves (not to mention the problems of dealing with the Others), allegiances varied. Yet group identifications helped them deal with shortages (tragedies of the commons) and put through collaborative endeavors (such as hut or raft construction). Once cooperation was under way, it tended to stabilize in accordance with the Lockean starting point in tit for tat, and those within the group could cohabit in harmony. When external threats arose, however, then the very same strategy dictated a refusal to be the first to cooperate, as in a Hobbesian state of "war."

The prisoners' dilemma and its resolution with tit for tat are only schematic tools for understanding the state of nature, but I suggest that they do at least begin to help us see how they can be generalized to cases involving the forty-six survivors on the beach who continue to look for negotiated solutions to their evolving situation. And it's not only *Lost* that can be seen in this light. There's also life off the island, not simply for the Oceanic Six, but also for the rest of us. As we've already heard Hurley say, "We're all in this together."

NOTES

1. We modernize the spelling and cite in brackets the pages (here p. 89) of Richard Tuck's edition of Hobbes's *Leviathan* (New York: Cambridge University Press, 1991).

2. See his second *Treatise on Government* (1690) of which the standard critical text was edited by Peter Laslett (Cambridge, UK: Cambridge University Press, 1960), sects. 6 and 27 respectively.

FRIENDS AND ENEMIES IN THE STATE OF NATURE

The Absence of Hobbes and the
Presence of Schmitt

Peter S. Fosl

Despite the sublimity and beauty of the island onto which
the survivors of Oceanic Airlines flight 815 have fallen, one
would be hard-pressed to describe the setting of *Lost* as a
Garden of Eden, a Xanadu, or a paradise. That's because of
the inhabitants already living there, the ones who come to be
called "Others" and who emerge from the jungle to assault,
abduct, and kill the castaways. It's also because on the island
lurks a terrifying Smoke Monster, apparently supernatural
forces, and, from time to time, the armed henchmen of a
very determined billionaire. Precisely because of the island's
bizarre nature, the island is a metaphor for the human condition, dramatizing the way that reason and passion battle for
control in modern society. We find ourselves rooting for the
good guys and seeing ourselves in them. But what exactly do
these "good guys" stand for, and what does that tell us about
our own political ideals?

Locke: Reason, Rights, and Torture

It's no accident that the names of a number of the most prominent characters on *Lost* allude to early modern philosophers who thought about what people would be like in a "state of nature," beyond the reach of human civilization, in a state of natural freedom, a place without government or much of any kind of social institution. I'm, of course, referring to the French philosopher Jean-Jacques Rousseau (1712–1778) and to the English philosopher John Locke (1632–1704). Although the characters on *Lost* who are named after these philosophers don't precisely represent the philosophers' philosophical theories, their prominence does, I think, give us a clue to the meaning of the show.

In order to understand human society and, in particular, the nature of legitimate power and authority, Locke developed his vision of the state of nature. In the Lockean vision, each person is naturally *free*—absolute lord over himself or herself, free from external authority. Each free individual is also *equal* to every other, with no artificial social hierarchies to establish privilege and subordination. Moreover, each is—and this is important—*rational*, born with innate, natural capacities to reason. Reason is important for Locke, because it allows people to apprehend a set of *natural rights* that also exist prior to society and therefore provide not only guidance for societies, when they come along, but also an independent standard by which any society can be judged. Among the most important natural rights that Locke identified are those of life (or security of one's person), liberty, and property.

Governed society comes along, according to Locke, as people realize that in the state of nature, they're vulnerable and likely to have their rights trod upon. Recognizing this problem, people get together and, by mutual *consent*, set up a contingent authority over themselves to secure the rights they possess naturally, as well as other new rights that might be conferred by government. By contrast, illegitimate governments derive their authority not from consent but by conquest and coercion. This distinction makes democracies legitimate forms of government and dictatorships illegitimate. The flip side to government by consent, of course, is change of government by consent (the repudiation of authority). Characteristic of governments by consent, then, is that they can be changed by the will of the people, and—what was especially radical to early modern thinkers—rebellion against them is legitimate when the government fails to secure natural rights or itself violates those rights.

Jack's rising to a position of authority among the survivors of Oceanic flight 815 in season 1 seems, at first, to follow the Lockean model in a fairly straightforward way. Although no formal vote is ever taken, Jack does not acquire authority by conquest or domination. Jack's leadership receives acknowledgment and consent through his bringing security to the survivors' bodies with his medical care, through his issuing directives that are followed and that produce rational order, as well as safe habitation. And, let's not forget, Jack organizes the group's defense against Ethan Rom (an anagram for "Other Man") and the Others when Ethan abducts the pregnant Claire (Jack's half-sister) along with Charlie. Jack Shephard is, as his name implies, their shepherd. Ana Lucia, the former cop and officer of state power, similarly rises to authority through her ability to provide (a bit of) security to the tail section survivors. Unlike the castaways of *Gilligan's Island*, the Oceanic survivors need real protection.

To a remarkable degree, people follow Jack's directives only because they consent to them. There is almost no coercion, and those who wish to go their own way—for example, Sawyer, Kate, and Locke—are free to do so. In fact, deviations from this principle of uncoerced authority seem shocking (such as when Locke ties up Boone to prevent him from telling the other castaways about the hatch). There are no police, no courts, no surveillance, no informants, and no prisons among the survivors or at least among the fuselage survivors. Indeed, on the whole, aside from the position of Jack as "leader," freedom and equality are maximal.

But this liberal edifice isn't without its cracks. When I speak of *liberalism* in this chapter, I am not speaking of liberalism as opposed to *conservatism* in the way those terms are used in contemporary U.S. political discourse. Rather, I mean liberalism as the political philosophy that values liberty and equality and aims to eliminate conflict and secure rational peace. Returning to *Lost*, consider the recurring issue of torture—in particular, Sawyer's torture, which seems a decidedly serious violation of the liberal political idea of human rights, especially because Sawyer is not one of the Others. Like the American republic in the wake of September 11, 2001, *Lost* finds itself both endorsing and fretting about the use of torture. By implication, we might wonder whether, like the American republic, *Lost* isn't fretting about how far it's willing to endorse liberal ideals.

This anxiety unfolds in the frequency with which torture is used, and it also appears in the way the show almost simultaneously regrets and excuses torture's application. Here's the general template *Lost* follows: when those on the island resort to torture, they do so with clearly liberal justifications for its use; their use of torture, however, almost invariably fails in its objective, and those who engage in torture suffer the pangs of guilt afterward. When, alternatively, people besides the survivors, on and off the island, and in survivor flashbacks engage in torture—for example, Sayid's torture of a woman in Iraq—the conduct is more unambiguously wrong, although even then the show does its best to present mitigating circumstances when torture is administered by someone (such as Sayid) who will become a survivor.

When Sawyer is finally subjected to torture (at the hands of an American-trained Iraqi), he is (mistakenly) thought to be hoarding medicine that could save Shannon's life, medicine that arguably doesn't belong to him in the first place. Sayid tortures Ben because the survivors suspect him of being one of a group that has already assaulted them, threatened their lives and liberty. (The survivors' suspicions are, of course, correct, but Ben never cracks.) Ana Lucia confines Sawyer, Jin, and Michael in a kind of prison and threatens Nathan with torture. She does so, however, only when she comes to believe that they also threaten fundamental Lockean rights to life and security. (It turns out that she's wrong; none of them pose genuine threats, and her actions lead to Nathan's death.) Dogen's torturing Sayid also seems motivated by his concern that Sayid may be a threat.

The challenge that Ana Lucia presents to the liberal social order of the survivors extends beyond her willingness to torture. In her gun-wielding, physically abusive, interrogating, incarcerating, and threatening conduct, we see a streak of the tyrant. Indeed, as philosophers have long recognized, it's common for those who rise up in the name of the well-being of "the People" to become tyrannical.

Yet, when the group insists on stopping in the jungle to camp at a water source, Ana Lucia, unlike a tyrant, yields to their will. Moreover, Ana Lucia's coercive behavior with Libby and the rest of the group occurs only after she kills Shannon and has reason to believe that she has placed herself outside of their society and perhaps even at war with it. After Eko convinces Jack and Locke that Ana Lucia is not their enemy and after she herself talks things through peacefully and honestly with Sayid, she is reincorporated into the survivors' society. Her violent, dictatorial, and illiberal conduct toward the survivors then comes to an end. Anyway, she pays for her violation of the liberal order with her leadership and with her life. Near the end of the series ("Dr. Linus"), even tyrannical Ben—after having violated many people's rights and killed Locke and Jacob—on expressing remorse and vulnerability is reincorporated into the survivors' community. But he has paid a price, too, a terrible price, for his violation of the liberal order in the death of his daughter, Alex.

Rousseau and Hume:
Friendship and Feeling

One might also, perhaps, point to Sawyer as an illiberal element of survivor society, but it's an accusation that is similarly limited. Sawyer does, yes, adopt a dictatorial posture after he cons the rest of the survivors into turning over their guns ("The Long Con"). Then again, that posture is a reaction to Jack's stealing the guns from him, violating his natural right to have possessions. In any case, Sawyer's posture, like so much of Sawyer, is an act. He never really exercises dictatorial control over the group, and he gives up much of his weaponry and medicine quickly and willingly, partly in honor of a peaceable bargain he made with Jack while playing cards.

More important, Sawyer gives up the goods as a result of the way his feelings and passions play on him. His sexual desire allows Ana Lucia to acquire the gun that Michael will use to shoot Libby, and through his consequent feelings of pity and guilt, he turns over the medicine that might save Libby's life. Sawyer's killing Anthony Cooper and Tom does show an illiberal willingness to violate the right to life, but neither seem premeditated and rather show us how powerful Sawyer's emotions are. In any case, this recognition of the power of feeling to bind and separate people is no trivial matter. In fact, it's central to the way a number of other early modern thinkers justified their liberal political theories.

The feeling of pity that drives Sawyer, for example, illustrates an important element of the political theory of Jean-Jacques Rousseau, as well as of Rousseau's sometime friend and contemporary David Hume (1711–1776). For Rousseau (a thinker who was considered one of the seminal theorists of the French Revolution and was associated with positive images of the "noble savage" leading a natural life uncorrupted by society), fellow feeling and the feeling of pity underwrite liberal society as much as reason does for Locke.

In the *Social Contract* (1762) and *Discourse on the Origin of Inequality* (1755), Rousseau developed a vision of the state of nature in which people enjoy the natural freedom to pursue the good and noble desires that are natural to them. The establishment of a government by consent for Rousseau, as with Locke, expands human freedom—but not simply by constructing a rational order that secures and elaborates natural rights. For Rousseau, the agreement that creates the state also creates an utterly new social being, something greater than the mere sum of the individual parts that compose it. It creates a collective thing that fuses individuals together into a larger whole, what Rousseau called the *general will*.

We see the emergence of this collective in "White Rabbit" when Jack ends a fight that's broken out among the group, gathers them together, and lays down their founding principle: "If we can't live together, we're going to die alone." The collective is also evident whenever the survivors refer to themselves as "we" and "us," and when Locke proclaims in an emotional speech in season 3 that he will retrieve those captive to the Others and bring them "home" ("I Do").

The Scottish philosopher David Hume thought the "state of nature" a pointless fiction and didn't believe in the "general will."[1] Yet he did share with Rousseau an important idea. Hume powerfully argued that what binds people together isn't only reason's calculation of personal interest or "self-love" but also various other-regarding feelings or sentiments. Human beings are "mirrors" to one another, wrote Hume, in that through "sympathy" they take on the feelings of others—feeling, in a sense, their pains and pleasures. Rousseau, for his part, held that each human being has pity, something that will "mitigate, in certain circumstances, the ferocity of his egocentrism . . . by an innate repugnance to see his fellow suffer."[2] In the show's social dynamics, the force of pity and sympathy are as prominent as they are powerful.

It is pity to which Juliet appeals when she asks Jack to help save Colleen. It is pity to which Ben appeals when he says he wants Jack "to want" to help him. Pity again when Eko carries wounded Sawyer through the forest. Even pity when Jack euthanizes U.S. marshal Edward Mars shortly after Sawyer's pity-driven attempt at a mercy killing fails ("Tabula Rasa"). Juliet's pity leads her to help Sun and contributes to her defection to the survivors. Alexandra's pity drives her to risk her beloved Karl, sending him to help the survivors. Kate's pity pierces the barrier of hostility separating her from Sawyer when she reads the letter she believes he wrote to the con man who destroyed Sawyer's family ("Outlaws"). Kate also appeals to Jack's pity when she begs him to operate on Ben so that the Others won't kill Sawyer.

Who Needs Hobbes?

Indeed, Kate becomes an especially important vehicle for a number of the liberal philosophical claims of *Lost*. Not only is Kate an erotic focus, evoking the desires of many of *Lost*'s central male characters (Sawyer, Jack, Ben)—especially through her distinctive proclivity for showering onscreen—her words and deeds also carry a specific kind of philosophical freight.

Kate advances the idea that people are not entirely selfish, that it's sentiment and feeling that bind people together, and that the collective surpasses the individual. The title of the episode "I Do," for example, doesn't refer only to Kate's failed marriage to police officer Kevin Callis and her choosing Sawyer. It also refers to the crystallization, in the face of her enemies and the adversity she now faces, of her fierce commitment to the survivors, even at the cost of her self-interest. Yet the dramatic scene in "I Do" where Jack's last-minute intervention saves Sawyer from execution isn't the first time Kate has put others before herself.

Previously, in "Every Man for Himself" (note the title), Kate refuses to climb free of the Hydra station cage, ignoring Sawyer's plea for her to look to her own interest and escape. By staying with Sawyer, Kate directly repudiates the selfish principle articulated by the episode title, embracing instead the principle Jack had established for the collective at its very founding moment (that's right, "live together, die alone"). As if having already made this point to Sawyer in "Every Man for Himself" wasn't enough, Kate in "I Do" literally screams her affirmation of the principle to Jack across the span of their separation, reminding him and us what the social order of the survivors is all about or, at least, is supposed to be all about.

Again, Kate's stalwart refusal—like Pickett's fury, like Sawyer's defiant kiss at the work site, like Juliet's insubordinate enlistment of Jack's surgical skill for Colleen, like Michael's desperate efforts to save his son, like Charlie's wild attempt to baptize Aaron, and like many other events in the series—illustrates the ever-present power of passion to join people and to cause individuals to risk themselves for the sake of those to whom they are bound.

Kate's conduct, however, also repudiates the doctrines of an early modern philosopher tellingly not named on *Lost*, one whose striking absence among the characters is explained by this repudiation. Thomas Hobbes (1588–1679) preceded Locke and Rousseau as a philosopher of human nature, government by consent of the people, and the authority of the state. A giant of that period, Hobbes is nearly always mentioned in the same breath with the other two, so his absence from the highly literate nomenclature of *Lost* seems hardly accidental.

Like Locke and Rousseau, Hobbes in his *Leviathan* (1660) and *De Cive* (1651) imagined human beings existing in a state of nature without government. Unlike Rousseau, however, the condition Hobbes imagined was a pitiless one, a world without fellow feeling, populated by wholly selfish beings, where each was enemy to every other in what Hobbes described as a "war of all against all" (*bellum omnium contra omnes*). If Hobbes was different from Rousseau in attributing no pity to humans in the state of nature, he differed from Locke in rejecting the idea that the state of nature includes any natural rights or natural laws, except for the right of self-defense and the law of survival.

You see, for Locke society is something like a farm or a garden—a methodized and corrected natural order. Lockean government, like a farmer, nurtures and cultivates the soil of human nature and natural rights in a way that is consistent with the laws of nature so that human beings will flourish peaceably and rationally. For Rousseau, the invention of society is more like the invention of human flight. Like an aircraft, according to Rousseau, society must honor nature and nature's rights (lest it crash in terrible corruption), but the delicate invention of society nevertheless allows us to transcend nature, to take a higher, enlarged view of our world and ourselves.

For Hobbes, by contrast, the state and society exist largely in order to limit, control, and oppose nature. People flee the state of nature because life there is, in Hobbes's famous phrase, "solitary, poor, nasty, brutish, and short."[3] Like wild beasts that must be broken and bridled, humans must, according to Hobbes, be coerced by threat of violence to recognize the rule of law and the rights of others. The social order satisfies more selfish desires than does the state of nature (and that's why people choose it) but only as a consequence of limiting those desires. Like a caged animal in a zoo, the beast can remain well fed, peaceful, and long-lived only by being contained.

The state of things among the survivors themselves is decidedly not Hobbesian, as Kate affirms. In the absence of the coercive powers of the state, the survivors don't return to a war of all against all, where the strong take what they want when they want it from the weak. People on the island don't steal, rape, and murder as they please, acting strictly as individuals. They recognize the rights of others, but not from fear of punishment. And they don't devolve into the sort of savagery depicted in William Golding's *Lord of the Flies* (1954). The survivors of Oceanic flight 815 are social beings, through and through, woven together by bonds of reason and feeling.

On the other hand, at first blush there does seem to be something Hobbesian about the survivors' relationship with the Others. The survivors may not be Hobbesian among themselves, but their relationship with the Others is nothing if not struggle and conflict. This probably shouldn't be surprising, because many have argued that while Hobbesian theory may not describe human individuals very well, it does accurately describe the relations among nation states. The Others, in particular, seem to take what they want from the survivors (notably, the survivors' children). Their gassing the people of the Dharma Initiative; their tossing their victims' bodies into an open pit, leaving them unburied; their taking over Dharma property; their ruthless disregard for the rational resolution of disputes; and the complete absence of pity and sympathy from them all exhibit their Hobbesian qualities.

Yet, despite these apparent indications, trying to see the relationship between the Others and the survivors through a Hobbesian lens doesn't entirely work. In the first place, the Others don't simply take because they can, and they don't assert their claims as matters of raw power and desire. They advance a moral justification for their actions, maintaining that they are the "good guys." Second, curiously, Ben honors the Others' agreement with Michael to provide him with a means off the island with Walt if Michael will successfully lead a specified group of the survivors into a trap—and Ben does so in the absence of any coercion ("Live Together, Die Alone"). If this is the case, then, perhaps no one on *Lost* is named Hobbes because the show rejects the Hobbesian vision. So, how should we understand the Others?

It's important to remember for the sake of my argument that Hobbes, despite his differences with Locke and Rousseau, was still a liberal philosopher. That's because even though he rejected the liberal idea of natural rights beyond self-defense, as well as the idea that people are bound together by feelings like pity and sympathy, Hobbes shared with the other liberals the same goal—namely, overcoming the conflict of the state of nature through a government founded on the consent of the governed. For the early modern liberal philosophers, government and society are artifices, technologies, invented to put an end to conflict and war and to replace them with peace, reason, happiness, and order. Conflict, struggle, and war are, for liberal political thinkers, problems that can be solved, problems that ought to be solved.

But recognizing this common trait among liberal philosophers is just what makes it possible to realize the persistently illiberal character of *Lost*, despite its pretensions, even its aspirations, to the contrary. In many ways, *Lost* pretends to defend a liberal, Rousseauian, and Lockean social order and to reject cynical Hobbesian ideas about human nature and political authority. Like the Smoke Monster that emerges from the island's idyllic forests, however, something even darker than Hobbes's philosophical vision slithers through the narrative of this popular American TV show.

About Schmitt

Rather than to Hobbes or any of the early modern liberal political philosophers, it's to a more recent intellectual whom we should turn in order to understand the philosophical claim that *Lost* makes about human societies. Carl Schmitt (1888–1985) was known as the "crown jewel" of the Nazi jurists. And despite his unapologetic service to Adolf Hitler's regime, Schmitt's philosophical work, especially *The Concept of the Political* (1927), has remained important, bizarrely enough enjoying a recent flurry of interest among left-wing philosophers.

Schmitt's central thesis is that an "enemy" is necessary to the formation and development of society. If liberal political theory is defined by its goal of eliminating conflict and securing a rational peace, Schmittian-Nazi theory is defined by its embracing conflict and war as not only desirable, but essential. This thesis becomes incarnate in the survivors' relationship with the Others.

The ancient Greek philosopher Aristotle (384–322 B.C.E.) regarded friendship, even love (*philia*), as crucial to the political order, and he characterized a friend as someone who (1) gives pleasure, (2) is useful, and (3) makes one a morally better person.[4] For Schmitt, by contrast, a friend is a member of one's own political group, an ally set against a common enemy. Whether anyone is an enemy or a friend is the most basic of political decisions, and to be a member of a polity is to be on one side of a struggle against people on one or more other sides: good guys versus bad guys, Swiss Family Robinson versus the pirates, Americans versus the terrorists, the United States versus the USSR, the United States versus Iran, the United States versus Saddam Hussein, the United States versus al-Qaeda, the Bloods versus the Crips, the University of Kentucky Wildcats versus the Louisville Cardinals, Republicans versus Democrats—us versus them. Subsequent political decisions, for Schmitt, turned on the question of whether a course of action would help one's friends and harm one's enemies. Helping friends and harming enemies is, in fact, the fundamental project of the polity. Put in terms of early modern liberal theory, the state of nature, so far as it exists among social groups, should be preserved.

Lost seems to take a similar view. Although the survivors among themselves often operate according to many liberal conceptions of social order, if we look closer, especially at their relationship with the Others, we find that those liberal pretensions don't run very deep. The survivors of Oceanic flight 815 don't simply form a society because of the infelicities of the state of nature, because of the difficulties of their relationships with one another, because of their struggles with the natural world, or even because of their fellow feelings. They bond together as a society *in opposition* to another society, to an *enemy*. Their strong, unifying leaders rise to authority as warrior chieftains. Jack isn't only the first among equals; he is their Führer. The enemy they face, moreover, seems hopelessly nonliberal. Ben, Jack's anti-Führer, seems to be feared as a ruthless dictatorial leader who, if Juliet is to be believed, can be deposed only by killing him. Tom (perhaps a reference to Thomas Hobbes, after all?) is especially loyal to Ben, refusing to negotiate when Jack and the search party that is sent to retrieve Walt confront the Others in the forest ("The Hunting Party").

Season 3 of *Lost* begins by showing us things from the Others' point of view. This affords us more understanding of their conduct—but not much. And, more important, we see as season 3 opens no efforts (perhaps no capacity) on the part of either group to embrace the other; to offer hospitality; to find ways of forging bonds of fellow feeling, friendship, and sympathy; to resolve conflicts peaceably and rationally; to solve problems collectively; to formulate a rule of law to regularize interactions; to share and cultivate the abundant resources that surround them; and to join in defense against the black Smoke Monster and the polar bear. Nothing of the sort is attempted. Nothing of the sort seems possible. Yet why don't the Others send a rescue party with medicine and food to the crash survivors? Why don't they escort the survivors back to the safety of their compound and offer them help, care, shelter, and the chance to join their community? Because that sort of offer is impossible to imagine in a Schmittian political universe such as *Lost*. Others are "bad people," enemies, and like the cannibals that Robinson Crusoe and Friday fight, the only language the enemy can understand is brute force.

Like the American republic, this television show crash-landed on views of human nature and society current among

Nazi intellectuals more than sixty years ago. If Frankenstein's monster symbolized the repudiation of early modern utopian dreams of reason and love, the Dharma Initiative, which our heroes come to hate, is progressive and even utopian (*dharma* means "natural law" and "higher truth"). So far as I can tell, however, this show hasn't presented anything better to surpass liberal politics. Instead, *Lost* argues that because *dharma* fails to stop the return of the repressed from the forest's heart of darkness, our best chance for survival is to cast off utopian naïveté and embrace the Schmittian law of the jungle. In short, our best chance against the bad guys, the "evil ones," is to "blow them all to hell," as Führer-Jack nakedly puts it in "Greatest Hits." Even when the enemy surrenders, they don't really surrender, as Sawyer opines after he (murderously) blows Tom away. The only good Other is a dead Other.

Americans flatter themselves as being liberal and democratic in their political ideology. If at times they are given to violence, even extreme violence, they see the violence as unfortunate but justifiable, justifiable invariably because it's somehow necessary to secure their Lockean rights to life, liberty, and property. Sure, sometimes they feel a pang of guilt afterward, but, as they see it, whatever wrongs they commit are anomalous and nowhere near as bad as the others'. More often, Americans find their conduct to have been animated by pity and compassion, saving the world from the "evil ones." Like the survivors, they see themselves as beautiful and sexy, racially diverse (to a point), superlatively technical and scientific (especially in medicine), yet also deeply spiritual. On the whole, they bring good things to life. Americans are the "good people."

This liberal self-image, however, periodically crashes for Americans when faced with some other. Classically liberal in their self-understanding, Americans nevertheless have come to see others through Schmittian eyes. With an almost tiresome predictability, they imagine others to be dangerous, cunning, illiberal, and subhuman murderers, capable of understanding only force, sprinting to assault them even before they've crawled from the wreckage.

If movies such as *The Invasion of the Body Snatchers* (1956) and *The Creature from the Black Lagoon* (1954) and the giant insect movies of the 1950s incarnated American anxieties about communism, the Others of *Lost* incarnate American anxieties about the "enemies" the United States faces today. While the source of anxiety has changed, the response to it has not. In the face of problems posed by Islamic militant jihadis, the Taliban, the Palestinian resistance, Iraqi insurgents, Iran, North Korea, North Vietnam, communists, Black Power, Native Americans, Sith, or Mordor, the solution has so often been the same gruesome final solution: kill them all.

What's as astonishing, however, in the text of *Lost*, like the text of American culture, is that this dim view of "our" society's relationship to others persists even as we learn that the others are in many ways—in their thoughts, in their reading, in their bodies, in their history and ideas, in their manner, in their emotional lives, and so on—not, in fact, terribly other. As season 3 opens, we find that the Others read Stephen King, speak English, share the same biological features, share the same histories, play the same sports, suffer the same sorts of needs and feelings and desires as those that characterize the survivors. As Shylock puts it so well in Shakespeare's *Merchant of Venice*, "If you prick us, do we not bleed? If you tickle us, do we not laugh? If you poison us, do we not die?"[5] So, why, then, are the Others conceived as irredeemably other? Why do they remain others even after we discover they are not? Why does *Lost* chant with the French philosopher Jacques Derrida (1930–2004), even in the face of its own evidence to the contrary, "*tout autre est tout autre*" ("every other is totally other")?[6]

There seemed, in the logic of *Lost*, little to be hoped for besides continuing war between the Others and the survivors—and, as Ben proves right about Naomi, a new war with a new group of others, let's call them other-Others, people from Widmore's ship, the ship that Charlie figures out isn't Penelope's, just before he (pointlessly?) dies. Prior to the series finale, *Lost* seemed poised to follow the well-worn courses laid out by many narratives endorsed by American culture: another absurd showdown, a final confrontation between opposing hero-leaders (Ben and Jack/Jack and the Smoke Monster), the reestablishment of the dominion of the really "good" people with an act of redemptive violence. Another possible resolution available to *Lost*, or course, is escape from the state of nature through an act of transcendence. I toyed with the possibility of some deus ex machina like rescue helicopters or a friendly ghost (Walt or Jacob or Jack's dad) or an act of magic along the lines of Locke's surviving the mass grave, without any real resolution to the survivor's conflict with the Others and Widmore.

Alternatively, I had hoped for something better than the standard fare. My hopes looked for something like the eruption of some sort of feeling or passion that would shatter the stony fascistic order under which *Lost* had labored, consigning what in the show's future would perhaps be called the "Other War" to the rubbish heap of the three-toed colossus and other monstrosities.

The unlikely appearance of erotic love between the beautiful, spoiled, blond American, Shannon, and the swarthy, brooding Iraqi soldier, Sayid, signaled for me the possibility of reconciliation among enemies, of the overcoming of deep conflict through bonds of feeling. The attraction between Jack and Juliet and between Sawyer and Juliet exhibited something of the same. Might bonds of feeling, the desire for something besides war, and a recognition of what they share in common somehow appeal to what Abraham Lincoln called the "better angels" of human nature and reconcile the survivors of Oceanic flight 815 and the Others (and the other-Others)? Might the warring groups find a way to forge a democratic collective or a federation of ordered liberty, or perhaps even an Eden-like green world of peace and harmony, based on Aristotelian friendship and good old-fashioned love? Might they somehow come to help one another to get off the island? I confess to have harbored these hopes, but my understanding of the political ideologies popular among Americans today left me profoundly doubtful that my hopes would be realized.

My fear, given the currency of neofascistic ideas, was that any attempt to establish community among the combatants would die, like Shannon, in a hail of bullets, fear, and ignorance. Even worse, I worried that the dream of peace among the island's inhabitants, like the dream of peace between the United States and its adversaries, would asphyxiate in the gas chambers of Schmittian political philosophy and its terrible imperative to find in others not fellow human beings with whom one can sustain a common life, but an enemy to kill before that enemy kills us.

The Final Solution

Were my fears realized? Yes and no. The war continues, silly, boring supernatural devices are indeed deployed. And just when the Others cease to be so "other," another adversary, Team Widmore, reasserts itself. True, James and Juliet begin a love affair, overcoming their otherness. The survivors become assimilated into the Dharma Initiative. Even Ben becomes humanized, an object of understanding and sometimes sympathy. Of course, the show seems itself to become lost, stumbling through time, place, and various science fictions, abandoning the unities that had given the show focus. But at least the boundaries of otherness become blurred. For a time, even Widmore recedes into the background.

I began to worry, though, watching the episodes where the survivors are delivered from the repetitions of the island's space-time continuum by embracing nuclear weapons. As I feared, violence and destruction showed themselves to be irrepressible in *Lost*. Just as war seems on the verge of ending, the survivors find their way to a temple where a dopey ancient contest lumbers on. At the very instant that Ben is accepted by Ilana and reincorporated into her community, the phallic periscope of Widmore's submarine breaks the surface and casts its threatening, covetous gaze on the island.

When Smoke Monster Locke travels to Hydra Island to confront Widmore, he announces that war has come to the island. Yet this isn't quite right. It's not that war has finally reached the island. Rather, it's simply that the island war has, like the smoke, taken on a new shape. Indeed, Smoke Monster Locke's announcement signifies only that Widmore's war against Ben for possession of the island has become incorporated into the higher-level war, the background war, the primordial war, the war to sustain all wars, the war that makes the ultimate division between the camp of friends and the camp of enemies. I mean, of course, the struggle between Jacob and the unnamed Man in Black.

In medieval philosophy, thinkers such as Thomas Aquinas (1225–1276) found the idea of an endless series of causes and effects, stretching back into time, absurd and unacceptable. Instead, they reasoned, the chain must come to an end. There must be a first cause. So, it seems, in *Lost* the series of wars with "others" can't go on forever. As soon as the boundaries separating two groups break down, another "other" emerges, then another, and so on. But as for the medievals, so for *Lost*, the process must end somewhere. The series has, after all, reached its end, and it has done so in the divine.

One option for bringing the series of otherings to an end— the option for which I had hoped and for which modern, liberal political theory has aspired—is to overcome otherness and realize a peaceful common life through bonds of fellow-feeling, friendship, and love; through the recognition of common humanity; and through respect for universal human rights. In flying to the superhuman or divine, *Lost* does more than appeal to a cheap deus ex machina. It repudiates the modern liberal option and embraces not only the mouldering incense of religion but also the black smoke of death. Rather than achieve modern, liberal, reasoned peace, we're returned to a war of quasi-biblical proportions. The island becomes something far different from the "state of nature" of which Locke and Rousseau had mused. It becomes a technology, a stage (or a staging area), a petri dish, and an artifice for bottling up cosmic evil and ultimately, once the business of purgatory is complete, for leveraging the transition to some sort of pretentiously universalist afterlife.

This move toward the supernatural repudiates modern liberalism because if nothing else, modern liberal social contract theories were advanced to supplant medieval political theorists' reliance on the divine as a basis for social order. In the liberal state of nature, people instead are thrown back on themselves, and they ground their social authority on their own design and their own consent. In the last throes of the series, by contrast, we find that people are not on their own. They don't give consent for what befalls them. Their wills, their lives, and their circumstances have been manipulated by powers beyond them.

As it was in ancient Greek mythology, the story of Jacob and his brother positions the survivors as the playthings of the gods (or, anyway, of superhuman creatures). The early modern liberal philosopher Immanuel Kant (1724–1804) had argued that people ought to be autonomous and treated as ends in themselves, never as mere means. Yet, as *Lost* winds down, people on the island are treated more like Job in that odious story from the Bible—that is, as guinea pigs, as the subjects of a test, as the means to resolve a bet, as beings whose natural rights are of little (or, anyway, subordinate) concern. Jack, learning more about who's been pulling the strings than Job did, remarks (in "Ab Aeterno" and "The Package") that he now sees that there has been a "reason" for everything that has happened—that is, a reason beyond his own or any of the survivor's reasons. Jack doesn't seem to recognize, however, or even consider that the reason things have happened as they have, from a modern liberal point of view, is objectionable and itself grounds for rebellion.

Who is Jacob, anyway, to determine the course of people's lives, to interfere with their freedom? Who is he to select candidates to assume his position as sentinel of the island, manipulate their lives, expose them to countless dangers, and separate them from their loved ones and their property? If he, like his brother, is only an invention of the islanders' imaginations, then he exposes the islanders' Schmittian need for an enemy to be fought and killed. If he's actually a manifestation of something divine, then the freedom and self-determination of the islanders have been undermined by divine manipulation. Either way, the islanders' strategy for confronting the state of nature is by no means liberal in the classical sense of the word. All of this leads me to ask why, in a show like this, in a time and place like ours today, are such illiberal courses taken to offer resolution? The answer, as I see it, lies in the background social-political ideology not only of the show but of the American society that has produced it.

The conclusion of the show weaves together two different forms of redemptive violence that are characteristic of Schmittian and Christian ideology. First, there is what I might call "Schmittian violence"—that is, war and the extermination of the other, here the evil brother who becomes Smoke Monster Locke. Second is what might be called Christian violence, the violence of human sacrifice for the sake of redemption, the Jesus-Aslan moment that requires the hero to die, and preferably die at the hands of his or her enemy, in order to save the "good people." In the most ideal cases, the Christ-figure who submits to death is later resurrected (like Optimus Prime in *Transformers: Revenge of the Fallen*, 2009), just in time to lead everyone to the promised land. Jack, of course, executes both forms of violent resolution. He manages both, as a Schmittian hero, to kill off his enemy (with Kate's help) and, as a Christlike son of the Father, to die at his enemy's hand, to be resurrected, and to see his people enter something like the kingdom of God. In both of these acts of violence, the show finds its satisfaction, indeed a quasi-sexual satisfaction.

After Jack kills the Evil One, he enters a cave and inserts a stone into a hole, which then floods the chamber with life-giving wetness. Lying almost cruciform after having deposited his load in the cave, his side pierced just like Jesus', and then recumbent and spent among the bamboo shafts, Jack stares heavenward as if to say, "It is finished" (Jesus' final words before his death on the cross; John 19:30). The orgasmic imagery and symbolism of the closing scenes call to mind that the French refer to orgasms euphemistically as *la petite mort* ("the little death"). I can just picture Jack lying among the bamboo, looking up at the plane flying overhead while smoking a cigarette.

But it's not just human satisfaction that's at stake here. The Father and Christian shepherd's ushering the survivors happily into the afterlife stamps the islanders' wars, torture, and struggles with divine sanction and approval. To be saved and to find fulfillment, then, on *Lost* is to fight for the good side and to be victorious in its war. As left-behind Ben indicates, being contrite and forgiven is not enough.

It's both in this embrace of the necessity of violence and in this appeal to the divine that *Lost* exposes not only its own illiberal subtext but also something about the society that loves it so much. Americans, like the islanders on *Lost*, fancy themselves ultimately as the "good people"—people who fight on the side of divine righteousness and who deserve the rewards their violence has made it possible for them to amass. *Lost* panders to that fantasy. But the American demand for an enemy "other" to fight, as well as the great pleasure Americans take in doing so, suggests that their understanding of themselves as the "good people" may not be well founded. Despite their appeals to divine authority and despite their never-ending assertions of their justice and virtue, Americans just can't free themselves of the stench—can't free themselves of taking pleasure in the stench—of human smoke.

NOTES

1. David Hume, *A Treatise of Human Nature*, Book III, 1740.

2. Jean-Jacques Rousseau, *Discourse on the Origin of Inequality*, part 1, in *The Basic Political Writings*, trans. Donald A. Cress (Indianapolis: Hackett Publishing, 1987), p. 53.

3. Thomas Hobbes, *Leviathan*, chap. 8:

> Whatsoever therefore is consequent to a time of war, where every man is enemy to every man, the same consequent to the time wherein men live without other security than what their own strength and their own invention shall furnish them withal. In such condition there is no place for industry, because the fruit thereof is uncertain: and consequently no culture of the earth; no navigation, nor use of the commodities that may be imported by sea; no commodious building; no instruments of moving and removing such things as require much force; no knowledge of the face of the earth; no account of time; no arts; no letters; no society; and which is worst of all, continual fear, and danger of violent death; and the life of man, solitary, poor, nasty, brutish, and short.

4. Aristotle, *Nicomachean Ethics*, Book VIII and IX.

5. William Shakespeare, *The Merchant of Venice*, act 3, scene 1.

6. Jacques Derrida, *The Gift of Death*, trans. D. Wills (Chicago: University of Chicago Press, 1995), chap. 4.

IDEOLOGY AND OTHERNESS IN *LOST*

"Stuck in a Bloody Snow Globe"

Karen Gaffney

With every new season, *Lost* forced us to question what we believed about the show. The first two seasons gave us flash-backs, which, though a little unsettling at first, soon provided some comfortable context. Similarly, these two seasons established several fundamental notions about the Others; they were a bad, dangerous, deceptive group to be feared. Then the third and fourth seasons shook that foundation, bringing us flash-forwards and Others who become allies, not to mention a whole new group of people with unclear motives. Finally, with the fifth and sixth seasons, that foundation was not only shaken but also completely destabilized. The island disappeared, the survivors bounced around in time, and the bomb went off, prompting the flash-sideways. We could no longer depend on any basic notion of time, space, or reality. Who should we trust? Who's good, and who's bad?

In other words, the show progressively forced us to ask questions such as: How do we know what to believe? How do we know what's real? How are we taught to believe what we believe? A belief system is very powerful; for it to maintain its power, its inner workings can't be revealed. Yet I think *Lost* does just that. It reveals the process behind our belief system, or ideology.

Ideology: Drinking the Kool-Aid

To say that something is socially constructed is to say that it is created by society; it is not inherent, natural, or the norm. What is socially constructed *appears* to be the norm, however, because it is normalized, or taken for granted. No other way of looking at the world is even considered. This is how ideology functions. An ideology is a belief system, but in order for it to be effective, it must be perceived as the truth, rather than be seen as one of many possible belief systems. An ideology is like a pair of glasses you don't know you're wearing. You look through those lenses at the world as if that is the only way of seeing the world. Not only do you not know you're wearing glasses, you don't even realize that you might see the world differently through a different pair of glasses. An ideology ceases to function when it is seen as an ideology; to function properly, it must be subtly presented as "the truth" and taken for granted. An ideology you're aware of loses its power to construct your worldview. Like a pair of glasses, such an ideology can be removed.

The philosopher Louis Althusser (1918–1990) called the process of individuals becoming indoctrinated into an ideology *interpellation*. For interpellation to work, an ideology must be presented as a given so that it will be believed and taken for granted. Althusser described two different methods of controlling people: the repressive state apparatus (RSA) and the ideological state apparatus (ISA). RSAs function by force, such as the police or the military. RSAs can literally control people by placing them in jail. For example, in the first half of *Lost*'s third season, the Others imprison Kate and Sawyer in outdoor animal cages. This method of control is tangible and easy to see. In contrast, ISAs, such as religion, school, and the family, operate based on the power of ideology. People are interpellated into a particular ideology and then take that belief system for granted as the only way of thinking, without even realizing they were interpellated in the first place. Rather than being placed in a literal jail, they are placed in a figurative jail, an ideological jail, without knowing it. Continuing with the earlier example, not only is Sawyer imprisoned in a literal cage, but he is also tricked into believing that a device is monitoring his heart rate and will kill him if his heart beats too quickly ("Every Man for Himself"). The actual jail confines his movements to a certain degree, but then Sawyer himself contains his movements that much more for fear of triggering the device. He is taught to believe that the device exists, when in fact it never did. He is interpellated into an ideology that controls his movements and makes him paranoid.

In the final season, Sawyer provides a perfect metaphor for the process of interpellation. When he is talking to Kate about the plan to outwit Locke (the Man in Black) and get off the island, Sawyer says that Claire shouldn't be included, but Kate's entire reason for returning to the island was to find Claire and bring her back, so that Claire could raise Aaron. Of course, that was before it became clear that Claire wasn't exactly herself, having been "infected" with the same dark force (connected to the Man in Black) that infected Sayid. In describing the change in Claire, Sawyer says that she's been "drinking Locke's Kool-Aid." ("The Last Recruit") In other words, she has been interpellated into Locke's ideology; she believes whatever he tells her. In an earlier episode, Locke tells Kate about this process, saying, "I gave her something to hate." ("Recon") Claire was angry about losing Aaron, so Locke told her the Others had him; if he could funnel her anger toward the Others, then that would only help him. Again, Claire was interpellated into Locke's ideology, and this situation reveals how anger and fear are fundamental to that process.

Furthermore, on many occasions, the show gives an explicit nod to the concept of ideology. Consider the third season episodes "The Man behind the Curtain" and "Through the Looking Glass." The first, of course, is a reference to *The Wizard of Oz* and how Oz is ultimately an ideology constructed by "the man behind the curtain." The second is the title of a sequel to another major children's work, *Alice's Adventures in Wonderland*. Both stories explicitly question fundamental notions of time, space, and reality. Ultimately, though, I find the two most compelling examples of ideology to be "pushing the button" in the Dharma Swan station and then, of course, the representation of the Others.

Ideology and the Dharma Initiative: A Snow Globe

Early in the series, the survivors from the front section of the plane come across a hatch in the jungle. After considerable effort, they open it and find an extensive underground shelter, part of what's called the Dharma Initiative, complete with electricity, running water, food, weapons, and a social experiment that would make B. F. Skinner proud. They also find a man down there named Desmond, who insists that a series of numbers must be entered into a computer every 108 minutes in order to prevent the end of the world.

Jack's initial skepticism reflects his resistance to the ideology of pushing the button ("Orientation"). He says to Desmond, "It says 'Quarantine' on the inside of the hatch to keep you down here, keep you scared. . . . Did you ever think that maybe they put you down here to push a button every one hundred minutes just to see if you would? That all of this, the computer, the button, is just a mind game, an experiment?" Desmond responds, "Every single day." This conversation reveals that Desmond's skepticism still doesn't stop him from pushing the button and that Jack recognizes how fear plays a role in adopting a certain ideology.

Despite Jack's skepticism, when Desmond runs out of the hatch and disappears into the jungle, the survivors immediately begin to take shifts to make sure the numbers are entered and the button is pressed. But why? They have no clear evidence that anything bad will happen. If anything, the enterprise seems absurd and irrational, yet they become immediately interpellated into its ideology. Despite some disagreement, the survivors collectively buy into the ideology of the hatch, and once they start doing so, it becomes incredibly difficult to stop. The show's representation of the Dharma Initiative reveals how ideology operates. The audience does not take the ideology of the Dharma Initiative for granted as a given, which is how ideology must operate to maintain its power. Instead, the show forces us to be skeptical and constantly aware of the process and power of ideology.

Initially, Locke is passionate about "pushing the button," but when Mr. Eko and he discover another hatch in the jungle (underneath the question mark), Locke immediately replaces one ideology with another ("?"). They watch a videotape that explains this station's purpose, to "observe and record" the activities of the Dharma participants (via the multiple television screens). The tape instructs them:

> You and your partner will observe a psychological experiment in progress. . . . These team members are not aware that they are under surveillance or that they are the subjects of an experiment. . . . What is the nature of the experiment, you might ask? What do these subjects believe they are accomplishing? . . . You as the observer don't need to know. All you need to know is that the subjects believe their job is of the utmost importance. ["Orientation"]

Locke now decides that they were tricked into believing that pushing the button matters, when in reality they are "rats in a maze." While Locke was initially interpellated into the ideology of pushing the button, he is now interpellated into an opposing ideology that pushing the button is, as he says, "meaningless." Perhaps surprisingly, although Locke is critical of himself for having been so quick to believe the first ideology, he unquestioningly and immediately subscribes to the second ideology. Mr. Eko, on the other hand, finds his initial belief in pushing the button affirmed by their discovery in this station. When Locke substitutes one ideology for another, he thinks he is making the transition from a lie to the truth, when in fact he is merely substituting one constructed ideology for another.

Tellingly, when Desmond attempts to abandon the ideology of the island, he cannot. He sets sail only to be pulled back to the island, and when he realizes where he is, he says, "This is it. This is all there is left. This ocean and this place here. We are stuck in a bloody snow globe. There's no outside world. There's no escape." ("Live Together, Die Alone") His words neatly describe the insidious nature of ideology; one is trapped in a worldview. Theoretically, if one becomes aware of that worldview, then there is an opportunity to change it, but Desmond's experience reveals the difficulty of making that change. Locke could easily change his worldview from finding meaning in pushing the button to finding it meaningless, but both of those ideologies still function within the larger ideology of the island, because Locke so passionately wants to believe in the island and discover its secrets. When Desmond, however, literally tries to extricate himself from this larger ideology of the island, by trying to leave, he cannot, signifying once again the ideology's power.

Lost invites us to examine the process of how ideology works and how, in particular, people buy into an ideology that is socially constructed without thinking that it is socially constructed. Furthermore, because the show makes explicit the process of how ideology functions, that concept can be used as a theory for analyzing how the show depicts the socially constructed ideology of otherness.

The Others

The notion of otherness works on an ideological basis. To identify someone else as an "other" is to identify that person as marked in some way, whether it is based on skin color, religion, language, gender, sexual orientation, or some other category of difference that we use to divide people. Marking someone as other indicates a power relation, because the one who has the power to identify someone else as other is by definition normative, not-other, and unmarked. Perceiving someone else as other then becomes a process of identifying that person as inferior. Although the basis for otherness is often perceived as natural (such as race), it, like all categories of difference, is socially constructed, and one must be interpellated into a certain ideology in order to identify otherness.

Lost makes the notion of otherness explicit by depicting a group literally referred to as the Others. Throughout the series, perceptions of the group known as the Others constantly evolve and morph, reflecting the slipperiness of the very notion of otherness. For otherness to function, it must be slippery, and it must adapt to new moments. If it is static, it will lose its power.

The six seasons of *Lost* collectively reveal and then dismantle the ideology of otherness. Initially, the show depicts the multiple ways in which otherness operates, how it both creates fear and is created by fear, how it serves as a divide-and-conquer strategy, how it creates an "us versus them" mind-set, and how those who are associated with otherness are linked to savagery and to a lack of civilization. In the first two seasons, the survivors generally feared the Others, bringing the audience into that fear; the third and fourth seasons complicated matters by introducing sympathetic Others who became allies (such as Juliet). The fifth and sixth seasons took that complexity much further and brought in many new characters whose alliance with the Others was unclear, culminating in a conclusion where the Others actually seem to be good. Ultimately, the line between the survivors and the Others was entirely blurred and transcended.

Fearing the Others: "Run, Hide, or Die"

Consider how, in the first season, characters who have encountered the Others describe them to survivors who have not directly encountered them. Rousseau explains what happened to her when she was shipwrecked on the island sixteen years ago, specifically being pregnant and delivering the baby herself:

> Rousseau: The baby and I were together for only one week when we saw black smoke. A pillar of black smoke five kilometers inland. That night, they came. They came and took her. Alex. They took my baby. And now, they're coming again. They're coming for all of you.
> Jack: Who's coming?
> Rousseau: The Others. You have only three choices: run, hide, or die. ["Exodus: Part 1"]

The repetition of the word *they* is striking. That repetition focuses on a separation between "us" and "them," with "us" being the plane crash survivors and Rousseau and with "them" being this anonymous group literally called "the Others."

In the second season, when Ana Lucia, a survivor from the back of the plane, describes the Others to Michael, a survivor from the front of the plane, she reinforces that "us versus them" mentality. When Michael demands to know what happened to Ana Lucia and the survivors from the back of the plane, she says, "They came the first night that we got here. They took three of us. Nothing happened for two weeks. Then they came back and took nine more. They're smart. And they're animals. And they can be anywhere at any time. Now we're moving through the jungle, their jungle." ("Abandoned") Like Rousseau, Ana Lucia repeats the word *they* in order to reveal a profound difference between "us" and "them." She also describes them as "animals," which is a conventional way of dehumanizing a group and constructing its members as "other." Rousseau and Ana Lucia are incredibly fearful of the Others because the Others have posed a direct threat to them. This notion of the Others as a threat is important. Rousseau and Ana Lucia, however, are talking to fellow survivors who have not directly encountered the Others. Through their descriptions, Rousseau and Ana Lucia's fear spreads to the other survivors, who become extremely fearful as well, reinforcing the power of fear in the context of otherness.

Similarly, when Ana Lucia and her fellow survivors examine bodies of dead Others, she again reinforces the divide between "us" and "them." Ana Lucia says, "They're out here in the jungle with no shoes, nothing in their pockets, no labels on their clothes. These people were here before us." ("The Other 48 Days") In connection with Ana Lucia calling them animals, this last scene depicts the Others in stereotypically native and uncivilized ways. The brutality of their actions and their lack of predictability reinforce this perceived savagery and work together to build the fear that both Rousseau and Ana Lucia express. These two women successfully use fear in persuading the crash survivors from the front of the plane that the Others exist and are to be feared.

Rousseau and Ana Lucia have already been interpellated into an ideology of fearing the Others based on their past experience, and they in turn share that fear so that it takes on legendary qualities. Ironically, although clothing may seem to mark the Others, the survivors' own clothes are ripped and dirty and otherlike, so that it becomes very difficult for the survivors to determine who is an Other based on appearance, which confirms the socially constructed nature of the category.

Recognizing the Others: "There's a Line"

Despite the fact that Michael, Sawyer, and Jin have been interpellated into the ideology of otherness by Rousseau, they still don't recognize the Others when the two groups come face-to-face for the first time. Such a lack of recognition highlights the slipperiness of otherness. When the crash survivors leave the island on a raft, they soon encounter people in a motorboat and expect that these people will rescue them. Their hopes and expectations are dashed, however, as, to their horror, the people in the motorboat shoot one of them, kidnap the child Walt, and blow up the raft ("Exodus: Part 2"). Perhaps because the survivors have temporarily left the island, they leave the ideology of the island behind. It's as if the survivors on the raft have totally forgotten about fearing the Others; they seem naive and innocent, perceiving anyone coming toward them in a boat as a potential rescuer. That perception quickly changes, however, and they realize that their supposed rescuers are in fact the Others.

When Sawyer again encounters the man he believes to be the head Other (Tom), his innocence is lost ("The Hunting Party"). Sawyer, Jack, and Locke encounter Tom, knowing full well that he is an Other. Interestingly, Tom expresses his feeling of ownership over the island, depicting the survivors at first as disrespectful guests. He asks, "You go over a man's house for the first time, do you take off your shoes? You put your feet up on his coffee table? You walk in the kitchen and take food that doesn't belong to you? Open the door to rooms you got no business opening?" This last reference is, of course, to the hatch that the survivors blew open, entered, and now occupy. That hatch revealed the Dharma Initiative, which helps the audience see the way ideology functions. Tom then says, "This is not your island. This is our island. And the only reason you're living on it is 'cause we let you live on it." To the Others, the survivors are intruders, invaders who are at their mercy.

Tom's words lack context. One could interpret the Others' perspective as being that of indigenous peoples who are invaded by colonizers and are trying to protect their land. Conversely, one could interpret the Others' perspective as that of a nativist, anti-immigrant group seeking to maintain racial purity. The only real difference in these two interpretations is the power dynamics, because the power lies with the colonizers in the first example but with the nativists in the second example. Tom's words are also important because they invoke the notion of privilege and entitlement, claiming something as "ours" and controlling access to it. Furthermore, while Jack, Sawyer, and Locke perceive Tom as savage and uncivilized, he is accusing them of not knowing their manners, of essentially being uncivilized.

In this scene, the power dynamic shifts from Jack, Sawyer, and Locke to the Others. Jack first tells Tom that he refuses to become interpellated into the Others' ideology. He doesn't believe that the Others rule the island. Instead, Jack says, "I think you got one guy up there with a gun. I think there are more of us than there are of you." Of course, Jack's perception is short-lived, because Tom calls out, "Light 'em up," and Jack, Sawyer, and Locke become surrounded by a circle of people with torches. They are outnumbered, and Tom was correct that the Others did have control of the situation. He takes this power further by demanding that Jack, Sawyer, and Locke return to their camp, never to enter this territory again. He says, "Right here, there's a line. You cross that line, and we go from misunderstanding to something else." He describes "a line," which is essentially a border. The notion of the border is key in creating, maintaining, controlling, and protecting that power. Jack and the other two survivors here are shocked when they realize how greatly the Others outnumber them. That sense of feeling outnumbered and the way the survivors are surrounded just fuel their fear, which in turn furthers their ideology of otherness.

In the context of this moment in the series, the distinction between the survivors and the Others seems clear, impermeable, and immutable. Yet taking the final season into consideration and looking at this scene in retrospect, we can see how that supposed distinction between the survivors and the Others dissolves when it becomes clear that these three survivors—Jack, Sawyer, and Locke—are indeed candidates to succeed Jacob. In this way, as we will see, the show reveals how the ideology of otherness is constructed and then proceeds to dismantle that construction.

Another important aspect of the ideology of otherness is depicted in the second season: namely, the way in which it serves to divide and conquer. When the survivors who were on the raft make it to shore, they are, of course, incredibly fearful of the Others, so fearful of the Others, in fact, that when they see a group of people approach them on the beach, they assume they are the Others. In turn, this group of people assumes that the raft survivors are the Others ("Orientation"). The irony is that none of them are Others (they are all survivors of the plane crash); it's simply that they were in different parts of the plane and have crashed on different sides of the island.

In this scene, the men on the raft are approached by a group that appears otherlike. After all, they have giant sticks that they carry as weapons, and they are dressed in torn clothing. In turn, the men who were on the raft also appear otherlike; their clothing is ripped and dirty. Each group perceives the other group as the Others and therefore reacts with not only hostility but also sheer violence. Ultimately, though, the members of each group realize they are in fact fellow survivors of the crash, so they band together to fight against the "real" Others.

This complex series of shifts in perception raises another key issue: the way that the ideology of otherness can divide and conquer those who could have potential alliances. This divide-and-conquer strategy is successful at pitting groups against one another and preventing them from working together to fight against the power structure. The two groups of survivors have been taught to believe that the Others are incredibly dangerous, so their suspicion of one another hampers their ability to create an alliance, at least initially. Of course, the revelation in the sixth season that many of these survivors were or are candidates completely defies this survivor versus Other split.

Even before there was any hint of this revelation, it was clear early on that the Others weren't simply "Others"; they were somehow using a performance of otherness to perpetuate fear. In the second season, Claire, Rousseau, and Kate find the underground medical facility that was used for pregnant women ("Maternity Leave"). Kate comes across a locker with brown, ragged clothes and a cap, much like those worn by the Others. She even discovers a bottle of theatrical glue and a fake beard. Later, in "Live Together, Die Alone," when kidnapped by the Others, Kate refers to the fake beard on one of the Others, and he removes it, confirming her suspicion. It seems as if the Others are dressing up in stereotypically "otherlike" ways to perform and to be perceived as savage and uncivilized when in the presence of non-Others, but when they are not trying to manipulate any non-Others, they have an almost suburban, middle-class existence, complete with book clubs and football games. Again, in retrospect, this was perhaps an early clue that if they must dress up to be perceived as savage, then maybe they aren't actually savage after all, that they are in fact, as Ben says, "the good guys" ("Live Together, Die Alone").

Becoming the Others: "The Good Guys"

While the first two seasons clearly construct the ideology of otherness to depict the Others as manipulative, dangerous, rightfully feared, and savage, starting with the third season that construct becomes much more complex and slippery. Season 3 introduces us to the Others' suburban lifestyle in the Barracks and particularly to Juliet, whose motives are unclear but who ultimately becomes an ally with the survivors, breaking down the previously more obvious survivor versus Other division. Later that season, Naomi from Charles Widmore's freighter parachutes onto the island, raising questions about not only her motives but the motives of those on the freighter and their relationship with the Others. In the fourth season, we're introduced to several new characters from the freighter (Miles, Daniel, Charlotte, and Frank), whose motives are also unclear. Are they the enemies of the Others? Or allies? How do the survivors fit in? Juliet's sarcastic comment to Jack reflects the increasing complexity of the depiction of the Others. As she says, "It's very stressful being an Other." ("The Other Woman") Furthermore, season 5 reveals the complex factions within the Others; they are far from the monolithic group they first appeared to be. We see, through flashbacks, the evolving struggle for leadership of the Others between Charles Widmore and Ben Linus, ultimately leading to Ben banishing Charles from the island. Not only are the factions becoming clearer, especially through Charles sending the freighter and later the submarine to the island, but Juliet also makes another witty comment that reflects how the Others need to learn to be Others, which resists the idea that the Others are a natural group that automatically knows how to be Others. When Juliet tells Sawyer that she learned Latin in "Others 101" ("Jughead"), it ultimately reflects the socially constructed nature of the Others.

Finally, with season 6, instead of the show merely continuing to reveal the inner workings of the ideology of otherness, it actually dismantles that ideology completely through two important developments. First, not only do we realize that many of the survivors are in fact candidates brought to the island to succeed Jacob, but two of those survivors, Jack and then Hurley, actually become Jacob's successors, completely transcending the boundary between survivor and Other. Second, it becomes clear that Ben was right all along about the Others being "the good guys." Jacob's sole focus was on protecting the island. Richard served as his intermediary, and he worked with the evolving group of Others to identify candidates, protect them, and, at times, test them. Granted, the Others sometimes thought they were following Jacob's instructions when in fact they were being manipulated by the Man in Black (who could take the form of dead people such as Christian Shephard and Alex). Ultimately, though, during the course of every season, *Lost* has revealed the way the ideology of otherness is socially constructed and then, finally, taken apart, piece by piece.

"Lost"

When one is interpellated into an ideology, one has an understanding of one's place; in a sense, one is not lost. For example, if you are inside a snow globe, and you think that snow globe is the whole world, then you wouldn't think you were lost. Being lost seems to imply not having a clear worldview, such as when Desmond recognizes he's stuck in a snow globe and how that's not the whole world. Someone who is lost is aware of an ideology at work and so questions his or her perceptions.

Even though *Lost* forces us to be skeptical and aware of the power and process of ideology, there have been a few fascinating moments where we, the viewers, are interpellated into a particular ideology without realizing it, and we think we're "found." In the opening episode of season 2, we see a flashback to Locke, Jack, and Kate blowing up the hatch ("Man of Science, Man of Faith"). That scene is juxtaposed with the actual beginning of this episode, where we hear a beeping and see a man get up, type on an old computer, and play a record. Despite the juxtaposition of the hatch explosion and this scene, the viewer does not automatically assume that this latter scene is occurring inside the hatch. We then hear an explosion and the record player skips and some dust filters down from the ceiling. The camera winds its way through some passageways, up a long shaft, and then turns 180 degrees. We see Locke and Jack staring down. We were in the hatch and didn't know it.

We were interpellated into an ideology of believing that we were off the island when in fact we were deep in the Dharma Initiative. For a few moments, we thought we knew where we were; we thought we were "found," and then, just as quickly, we're lost again when we realize that those two scenes are the same place, and we're left with questions about Desmond, the hatch, and our perceptions.

The show repeats this clever move in the opening of the third season, when we see a seemingly typical suburban scene of a woman baking muffins and hosting a book club meeting ("A Tale of Two Cities"). As in the first example, our notion that we are off the island is again disrupted when the survivors' world collides with this one. In this second example, we slowly realize we are very much on the island when we hear an explosion of some kind and realize that a plane is crashing, Oceanic flight 815. Instead of being in the midst of a far-off suburban book club, we are with the Others.

Although one might think that the audience couldn't be interpellated into the same belief system twice, it happens easily. Such is the power of ideology. Furthermore, *Lost* repeatedly makes this process explicit; it is always drawing attention to the very nature of how we know what we know and how we decide what to believe. The show explicitly engages with what it means to be "lost" in an ideological sense, of not feeling grounded in a particular worldview. What is so interesting about the third season's opening is that despite so many encounters with the Others during the second season, we still didn't recognize them in the opening moments of this episode. The notion that the Others are difficult to identify runs throughout the early part of the series and only reinforces the slippery nature of otherness and the constructed nature of ideology.

As the seasons progress, the show plays with our perceptions even more. Every time we think we know where we are, the next moment loses us again. We had come to expect that scenes off the island were flashbacks, because the first two seasons and most of the third did that very consistently. Yet at the end of the third season, we start to see flash-forwards. Then, in the fourth season, the episode "Ji Yeon" juxtaposes flashbacks of Jin getting a giant panda for a new baby with flash-forwards of Sun delivering her baby. In an initial viewing of the episode, it's not at all clear that some of the scenes are flashbacks; the viewer tends to assume that they are one single story. Then, when Ben turns the donkey wheel and makes the island disappear, not only do the flash-forwards continue, but some of the survivors are also bouncing around in time on the island.

Fundamental notions of time and space are disrupted more and more as the series progresses, culminating in the final season's scenes of the flash-sideways world. We realize that we can't count on any definite notion of reality, time, or space. We have learned that every time we think we're grounded, the ground collapses under us, keeping us constantly "lost." Yet this lack of stability forces us to be aware of the way ideology operates and to recognize that we cannot trust our perceptions to tell us that what we see is in fact real. *Lost* makes us aware that we're wearing glasses, that we're being presented with something that is socially constructed, and that there are a variety of glasses or ideologies out there. With every new episode, we get a new pair of glasses, and we know we're getting them because the show makes that explicit.

Ultimately, *Lost* reveals to us the way that ideology operates. It shows us how otherness is socially constructed and the purpose it can serve in instilling fear, maintaining the status quo, and creating a divide-and-conquer mentality; it also reveals that this socially constructed category of otherness can be completely dismantled when the boundary between groups dissolves and the motives of these groups merge. Yet although there is a definite level of resolution in the finale when it comes to the Others, the series leaves several questions remaining, such as the ultimate meaning of the island, the light, and the flash-sideways world. This lack of resolution reinforces the way ideology operates. For ideology to function, it cannot be finite and resolved; instead, it must constantly shift. Over its six seasons, *Lost* did an impressive job of revealing how that process works, repeatedly forcing us to question how we know what we know. In the end, *Lost* showed us what it's like both inside and outside the snow globe.

PART FOUR

N IS FOR NECESSITY

ESCAPING THE ISLAND OF ETHICAL SUBJECTIVISM

Don't Let Ben Bring You Back

George Wrisley

Knowing about all of the evil Ben Linus will commit as an adult, Sayid is given the opportunity to kill him when Ben is a child. He takes it, shooting the young Ben. In Sayid's mind, he is executing a monster. Kate, however, despite also knowing who this boy will become, is horrified by Sayid's action. In her mind, Sayid is executing an innocent child. Who is right? It is difficult to say.

In contrast to most movies and TV shows, where good and evil are clearly and unrealistically demarcated, *Lost* illustrates the ethical complexities of real people and the situations in which we find ourselves. Life's questions are challenging because, as *Lost* demonstrates, things are rarely black and white. It can be extremely hard to know what to do or whether something is right or wrong.

Given inevitable disagreements among us, and given our natural desire for answers, it's easy to unreflectively assume that the answers to ethical questions are merely a matter of opinion. Thus, someone might say that it is right for Sayid to shoot Ben because he thinks Ben is a monster, but it would be wrong for Kate to shoot Ben because she thinks Ben is an innocent child. Or someone might say that it is right in Michael's eyes to shoot Ana Lucia, and it's wrong in Jack's eyes.

When people say these kinds of things, they may mean that there really is no objective moral truth—no right or wrong that we could discover that is independent of our feelings of approval or disapproval. In other words, it's all relative.

Subjectivism is the view that right and wrong are relative to an individual. *Cultural relativism* is a related view, according to which it is not only the individual, but the culture to which an individual belongs, that determines right or wrong. Both subjectivism and cultural relativism are very popular today, especially among young people who are trying to avoid judgmental attitudes. Yet on closer examination, is either view viable? The ethically charged situations in *Lost* provide an excellent testing ground for these views.

How Important Are Jack's or the Man in Black's Approval or Disapproval?

According to the most basic form of subjectivism, when I say, "It was wrong for Sayid to shoot young Ben," I am simply describing my attitude or how I feel. I really mean something like "I disapprove of Sayid's shooting young Ben." What makes the judgment true is simply the fact that I have the attitude that I say I have in the moral judgment. Thus, under subjectivism, it is not any aspect of the shooting itself that I am describing by calling it wrong. The sentence "Sayid's shooting young Ben is wrong" has the same grammatical form as the sentence "Jack's hair is dark," but the similarity is misleading. The description of Jack's hair ascribes a certain property to Jack's hair, but what appears to be a description of Sayid's *action* does not actually ascribe any properties to that action. Rather, the ethical judgment is a claim concerning the subject's own attitudes.

Similarly, according to the most basic form of cultural relativism, when I say, "Ben's betraying Widmore to the Man in Black was wrong," I am simply describing my culture's attitude toward betrayal in situations similar to Widmore's. I really mean something like "My culture disapproves of Ben's betraying Widmore to the Man in Black." What makes the judgment true is the fact that my culture does disapprove of such betrayal. Thus, as with subjectivism, it is not any aspect of the betrayal itself that I am describing by calling it wrong. I am merely describing my culture's disapproval.

As you will surely notice, subjectivism and cultural relativism are very similar. The main difference seems to lie merely in what each view takes ethical judgments to be describing. That difference, however, will become important when we look at possible objections to each view.

Tolerance and the Importance of Disagreement

Before looking at possible problems with subjectivism and cultural relativism, let's consider what might motivate a person to hold either position. A possible motivation for endorsing subjectivism or cultural relativism is the desire to avoid intolerance and closed-mindedness concerning others' views, while promoting diversity. It seems clear that people within and across cultures sometimes disagree, for example, about the best way to live, which religion is the true religion, and what actions are right and wrong.

Think about the differences among *Lost*'s characters. For example, Sayid comes from war-torn Iraq, Locke is an individualistic American, and Jin was raised in a traditional Korean family that prizes honor and respect. We can easily imagine the negative consequences that would result if Sayid, Locke, or Jin acted intolerantly by imposing their views on the other survivors. In this way, intolerance seems directly related to ethical objectivism. If the rightness or wrongness of an action were independent of any individual's or culture's attitudes, then someone might feel justified in trying to impose what he or she sees as the one true morality on others. It seems that subjectivism and cultural relativism diffuse this worry by giving various people or cultures the right to their own views.

In response to this motivation, we should note, first, that although intolerance and closed-mindedness should be discouraged and avoided, neither necessarily goes hand in hand with objectivism. It is true that those who are intolerant often claim they are in sole possession of the truth. In other words, intolerant people often try to use objectivism to justify their intolerance. Yet this doesn't mean that objectivism actually does justify intolerance. In fact, it is certainly possible to think morality is objective and still hold that we should be tolerant and open-minded about the views of others.

For example, Jack adamantly believes that it is best to move to the caves when water is discovered there. Yet he still respects the decision of the survivors who want to remain on the beach. You can believe you are right, while at the same time acknowledging that you shouldn't force others to go along with you.

You can also believe you are right even when you know you may be wrong. For example, Mr. Eko, although firmly committed to pushing the button, realizes that it might actually be pointless. Willingness to recognize that we may not have the whole truth is the wisdom that the ancient Greek philosopher Socrates (469–399 B.C.E.) most extolled. Socrates learned that he was the wisest man in Athens because he alone knew that he did not know. Realizing that you could be quite wrong about what you think you know is the first step toward becoming a philosopher.

Furthermore, subjectivists and cultural relativists can be intolerant. Suppose the Man in Black is a subjectivist, believing that his own personal beliefs justify all of his actions. Then it is morally right for him to murder all of the candidates and to force Jacob to cooperate with his plan. We can even imagine the Man in Black joining a society of other likeminded individuals who decide to take over the world. There is nothing in subjectivism or cultural relativism that implies one must be tolerant of others.

Nevertheless, there is an argument that one might offer in support of subjectivism or cultural relativism or, at least, against objectivism. It goes like this: People within and across cultures disagree about what is ethically right and wrong. For example, it would be easy to find fans of *Lost*, both within our culture and outside it, who disagree about whether Sayid should have tortured Sawyer. Such disagreements also occur across time. For example, the ancient Athenians regarded slavery as morally permissible, as did Southern plantation owners in nineteenth-century America. Today, many countries around the world regard slavery as morally wrong.

What are we to make of such extreme ethical disagreement? Subjectivists and cultural relativists argue that because there is ethical disagreement across cultures and across history, there is no objective truth about whether any action is right or wrong. Right and wrong are relative to individuals or cultures. Let's call this "The Argument from Disagreement" and lay it out explicitly:

> Premise: There are ethical disagreements within and across cultures and history.
> Conclusion: Therefore, there are no objective ethical truths. Ethical truth is relative to either an individual or a culture.

The first step in evaluating an argument is to ask how strongly the premise supports the conclusion. That is, does the truth of the premise imply the truth of the conclusion? If we look at the previous argument, it is clear that the answer is no. The main problem is that the premise has to do with what people feel or think, whereas the conclusion has to do with what actually exists.

Consider this analogy to see what this means. Think of the second season's finale. Mr. Eko and Locke disagree about whether the button should be pushed. Locke has come to believe that it is all a twisted psychological experiment and *nothing will happen* if they don't push the button. Mr. Eko, however, clearly wants to keep pushing the button. Let's assume that he believes the world will end if they don't push the button. Thus, Locke and Mr. Eko disagree about what will happen if they don't push the button. Clearly, their differing beliefs have no bearing on what exists, namely, what will or will not happen if they don't push the button. In a similar fashion, it is a mistake to draw a conclusion about the nonexistence of objective ethical truth from a premise concerning what people think and feel. There could be objective ethical truth despite ethical disagreement.

According to objectivists, the ancient Athenians and the nineteenth-century American plantation owners were simply wrong about slavery. They were wrong about other things as well. For example, a lot of ancient Athenians thought the world was flat, and they were wrong about that. A lot of nineteenth-century Americans thought that tobacco was healthy. They were wrong about that. Objectivists believe that being able to admit you were wrong is just as important as being tolerant.

Not only can we question whether the premise of the Argument from Disagreement guarantees the conclusion, we can also question whether the conclusion is what we might call the *best explanation* for the phenomenon of ethical disagreement across cultures and time. An alternative explanation for ethical disagreement is that although there is objective ethical truth, it is simply hard to gain access to. While the existence of moral truth may allow for agreement, it does not always go hand in hand with agreement. This is certainly the case with scientific truth. Think how long it took to discover that micro-organisms were the true cause of influenza. Why would it be any different for moral truth?

Imagine that the writers of *Lost* have in mind a detailed explanation of what *exactly* the source of the light is that Jacob's "mother" entrusts him to protect. Imagine further that all of the writers die and take the secret with them, having destroyed all record of what the light is. It could very well be the case that even the greatest *Lost* fan, one who is in possession of all extant information about the show and the writers' intentions, will be unable to discern what exactly the source of the light is. And this will be so, even though a definitive answer exists. Similarly it is the way with ethical truth: it may simply be that ethical truth is something that is very hard to figure out.

Notice that people do agree about certain fundamental ethical truths. Everyone knows that murder and cruelty are wrong and generosity and charity are right. What we dis-agree about is whether and to what extent particular instances count.

We should notice, too, that the conclusion of the Argument from Disagreement consists of two very different claims:

1. There are no objective ethical truths.
2. Ethical truth is relative to either a subject or a culture.

Although the truth of (2) implies the truth of (1), the reverse does not hold. There might be no objective ethical truth, and yet subjectivism and relativism could be false. Some other nonobjectivist view might be the correct one. So, even if the argument were a good argument, it would not by itself be an argument for subjectivism or relativism. Moving from (1) to (2) would require additional premises.

Subjectivists and cultural relativists often claim to be motivated by tolerance, arguing for open-mindedness and diversity among individuals and societies. Appealing to these values, however, presupposes that they are objectively good. So it seems that subjectivists and cultural relativists contradict themselves when they say that no values are objectively good.

You may be unconvinced by these responses to the motivation and the argument for subjectivism and cultural relativism. Yet, as we shall see, there are serious problems with the views themselves.

Why neither Hurley nor the Dharma Initiative Can Make It So

Even after Desmond pulls the plug on the light, the island is a veritable paradise in comparison to the crippling isolation of subjectivism. Subjectivism implies that whether you approve or disapprove of an action, you speak the truth if you truly describe your attitude. That is, if you approve of Sayid's shooting young Ben and you say, "Sayid was right to shoot young Ben," then it is true that Sayid's action was right. So, you cannot be wrong about your moral judgments. No one else can be wrong about his or her moral judgments, either. Each person is an isolated island of ethical certitude. Such infallibility of moral judgments is an unacceptable consequence for at least two reasons.

First, as we see in *Lost*, the ethical situations that we may confront in life are terribly complex and difficult—even if we aren't lost on an island. Can we actually expect infallibility from ourselves or others in such situations? If we are honest with ourselves, we will admit that there are a number of ethical issues that we are not sure about. If you are certain about abortion, then what about euthanasia or capital punishment? Or imagine that Locke could save Jack, Claire, Charlie, and Sayid from the Smoke Monster but only by pushing Hurley in front of them? Are you sure about the right thing for Locke to do? The point is that there are certainly times when we are unsure of the right action in a given situation. If we are unsure and subjectivism is true, then it is neither true nor false that an action is wrong until we "make up our minds."

Second, there are instances when we would not want to say that others are making true ethical judgments. For example, certainly some of the moral judgments of Stalin, Hitler, or Pol Pot were not true.

This brings us to another problem for subjectivism. If all that Jacob is doing when he makes a moral judgment is describing his attitude, and all that the Man in Black is doing is describing his attitude, it is unclear how they could disagree. That is, it seems that an important aspect of our ethical talk is to express disagreement with one another. Imagine if Jacob says that it was wrong of the Man in Black to kill their "mother." In response, the Man in Black says, "No, it wasn't wrong." They seem to disagree, but are they disagreeing if subjectivism is true?

Think of a nonethical analogy to descriptions of one's attitudes. If Locke describes his head as bald, and Jack describes his own head as not bald, are they disagreeing? No, because there is no conflict in Locke's describing his own head as bald and Jack's describing his own head as not bald. Moreover, they can actually agree with each other's descriptions. There would be a problem only if Locke described *his own* head as bald and Jack described *Locke's* head as *not* bald.

Similarly, under subjectivism there is no genuine disagreement when Jacob says it was wrong of the Man in Black to kill their mother and the Man in Black denies it. Because all they are doing is describing their individual attitudes, they can actually agree with each other. That is, Jacob can agree that the Man in Black approves of the killing, and the Man in Black can agree that Jacob disapproves of it. Again, this is a problem if we think that there can be genuine ethical disagreement.

To be fair, the subjectivist can say that what people disagree about when making moral judgments are the relevant nonethical facts. By "nonethical facts," I mean facts that do not involve evaluations such as *good, right, should,* and *approve* or their opposites. For example, Jacob and the Man in Black disagreed about whether the woman who raised them was in fact their mother. Disagreement about nonethical facts is important because our attitudes and other beliefs are often based on what we believe those facts to be.

Presumably, if you approve of Michael's shooting Ana Lucia, that approval is based on a number of nonethical beliefs. For example, your approval might be based in part on your belief that he had no other choice but to kill Ana Lucia in order to free Ben, and if he didn't free Ben, he would never see Walt again. Now, suppose I disapprove of Michael's actions. Initially, under subjectivism, it might seem that we cannot disagree with each other. It turns out, however, that I believe that Michael had other options for freeing Ben. He could have volunteered to guard him and then let him go. Thus, we disagree with each other, insofar as we disagree about the nonethical facts that inform our ethical attitudes. Such disagreement might surface in discussion of the action in question.

The main problem with this response is that we can still have different ethical attitudes, even though we agree on all of the relevant nonethical facts. Consider Jack's operation on Ben's cancerous spine and his exploitation of Ben's vulnerable position on the operating table as leverage to free Kate and Sawyer. What if we agree on all of the relevant nonethical facts? Although we cannot make an exhaustive list, let's say we agree that Kate and Sawyer will be killed if Jack doesn't try the ploy with Ben's life. Furthermore, we agree that Ben will probably die, even if the operation is successful. It's at least possible that we could agree on all such relevant facts, while disagreeing about whether it is wrong of Jack to use Ben to manipulate the Others. The point is that although our beliefs about the non-ethical facts may have an influence on our ethical attitudes, there may still be a disconnect between our attitudes and our "factual" beliefs. And if that is the case, then the disagreement that seems to be involved in all cases of one person saying, "Action X was wrong," and another person saying, "Action X wasn't wrong," cannot be accounted for by appealing to disagreement over nonethical facts.

Cultural relativism faces problems similar to those of subjectivism. It holds that an ethical judgment is true if it accurately describes a culture's approval or disapproval of an action. This avoids the first problem that subjectivism faced. That is, because it is the culture that either approves or disapproves of an action, an individual person can make mistaken ethical judgments, insofar as he or she *inaccurately* describes the culture's stance. Thus, if we take the survivors on the island to form a culture, then an action is right or wrong depending on whether they as a group approve or disapprove of the action. So, let's say that the group approves of blowing up the Others who are coming to take Sun and anyone else who is pregnant. If Rose were to say, "It's not right for us to blow up the Others," she is wrong because she is inaccurately describing the group's position. Thus, it is possible under relativism for individuals to be mistaken in their ethical judgments.

The problem, however, is that although the individual can be wrong, it's not possible for the culture to be wrong—cultures as wholes become infallible. This kind of infallibility is troubling for two main reasons. First, if the Dharma Initiative as a group approved of torturing Sayid, then within that society, it would be right to torture Sayid. If cultural relativism is true, then the Dharma Initiative cannot be wrong for torturing Sayid. If that is not objectionable, then think of Nazi Germany's Final Solution or ancient Greece's approval of slavery. They weren't wrong either, according to cultural relativism.

The second problem with cultural infallibility, and one that ties into the first problem, is that it makes it unclear on what basis an individual can go against his or her culture in order to try to make changes. For example, let's imagine that young Ben tries to petition for the rest of the Dharma Initiative not to torture Sayid. He is in a poor position to do so, because he is, under cultural relativism, automatically wrong in his view that it is wrong to torture Sayid. Thus, cultural relativism destroys the notion of reform and revolution. Let's look at how Martin Luther King Jr. worked toward trying to get our culture as a whole to see the truth concerning the wrongness of racism and discrimination. If cultural relativism is true, then Martin Luther King Jr. could not have been working to get others to see the truth concerning the wrongness of racism. At the time, our society at large still approved of discrimination in various forms, and thus, under cultural relativism, Martin Luther King Jr. was simply wrong. How could society ever progress, according to this view?

We have seen that the simple forms of subjectivism and cultural relativism lead to three consequences: infallibility of persons or cultures, inability to disagree with one another, and no possibility of ethical progress. Because these consequences are unacceptable, the views that lead to them should be rejected. The question then becomes: where do we go from here?

If Not on the Island of Ethical Subjectivism, Then Where?

Lost does not, in and of itself, show the untenability of subjectivism or cultural relativism. Nevertheless, with its excellent writing and its morally charged and sometimes morally ambiguous situations, *Lost* presents one opportunity after another for ethical analysis. Despite Jacob's playing the white piece and his brother the black piece, Jacob is not clearly purely good, nor is his brother inexplicably evil. It is difficult not to react with moral judgment to Michael's killing Ana Lucia and Libby, Ben's repeated betrayals of others, the murder of Ben's daughter, Alex, or the Man in Black's recurrent slaughter of those who stand in his way. Although our reactions may differ, they invite us to try to determine the truth of the matter.

Yet is that truth objective? When we see Ben betray and kill Jacob, and we judge that action to be wrong, what could it be that makes it wrong? Philosophers have long struggled with this question, and I cannot begin to answer it here. Instead, I leave you with some questions to consider.

If the simple forms of subjectivism and cultural relativism that we have examined don't work, is it possible that more sophisticated forms might work? What ways could they be modified to meet our objections? Perhaps when Jack accuses his father of moral wrongdoing in the operating room, he is not saying anything true or false or describing anything, but rather simply *expressing* his feelings. If that is so, how might that help subjectivism or cultural relativism?

If those views are beyond help, what basis might there be for objective moral truth? A number of philosophers have offered suggestions, but don't be too quick to turn to someone else for answers. When you watch *Lost*, and it provokes an ethical judgment, ask yourself, "Why do I think that?" and "Are those good reasons?" See how long you can keep challenging your answers with "Why?" and discover where it leads you.

LOST TOGETHER

Fathers, Sons, and Moral Obligations

Michael W. Austin

"You Don't Have What It Takes"

Put yourself in Jack's shoes. Imagine that you're in junior high school and you're trying to save a friend as he's being beaten up by some older kids. Now imagine that your father says, "You don't have what it takes," because he thinks that you should have stayed out of it. You grow up feeling that your father doesn't believe in you. In response, you're driven to overachieve; you even finish medical school an entire year sooner than everyone else. Yet that doesn't fix anything in you or in your relationship with your father. This is Jack Shephard's life before the crash of Oceanic flight 815.

"You're Not Wanted"

Put yourself in John Locke's shoes. You've grown up in various foster homes, never knowing your biological parents. Now, by mere chance, it seems, you've found them both. You develop a close bond with your father and then discover it was all a ruse so that he could get one of your kidneys. After the transplant that saves his life, your father shuts you out of that life. Even worse, he later attacks you, pushing you through a window and paralyzing you.

Given this, do Jack or Locke have any moral obligations to their fathers? Perhaps Jack and Locke don't owe their fathers anything (especially Locke!). Most of us haven't been conned out of one of our kidneys, paralyzed, and nearly killed by a biological parent. And even though our parents have said things that hurt us, as Jack's father did, we've probably benefited in numerous ways from the sacrifices they made on our behalf. In light of these sacrifices, do we owe our parents anything?

What Do Jack, Locke, and the Rest of Us Owe Our Parents?

According to the contemporary philosopher Jane English, we owe our parents *nothing*.[1] This sounds very strange, because it runs strongly against the traditional view in Western society, according to which we owe them respect, as well as letters, phone calls, visits, and financial help (if this is needed and possible). Even if our relationship with our parents is not intimate, honest, and trusting, it is traditionally thought that we owe such things to them because of the sacrifices that they have made for us.

Of course, it is the job of philosophers to scrutinize traditional assumptions, even when it comes to morality. Sometimes those views withstand philosophical scrutiny, and other times they don't. According to English, the traditional idea that adult children owe a debt to their parents doesn't stand up to critical analysis. We'll have to decide for ourselves whether she's right about this.

Following English's view, Sawyer owes his father nothing. As a child, Sawyer was in the house when his father first killed Sawyer's mom and then himself. Over the course of the series, we see how this has deeply impacted Sawyer and his choices in life. Many would agree that because of the actions by his father, Sawyer owes him nothing (or would owe him nothing had he survived his suicide attempt).

There are also good reasons for saying that Locke didn't owe it to his father, Anthony Cooper, to give him a kidney. Simply consider the level of sacrifice on Locke's part. And certainly after being conned out of a kidney and paralyzed by his father, there are reasons for thinking that Locke owes the man very little or perhaps nothing at all. Of course, this doesn't justify Locke's having Sawyer kill his father, but many would say that Locke didn't owe Cooper anything.

Jack's situation is somewhat different. Through a series of flashbacks, we are given a fuller picture of what happened between Jack and his father, Christian. During one flashback, Jack is in the operating room and loses a patient. As the circumstances surrounding the patient's death are uncovered during the show, we learn that Jack's father was initially performing the surgery. A nurse finds Jack and asks him to come to the operating room because Christian is drunk while at the operating table. In his impaired state, Christian accidentally cuts an artery, and the patient dies. Later, he calls Jack to his office and asks him to sign off on a report stating that the patient succumbed to the injuries sustained in the car accident. After Jack shows some resistance, Christian says, "I know I've been hard on you, but that is how you make a soft metal into steel. That is why you are the most gifted young surgeon in this city . . . this is a career that is all about the greater good. I've had to sacrifice certain aspects of my relationship with you, so that hundreds and thousands of patients will live, because of your extraordinary skills." Then, putting his hand on Jack's shoulder, Christian continues: "What happened yesterday I promise you will never happen again . . . this is not just about my career, Jack. It's my life." After this, Jack signs the report, and his father says, "Thank you, son. Thank you." ("All the Best Cowboys Have Daddy Issues")

Jack later revises his statement and comes clean about his father's mistake in the OR. One reason for Jack's change of heart is that he believes his father was insincere in their earlier conversation. Jack sees his father put his hand on the shoulder of the dead woman's husband in the same insincere manner that he did with Jack. Then, in a meeting with hospital officials, Jack learns that the woman was pregnant, a fact that his father chose to conceal from him. At this point, Jack reveals what actually happened.

Christian helps his son, but perhaps not in the way that Jack would like. The end of season 5 contains a flashback to Jack's first major surgical procedure. Jack makes a mistake, and if he doesn't fix it, the patient will be paralyzed. Christian tells him to stop and count to five after making the mistake.

Later, we find out that Jack is angry with his father and was embarrassed by what happened in the operating room. Here we get a glimpse into one of the main components of the story of Jack—his self-doubt—when he says to Christian, "Dad, I know you don't believe in me, but I need them to." In response, Christian says, "Are you sure I'm the one who doesn't believe in you, Jack?" ("The Incident") Even though this observation is true, and we see Jack grow in this during the course of the series, there is still a lot missing in the relationship between Jack and his dad. Commonsense morality tells us that Jack still owes Christian something, given what he's done for his son.

Yet Jane English would insist that Jack and Locke owe nothing to their fathers. Why would she make such a claim?

Philosophers are often very picky about language, with the result that much, though not all, of the writing in academic philosophy these days is notoriously dry and emotionally uninspiring. There is, however, a good reason for this. A desire for clarity and precision helps uncover the real issue in any philosophical discussion. When we finally get at the real issue, the hope is that a deeper level of understanding is achieved. Setting aside whether or not English's view is true, it is this search for understanding and clarity that leads her to the conclusion that we owe our parents nothing.

Is her view true, though? According to English, the sacrifices that our parents make for us do not create debts. Instead, those sacrifices tend to create a friendship relationship between parents and their adult children. For this reason, English thinks that using the term *owe* in the context of the parent-child relationship is out of place and in fact has the consequence of obscuring or even undermining the love that should ideally be the basis for the friendship between parents and their adult children.

"Hey, Freckles"

We can learn something about friendship from Sawyer and Kate and the other survivors of Oceanic flight 815. When we do a favor for someone, we often expect that the person will someday do the same for us if we call in that favor. If I help out an acquaintance, I expect that someday he'll return the favor, if need be. He owes it to me, given my previous act of assistance. English notes, however, that friendship doesn't work this way. True friends don't keep track of the sacrifices they've made for one another. Their motive is not to be repaid someday, but rather to give what they can to one another. Friends help one another simply because they are friends. This is why everyone loves Hurley as the series progresses. He's a true friend.

As relationships develop on the island, the survivors of Oceanic flight 815 who become friends don't keep track of the ways that they help one another. For example, at one point early in the show, Locke and Claire develop a friendship, and Locke builds a crib for Claire's newborn baby. In the context of a friendship like this, such actions aren't done in order to get something in return. Rather, they are done out of affection and care.

Similarly, Sawyer and Kate develop some sort of friendship. In the first episode of season 3, they end up in cages about twenty feet from each other, put there by the Others. Concerned for Kate, Sawyer throws her some food that he was able to get. Although at one point their relationship becomes romantic, their friendship remains after the romance ends. Given that they are friends, Sawyer and Kate don't keep track of the ways in which they've helped each other. The motive for helping out a friend is affection and in some cases even love, both romantic and nonromantic. We see this same sort of thing later (well, actually, *earlier*, thanks to the light flashes and time travel) in the relationship Sawyer has with Juliet.

"I'm Not One of His Friends"

After Jack reports his father's misconduct to the hospital, Christian flees to Sydney. Jack and his mother talk, and she urges Jack to go to Sydney and bring back his father. Jack tells her, "He doesn't want me to bring him back, I'm not one of his friends." ("White Rabbit") His mother responds that Christian doesn't have any friends, and because of what Jack did, he has to bring his father back. Jack ends up finding his father in a morgue, dead from an alcohol-induced heart attack. He then pleads his way onto flight 815 so that he can bury his father back in Los Angeles.

For English, Jack isn't obligated to bring his father back home. He *owes* his father nothing. The same applies to all other relationships between adult children and their parents. Yet it doesn't follow from this that an adult child can treat her parents however she wants to treat them, or that the sacrifices parents make are entirely irrelevant to the relationship. Ideally, the sacrifices that parents make on behalf of their children will ultimately help create a friendship between parents and their adult children. Friendships can and do begin in this manner.

The idea English rejects is that the sacrifices made by parents on behalf of their children *create obligations* that those children must fulfill as adults. The amount of parental sacrifice is irrelevant to the adult child's obligations to her parents, because this type of debt is not appropriate to friendship relationships. And the relationship between adult children and their parents should ideally be a friendship relationship. Not only does this mean that the amount and kind of sacrifices made by parents on behalf of their children are irrelevant to the adult children's obligations, but it also means that the biological relationship between parents and children is irrelevant, according to English.

So, if the plane leaving the island piloted by Lapidus in the last episode makes it back, and Claire is able to get herself together and raise Aaron, would Aaron owe her anything? English would say that if we assume that prior to Claire's death and presence in the church, Claire asks her son for some financial help to pay her medical bills, he would not have the obligation to do so simply because of the time, the physical labor, and the emotional effort that Claire gave to raise him. Yet if they have an ongoing friendship, a relationship in which there is mutual care, concern, and affection, then Aaron should and will help her out if he can. For English, whether there is an ongoing friendship will determine the obligations that Aaron has to Claire.

The Source?

No, I'm not referring here to the source, as in the glowing "heart of the island," but rather to the other possible source (or sources) of obligation in the parent-child relationship. According to the philosopher Henry Sidgwick (1838–1900), there is a different way to think about the obligations that children have to their parents:

> It would be agreed that children owe to their parents respect and kindness generally and assistance in case of

infirmity or any special need; but it seems doubtful how far this is held by Common Sense to be due on account of the relationship alone, or on account of services rendered during infancy, and how far it is due to cruel or neglectful parents. Most perhaps would say, here and in other cases, that mere nearness of blood constituted a certain claim: but they would find it hard to agree upon its exact force.[2]

Sidgwick offers a view that contrasts with that of English. His words reflect the traditional view that children do owe respect, kindness, and special assistance to their parents. Jack *owes* these things to Christian, in this view. Sidgwick is more tentative regarding the sources of these obligations, however, although he notes several possibilities: (1) the quality of the relationship, (2) the biological connection, and (3) as a debt of gratitude for parental services rendered during childhood.

Sidgwick is in agreement with English that the quality of the parent-child relationship itself plays a role in the existence and extent of the obligations that the adult child has to the parent. From this source, it looks like neither Jack nor Locke are obligated in any way to their fathers. A disagreement arises between Sidgwick and English, insofar as Sidgwick grants that the biological relationship and the services rendered by parents in the care of their children both play a role in dictating the existence and extent of these obligations. Do Jack or Locke owe their fathers anything based on these considerations?

Many people think that the biological connection that exists between parents and children is also a moral connection. If you are related "by blood," then you have some obligations to each other because of that kinship relationship. In this view, one need not think that Locke owes his biological father a kidney or that Jack owes it to his father to keep silent about his medical malpractice. Yet it seems that in this approach to the parent-child relationship Jack and Locke both do owe their fathers at least some respect, kindness, and care. Moreover, on the grounds that they are related by blood, Jack does owe it to his father to bring him back home from Sydney, as his mother told him to do. In the biological approach, those of us who have had decent parents do owe them phone calls, visits, and financial support (if they need it and we're able to provide it).

In opposition to the biological approach, it seems initially plausible that even when a biological relationship exists, if one's parents have seriously failed in their parental role, then this relieves an adult child of at least some of his obligations, as the case of Jack and his dad makes plain. And if biology is relevant to the obligations that parents and children have to one another, factors such as the quality of the relationship play a large role in the extent of those obligations. The significance of the quality of the relationship, rather than the biological ties, can be clearly seen when no such biological connection exists, as in the case of adopted children. Kate's love for Aaron is no less in quality or quantity because they are not biologically connected, but it is plainly evident in her commitment to his welfare.

The other approach alluded to by Sidgwick emphasizes the debt that adult children owe their parents due to the sacrifices made by the parents in raising the children. The contemporary philosopher David Mellow has developed an argument for the conclusion that adult children do owe their parents a debt based on gratitude.[3] Most parents have benefited their children in many ways that required major sacrifices on the part of the parents. Moreover, most parents have the right intentions and motives when making sacrifices on behalf of their children, such as the desire that their children have good and happy lives.

With these thoughts in mind, it is again clear that Locke would owe nothing to Anthony Cooper based on a debt of gratitude. As Locke puts it, his father "pretended to love me just long enough to steal my kidney and dropped me back in the world like a piece of trash . . . just like he did on the day I was born!" ("Orientation") Locke's biological father has made no sacrifices on Locke's behalf, ever. In this understanding of family obligations, however, Jack does owe his father something. Still, how much Jack owes Christian is unclear. We know that Christian is Claire's biological father, although he kept this to himself. We also know from a conversation that Christian had in Sydney with Ana Lucia that he loves and respects Jack but is unable to tell him. So it seems likely that during Jack's childhood, Christian did make some sacrifices with Jack's best interests in mind. If this is true, we can say that Jack does owe it to his father to go to Sydney and bring him back to Los Angeles.

"I've Done Everything You Wanted Me to Do!"

After the transplant surgery, Locke wakes up in the hospital room he shared with his father, and his dad is gone, having checked out and returned home under private care. Locke, after learning what has occurred, that his own father has selfishly manipulated the entire situation and conned him out of one of his kidneys, leaves the hospital and goes to his father's house. Bleeding from the spot where his kidney was removed, Locke is turned away by the security guard. Locke drives away, and in anger and despair he pulls over to the side of the road and weeps. The scene fades into Locke weeping in the same way at the hatch, which he has tried unsuccessfully to open. Locke cries out, "I've done everything you wanted me to do. So why did you do this?" ("Deus ex Machina") It seems like the island at this point in the series' second season has become a surrogate father for Locke. Given that his own father not only manipulated him but also tried to kill him, it makes sense that Locke would look elsewhere. Just as he did all that he could do to obtain his father's love, he has tried to do all that the island has asked of him to learn why it brought him to itself. This observation might sound like it belongs in a book titled *Lost and Psychology*, but this scene does have philosophical significance.

Locke's desire for his father's love, while perhaps too extreme, illustrates a need we have as human beings. For some reason, human nature is such that we long to have loving parental figures in our lives. If we don't have them, we deeply miss them, even as adults.[4] Children need their parents, especially early in life. Yet sometimes, of course, that need is not met. In such circumstances, adult children often continue to feel a need for a relationship with their parents and long for it when it is absent or somehow broken. We see this between Miles and his father, Pierre Chang, the head scientist of the Dharma Initiative. Miles claims not to care about his father or to have any desire to connect with him. Yet when Miles travels back in time and sees his dad playing with him as a baby in 1970s Dharmaville, something happens. A longing for connection emerges, and Miles reaches out to his dad, ultimately saving his life.

Parents also need their children and long for a close relationship with them, sometimes especially later in life. Given these facts, perhaps what parents owe their children and what children owe their parents rests not only on the quality of the relationship they share, the sacrifices that they make for one another, or the biological relationship that exists. Instead, what parents and children owe one another depends on the *needs* they have that parents and children are uniquely situated to meet for one another. Clearly, Jack and Locke both need more from their fathers than they received, although Jack and his father are reconciled in "The End." Yet both Christian and Anthony have failed to fulfill their parental obligations to their sons. It's also clear that the parents of adult children have a very human need that only their adult children can meet: the need for respect and love from one's children. Perhaps the recognition and true appreciation of this need can go a long way in telling us what Jack, Locke, and the rest of us owe our parents.

"Dead Is Dead" (or Is It?)

Many things made this television series special. Part of the attraction and the fun was that it was so different from real life. The smoke monster, polar bears in a tropical environment, Hurley's numbers, the hatch, time travel, the Dharma Initiative, all on an island with some very unique and powerful electromagnetic properties. Of course, the show was not primarily driven by its many mysteries, both solved and unsolved. As cocreator Damon Lindelof said in the series recap prior to the finale, "*Lost* is at its heart and soul a character study. We're fascinated as storytellers by what makes people the way they are."

One of the things, often one of the central things, that makes us who we are is our relationship with our parents. This is reflected in the lives of the characters of *Lost*. In this way, the show was very much like real life. Sun, Sawyer, Ben, Miles, Walt, Locke, and Jack are all shaped by their fathers. And although Locke and his father never reconcile, not even death prevents Jack and Christian from reaching a form of reconciliation in their relationship. As you know, in the series finale, Jack is brought to the church and opens his father's coffin, only to (again!) find it empty. But then we hear Christian say, "Hey, kiddo." Jack is at first shocked but comes to accept reality when Christian helps Jack realize that he's dead as well. Now better words, words that are more suitable from father to son than "You don't have what it takes," come out of Christian's mouth. He tells his son, Jack, "It's okay. It's okay. It's okay, son." Father and son express their love for each other and then head out into the sanctuary of the church to be with everyone else in order to move on into the next life, reconciled and together.

Lost left us with a hope of redemption and of forgiveness, even in that significant and sometimes strained relationship, the relationship between father and son.[5]

NOTES

1. Jane English, "What Do Grown Children Owe Their Parents?" in Onora O'Neill and William Ruddick, eds., *Having Children* (New York: Oxford University Press, 1979), pp. 351–356.

2. Henry Sidgwick, *The Methods of Ethics* (Indianapolis: Hackett, 1981), p. 248.

3. David Mellow, "Sources of Filial Obligation," unpublished paper.

4. For a fuller discussion of this and other issues related to family ethics, see my *Wise Stewards: Philosophical Foundations of Christian Parenting* (Grand Rapids, MI: Kregel, 2009).

5. I would like to thank Cameron Griffith, Brett Patterson, Jonathan Boyd, and Bill Irwin for their comments on earlier versions of this chapter.

SHOULD WE CONDEMN
MICHAEL?

Becky Vartabedian

If you're like me, one reason you looked forward to watching *Lost* each week was to find out which character we'd learn about in that week's episode. Flashbacks, flash-forwards, and trips into the flash-sideways world are captivating ways of telling us more about each of the characters. These flashes convey important experiences and—in many cases—reveal significant relationships with other characters. It is by this route that we learn of Locke's complicated relationship with Anthony Cooper, Desmond's enduring connection to Daniel Faraday, and Libby's life in an institution.

When it comes to evaluating *Lost*'s characters, we need a theoretical framework that can accommodate their complexity. Philosophy gives us a variety of theories that are *agent-specific*, counting a person and those affected by his actions to be just as significant as the rules or the principles he is following. The British philosopher W. D. Ross (1877–1971) gave us an agent-specific theory that sheds light on Michael's actions, relative to both his rescue of Walt and his return to the island aboard the freighter *Kahana*. While Ross's theory takes into account Michael's unique experience and reasons for acting on Walt's behalf, it also reinforces his connections with—and responsibilities to—those he left behind.

The Character

With its use of flashbacks, *Lost* is clearly concerned with why characters make the choices they do. We know that Michael's forced separation from Walt was a source of great personal pain. When Walt's mother dies, Michael must work to earn Walt's respect and trust. Furthermore, we know from his actions on the island that Michael places his son's interests above his own.

These factors help us understand Michael's desperation to recover his son when Michael is kidnapped by the Others. In the closing moments of season 2's finale, Michael leads Jack, Kate, Sawyer, and Hurley to the Others in exchange for Walt. As Walt and he putter away in a tugboat pointed in the direction of safety, Michael exchanges a long look with Jack, Kate, and Sawyer, who sit—bound and gagged—on the dock, now prisoners of the Others. Perhaps we condemned Michael's actions. Then again, perhaps we found ourselves sympathetic to Michael's situation. In fact, some of us might say that in a similar situation, we'd be inclined to make the same kind of trade.

The Theory

In *The Right and the Good*, Ross proposed that an adequate moral framework must "fit the facts" of our experience. For example, all things being equal we should keep our promises, but certain features of a situation may prevent us from doing so. This is the sort of flexibility that accompanies our experience of promise keeping, and Ross proffered a moral theory that can account for it. His system employs six principles that are flexible in their relative applicability to a situation but not in their nature. That is, while the principles themselves don't change, their functioning in any given situation might change. Ross's principles are as follows:

1. Fidelity. I should be true to my word.
2. Gratitude. I should not exploit the services of others.
3. Justice. I should distribute goods fairly.
4. Beneficence. I should strive to improve the situation of others.
5. Self-improvement. I should strive to become a better person.
6. Noninjury. I should avoid harming others.

Ross argued that these six principles are self-evident duties, requiring no demonstration or explanation. And our moral experience confirms that all things being equal, it is best to do our duty. Ross called these duties *prima facie*, a Latin term meaning "at first face." By this, he meant that one must follow the principles unless some relevant factor intervenes.[1]

The Button: How Prima Facie Duties Work

The flashbacks characteristic of *Lost*'s first three seasons provided us with unique access to each character's "moral memory." In fact, the flashbacks have the substance of reasons, in that they serve as a resource for our understanding and contextualizing a character's choices on the island. Through flashbacks, we learned both the how and the why of Michael's actions concerning Walt—flashbacks provided us with the content of experience that would bear on Michael's moral decision making.

In any given situation, one acts according to the weight of reasons. In doing so, Michael "sorts" among his prima facie duties. In the case where more than one prima facie duty is in play, the moral agent must thoughtfully decide which duty is the most important at that time.

Consider an analogy. Each individual is like a car having a motor with six gears. These gears run in neutral until we need to move forward. We judge which gear to use based on road conditions, the power of our motor, and our desired speed. Our gear selection and the subsequent movement of our "car" represent doing our duty.

Think of Locke's refusal to continue pushing the button. After watching the video at the Pearl station, he comes to see the Dharma Initiative as an insult to his intelligence and virtue. In this situation, Locke's refusal is a duty because he acts according to the principle of self-improvement. Yet note that the prima facie rightness of his action does not guarantee any sort of outcome, nor can we immediately evaluate the act. Whether the act is right or wrong depends on whether Locke accurately assessed all of the relevant intervening factors.

In the scenario at the dock, Michael's moral transmission shifts to beneficence in order to save Walt. Speaking broadly, the father-son relationship is governed by the duty of beneficence, so Michael is obligated to strive to improve Walt's overall situation. Just as Michael has this duty, Walt has a right to his dad's making this kind of effort on his behalf. The relationship between duties and rights is mutually reinforcing, and when other people are included in our moral considerations, we gain the language of "responsibility to" as part of this moral framework. In Michael's case, his responsibility to his son makes it possible to override his other duties in favor of saving Walt. And Michael's "actual duty"—Ross's designation for what we finally choose to do—involves injury to Jack, Kate, and Sawyer.

Saving Walt: Prima Facie Duties, Actual Duty, and Equilibrium

When Michael overrides his other duties in favor of beneficence to Walt, he does not eliminate his other duties. Ross explained that when we sort and act according to a prima facie duty, we are required by compunction—guilt—to make it up to those we might have wronged. Indeed, guilt is often a consequence when we put a prima facie duty into action. So Ross's theory does not give us a blank check to act however we want. Our relationships to others bind us to them by responsibility. Prima facie duties construct a system within which one is able to act, as well as be held accountable for one's actions.

When Michael acts out of beneficence for Walt, he knowingly acts *against* his duties of fidelity and noninjury to Jack, Kate, and Sawyer. We have good reason to think that Michael knows what he's done—consider his long look at them as an acknowledgment of guilt. This means that Jack, Kate, Sawyer, and the other castaways may rightly demand that Michael make amends.

Actual duties, when they require us to discern between two prima facie duties, demand what Ross termed a *moral risk*. Michael's actions at, and leading up to, the dock fit this bill. His decision seems to be based on his role as Walt's father, and the resulting duty emerges out of much of the baggage revealed in the flashbacks. Even though Michael has saved Walt, however, he's left a mess in his wake:

- He is responsible for the deaths of Libby and Ana Lucia.
- He is responsible for the imprisonment of Jack, Kate, and Sawyer and (at least) implicated in their torture.
- He is responsible for a great deal of confusion and terror faced by the remaining survivors of Oceanic flight 815.

These are the ripple effects of Michael's actions. Some ethical theories would condemn him because of these effects. Yet according to an ethic of prima facie duties, we would be careful to reserve final judgment until we can determine whether Michael makes amends.

Meet Kevin Johnson

In season 4, we learn that since leaving the island, Michael has been haunted by Libby's ghost. He has also confessed to Walt that he was responsible for the murders of Libby and Ana Lucia. In response, Walt turns away from Michael, and Michael attempts suicide twice, failing both times.

These "failures" are explained in a visit Michael receives from Tom (aka Mr. Friendly). Tom tells Michael that his suicide attempts have been thwarted because the island isn't finished with him yet. In order to pay his debt, Michael is to join the crew of the freighter *Kahana* and act as Ben's spy. Michael accepts this assignment and signs on to the *Kahana* under the alias Kevin Johnson.

While aboard the freighter, Michael learns of certain of the crew's evil intentions toward those Michael left behind. With Jin's help, Michael is able to construct and deploy a bomb to destroy the freighter. Michael gives Jin the crucial time he needs to get away from the bomb, and the freighter explodes. While Jin and Sun are separated across time and space (because the freighter's explosion coincides with Ben and Locke's moving the island), Michael is responsible for saving Jin's life. His debt sufficiently paid, Michael is "released" by the island and allowed to die in the explosion.

"Hey, Hurley . . . If You See Libby Again . . . Tell Her I'm Very Sorry"

Michael's work as Kevin was mandated by the island, and the island was evidently satisfied with it. Yet was Michael's work morally sufficient? Ross's theory demands that we examine whether Michael satisfies his responsibility to those he wronged.

It's worth reminding ourselves of the nature of these responsibilities. First, Michael must atone for the murders committed en route to rescuing Walt. Second, he must take responsibility for his direct betrayal of Jack, Kate, and Sawyer.

Finally, he bears some culpability for the situation facing other survivors of Oceanic flight 815 after the capture of Jack, Kate, and Sawyer. As we come to a conclusion about Michael, we ought to consider that he is doing those he wronged a favor by providing Ben with information. Furthermore, by saving Jin's life, he does something that those he wronged would have wanted him to do. Is this sufficient?

On the one hand, we might answer yes, that Michael, by acting on behalf of his (former) friends, is doing the best he can to make up for past actions. Michael's work behind enemy lines is the most productive thing he can do for the castaways. According to this view, although his actions aboard the *Kahana* are not completely praiseworthy, they still allow him to escape condemnation.

On the other hand, we could also claim that Michael does nothing to repair the problem he created. Although it is not clear what such repair would involve, a simple apology probably is not quite enough. In some ways, Michael's work on the freighter could be seen as his own selfish effort to achieve his goal of dying. This perspective may insist that the only way for Michael to pay his debt is to face the people he wronged and make up for those wrongs *on their terms*. Because he does not do this, we might conclude that Michael must be condemned.

Walt's rejection of Michael's influence confirms the notion that Michael was not justified in doing whatever he wanted in securing his son's release. Although Michael and Walt suffered no immediate consequences in their escape from the island, Michael's confession and Walt's subsequent spurning do show the ways in which Michael's choices negatively affect the relationship he was so keen to preserve. It is worth considering whether Walt's estrangement from Michael is punishment enough for his actions at the dock. That this consequence is devastating to Michael is obvious, but can suffering make reparation? It seems unlikely that these would be the terms set by the people whom Michael wronged.

We Never Really Go It Alone

We have considered the implications of Ross's theory of prima facie duties as they work out in Michael's postdock actions. As an agent-specific theory, an ethic of prima facie duties can accommodate the variety of reasons we bring to any action. Yet this perspective also reminds us that our evaluation of any action or set of actions is connected to satisfying or avoiding the set of responsibilities our actions creates. Ross's theory indicates that our evaluation must cope with the many nuances of applying a theoretical framework to a live situation.

Michael's actions, like many in *Lost*'s universe, remind us that we often come up against a hard case—one where matters of right, wrong, praise, and blame are difficult to discern. Although it may be the case that Ross's theory "fits the facts" of our experience better than some of the alternatives do, it may not fully determine moral responsibility.

One final point seems worth mentioning, particularly in light of Michael's absence from the show's closing scenes in the church. Consistent with *Lost*'s internal logic and with the moral framework I've described here is the insight that we never really "go it alone." Michael's tendency is to try fix the situations he's confronted with—he is a construction worker by trade, after all. His failure with Walt illustrates that there is a limit to the effectiveness of actions conceived and implemented on one's own. Ultimately, Michael exiles himself from the moral community.[2]

NOTES

1. Ross's claim regarding the adequacy of a moral theory can be found in *The Right and the Good*, ed. Phillip Stratton-Lake (Oxford: Oxford University Press, 2002), p. 19. The discussion of the prima facie duties is found in the same text on pages 20–21.

2. My thanks to Hamad Al-Rayes, Brock Bahler, Andrew Vartabedian, George Wrisley, and W. T. McRae for their comments on various versions of this chapter.

THE ETHICS OF OBJECTIFICATION AND THE SEARCH FOR REDEMPTION IN *LOST*

Patricia Brace and Rob Arp

People use objects such as cars and computers to get what they want, fulfill goals, or gain pleasures. Fair enough. On *Lost* (and in real life), however, people often use other people to get information, power, or sex. For example, prior to the crash of Oceanic flight 815, Charlie deceived Lucy Heatherton for drug money ("Homecoming"), and Sawyer seduced the unhappy wives of rich men ("Two for the Road"). The act of using a person like an object is called *objectification*. Such behavior strikes us as wrong because we think human beings are subjects, rather than objects; they should never be treated as instruments at our disposal. Yet on *Lost*, many characters go from blameworthy to praiseworthy by allowing *themselves* to be used as instruments for the benefit of the majority. For example, we admire Charlie when he undertakes a suicide mission to the Looking Glass station ("The Light House") and

Sawyer when he gives up his place in the escaping helicopter ("There's No Place Like Home"). *Lost* characters who stop objectifying others and start to objectify themselves experience a kind of redemption. Yet how can it be morally right to do to yourself something that you ought not do to others?

You Kant Take It with You

Followers of Immanuel Kant (1724–1804) ground moral decision-making in the conviction that persons are conscious, rational beings, capable of making their own free and informed decisions. Kant told us that we should always treat another person (and ourselves, too) as an end in itself and never as a mere means to an end. This implies that you should never objectify another person the way that Charlie and Sawyer do on occasion.

Kant was not saying that we should never treat people as means to our ends. After all, we have to use people for goods, services, and other things in order to live our daily lives. What Kant ruled out is treating a person as *nothing but a means* for such ends. From this perspective, morally right decisions are those that treat a person as an end, and morally wrong decisions are those that treat a person as a mere instrument or means to an end. This all makes common moral sense to most of us.

The episode "One of Them" introduces us to a fascinating character first known as the hapless balloon crash survivor, Henry Gale, and eventually revealed as the leader of the Others, Benjamin Linus. As the survivor of an abusive childhood on the island, Ben starts on a dark path that leads to the murders of his own father and the rest of the Dharma Initiative in the Purge ("The Man behind the Curtain"). Treated as an object his whole life, it is no wonder that Ben becomes a master of manipulation, objectifying everyone around him as he seeks the power promised to him by an alliance with the Others. Ben will almost always do what is necessary to achieve his own ends, which includes endangering the lives of innocents.

You don't need to be Kant to see that Ben's actions are immoral. Things get a little more hairy, though, when we consider other aspects of Kant's moral position. Given that persons are conscious, rational beings, capable of making their own free and informed decisions, Kant also insists that they must be considered *autonomous* beings.

The word *autonomy* comes from two Greek words meaning "self" (*auto*) and "law" (*nomos*), highlighting the fact that a rational person is "self-ruling." Kant took this to mean that our own informed decisions should be respected. Because a person's innate dignity and worth are tied to rational autonomy, some Kantian philosophers argue that what is most significant in making a moral decision has to do with whether a person's freedom in rationally informed decision-making has been respected. The idea here is that if a fully rational person chooses to engage in some action—as long as the action doesn't harm anyone else—then that person is fully justified in making this decision, even if the decision puts the person in the position of being used by another person or group of persons.

For example, Claire allows herself to be used as bait to help capture her kidnapper, the devious representative of the Others, Ethan Rom ("Other Man"). Turning to the real world, people join the army knowing that they may be sacrificed for the sake of winning a war. People working at a huge corporation know full well that the ultimate goal of the company is to make money, and that they may lose their jobs in a down-sizing.

When we use others around us to get the things we want, we violate the Kantian concept of moral sanctity. When we allow ourselves to be used as instruments for some greater good, however, we exercise our moral autonomy. And moral autonomy trumps moral sanctity. This is why, in Kant's view, our *Lost* heroes are redeemed.

Milling Around

Followers of John Stuart Mill (1806–1873) argue that an action is morally good insofar as its consequences promote the most benefit for the most persons affected by the decision. This view has been termed *utilitarian* because of the apparent usefulness (utility) to be found in generating as much satisfaction as possible in society at large. In opposition to the Kantian view that persons should never be used as a mere means to some end, the utilitarian view justifies treating persons as means whenever it achieves the greatest good for the greatest number. If saving a group of people from some evil-doer requires killing one or two people in the process, then, on utilitarian grounds, it is morally correct.

Sayid Jarrah makes for an interesting utilitarian. When Ben tells him that he must assassinate a number of people in order to help the survivors who remain on the island, he is content to cooperate ("The Economist," "The Shape of Things to Come"). If Ben had been telling the truth, Sayid's actions may have been justified on utilitarian grounds. Of course, Ben was not telling the truth, and when Sayid discovers this, he is filled with remorse. One problem with utilitarianism is that it is extremely difficult to acquire all of the information necessary for promoting the greatest good for the greatest number of people.

Although Ben objectified Sayid in the worst way, Sayid gets the opportunity to make things right. Traveling back in time, he meets Ben as a boy ("He's Our You"). By executing the young Ben, Sayid would prevent the deaths of the dozens (if not hundreds) of people for which Ben is responsible. The young Ben now becomes the means to Sayid's end. Kate, representing a more traditional moral perspective, is appalled at Sayid's action, but Sayid's action is fully justifiable on utilitarian grounds. If Sayid had been successful, he might have been redeemed.

The Virtue of Virtue

In contrast to Kantian and utilitarian positions, which emphasize the value of actions, there is a moral position dating back to Aristotle (384–322 B.C.E.) that places emphasis on the character of the person who performs the action. Because the concern is to promote a good or *virtuous* character, this moral position is known as *virtue ethics*. The central idea is that if a person has a virtuous character, then not only will that person likely perform morally right actions, but these actions will also likely have good consequences.

Whenever people on *Lost* are sick or hurt, they can count on Jack (who is caring and reliable) to treat them and usually with good results. Even though Jack does not always do the right thing, he is still a virtuous person. Sometimes you can get a demon to do the right thing, yielding good consequences—however, he's still a demon. Wouldn't it be better instead if we could turn demons into angels? Thus, virtue ethics can act as a kind of complement to the Kantian and utilitarian positions, rounding out our moral lives.

Followers of Aristotle conceive of virtues as good habits whereby one fosters a kind of balance in one's character. The idea is not to promote the "too much" or the "too little" but the "just right" in our characters, so that our actions and reactions to situations hit the mean between two extremes. A virtuous person has cultivated the kind of character whereby she knows how to act and react in the right way, at the right time, in the right manner, and for the right reasons in each and every moral dilemma encountered. The way in which one cultivates a virtuous character is through choosing actions that are conducive to building that virtuous character.

So, for example, if one wants to cultivate the virtue of self-control so that one can actually be a self-controlled person, then one needs to act with self-control, time and again, so that the virtue can "sink in." The more Charlie actually abstains from taking drugs, the more he cultivates the virtue of self-control. Likewise, the more Sawyer lies when asked whether he has done something wrong, the more he cultivates the vice of dishonesty.

Important virtues include honesty, courage, prudence, generosity, integrity, affability, and respect, to name just a few. Respect is the key virtue for our purposes, in terms of not objectifying people. The person who has cultivated respect for persons in his or her character naturally will not objectify another person. When one treats a person as an object, one deprives the person of his or her intrinsic dignity, value, and worth, which affects both the person doing the objectifying and the person being objectified.

Although the Aristotelian virtue of respect condemns treating others as objects, the Aristotelian virtue of courage enables one to willingly sacrifice oneself for some greater good. Probably the best example of the virtue of courage in *Lost* is Dr. Jack Shephard. Christlike Shephard, complete with the wound in his side and with that dogged symbol of fidelity, Vincent, next to him, ends the series by literally laying down his life to save the world, coming full circle from his mad-dash rescues of fellow Oceanic flight 815 survivors in the opening minutes of the "Pilot" episode.

In "What They Died For," when Jack volunteers to become the new Jacob, he is acting courageously. He knows he will die, but he is at peace with this consequence. In the finale, when he doesn't stop Desmond from uncorking the glowing golden hole of goodness at the Heart of the Island, he is in fact conning the Smoke Monster by his very inaction, something that even Sawyer can respect as a courageous action. The willingness to die for others is the ultimate in self-objectification and shows the highest level of courageous character.

Redemption Redeemed

The Kantian, utilitarian, and virtue theories we have presented enable us to see redemption even in the most complicated characters on *Lost*.

Kant and Aristotle would redeem Ben. In "Dr. Linus," when Un-Locke gives him the chance to kill Ilana, who was going to execute him for murdering Jacob, Ben hesitates and then tries to explain to her why he did it. In a tearful mea culpa, he pours out his deep shame and remorse for what he has done, invoking Alex's death, not the loss of his power, as the true tragedy of his life. He has a father's love for the girl, which epitomizes the Kantian concept of moral sanctity and belief in the *intrinsic* value of people. To reinforce this, in the flash-sideways world, we see how high school history teacher Dr. Linus gave up his chance at power over others (something Aristotle said cannot be a goal of complete virtue, because not everyone can achieve it) so that Alex, his student in this world, could get into Yale, securing her future. This was a heroic and unselfish act, showing that somewhere, deep down in his character, he is capable of both observing Kantian moral sanctity and applying Aristotelian virtue ethics.

Aristotle and Mill would redeem Kate Austen. From the very beginning of the series, we see that on the island the enigmatic Kate is usually the first to volunteer her help. Before we know "What Kate Did," we admire her. Kate is a respected member of the "A Team" of survivors, but in her flashbacks we see that she has been guilty of unethical objectification of others. On the island, Kate finds it hard to break the pattern of her old life. For every one of Kate's helpful actions, there is another self-serving objectification. An instance of Kate using people as means to her own ends occurs in "Born to Run," when the survivors build a raft in an attempt to find help. Desperate to leave the island, Kate schemes to get on the raft by manipulating those around her. The plan misfires badly, and her criminal past is revealed. This seems to be a turning point for Kate, who works hard to restore her reputation in the eyes of her fellow castaways.

In "Do No Harm," Kate delivers Claire Littleton's baby, Aaron, which creates a bond between her and the boy that will eventually prove stronger than any other relationship she has ever had. When Claire disappears in the episode "Something Nice Back Home," leaving Aaron behind, it is Kate who steps up to care for the baby. Becoming Aaron's mother gives her a sense of purpose she has never had before (something even Jacob recognized, giving this as the reason her name was crossed off his candidate list in the season 6 episode "What They Died For"). Instead of making self-serving decisions, Kate builds her whole life around the boy, and, in Aristotle's terms, it greatly improves her moral character.

When Kate returns to the island to save Claire, Kate combines the skills of her pre-island life with the protective streak that being a mother brought out in her. One of the behaviors that got her into trouble on many occasions was following after someone when she was expressly told not to do so ("The Hunting Party"). In the series finale, Sawyer even jokes about it, but in the end, this tag-along behavior allows Kate to save Jack so that he can complete his task. After unsuccessfully trying to shoot Un-Locke, Kate trails Jack, who has chased the newly corporeal Un-Locke to the literal cliff's edge. As Un-Locke is about to strike a death blow to our hero, a shot rings out and Un-Locke goes down. By killing one man, Kate saves herself and her friends: a fair utilitarian trade.

Finally, Kant and Mill would redeem Sawyer. He steps up and successfully maneuvers his group of survivors into the 1974 Dharma Initiative in the episode "LaFleur." As Kate did back in L.A., Sawyer finds a reason to be a better person. As Aristotle would say, the habits of virtue have become engrained in him.

For three years as the head of Dharma security, Jim LaFleur has earned respect from his peers and is in love with Other defector Dr. Juliet Burke. Because he has not revealed the truth of their identity and how they came to be there, in a sense he is exploiting the trust of the people in the Dharma Initiative for his own benefit. From the utilitarian perspective, however, he has become the leader—taken over Jack's role, in effect—and the subterfuge serves the greater good for his group. Instead of being a con and a manipulator, as we saw in season 1, when he selfishly hoarded the resources of the community for his own benefit, Sawyer is now a standard-bearer of morality, defending his friends and the Initiative as a peacekeeper. His defiant declaration in "The Long Con" back in season 2, "There's a new sheriff in town, boys," has finally come true. When he must choose between Dharma and the returned flight 815 survivors and later between camp Smoke Monster or camp Jacob, is he the righteous lawman LaFleur, the outlaw Sawyer, or perhaps something new—plain old James Ford?

Real World Island

As *Lost* unfolded, each of the survivors of Oceanic flight 815 grew and changed. We came to love them because they reflected all of the intricacies and the faults of people in the real world. They formed strong bonds in little communities, where each individual was forced, at times, to make tough decisions that affected the whole group. Although most of them objectified others, some discovered the immorality of objectification and found redemption by objectifying themselves, either for the person they objectified, for the greater good of the group, or for some higher ideal. If Kant, Mill, and Aristotle are correct, we would do well to follow their example.

PART FIVE

D IS FOR DESTINY

THE NEW NARNIA

Myth and Redemption on the Island of Second Chances

Brett Chandler Patterson

During its six-season run, *Lost* produced much speculation among its viewers about the meaning of the mysterious island and the overall trajectory of the series. Viewers noted the myriad allusions to other works of literature, from *Alice in Wonderland* to *The Wizard of Oz* to *Watership Down* and many others, including more weighty references to *Heart of Darkness* and *Of Mice and Men*. All of these references may be used as interpretive keys to unlocking the mysteries of a show that excelled at raising untold questions among its audience. From this long list of allusions, the one that is most telling and offers the most promise in connecting to the central themes of *Lost* episodes is C. S. Lewis's *The Chronicles of Narnia*. Damon Lindelof and Carlton Cuse, the primary creative force behind the mythology of the series, have noted that Narnia may bear the most influence on their work on *Lost*. Cuse has said that he hoped that what he and his partners were able to accomplish on their series is akin to what Lewis was able to do with Narnia.[1]

What does this tantalizingly short, yet revealing, comment tell us about *Lost?* Those who are familiar with C. S. Lewis's writings will see the parallels in myth building. Lewis drew on a tradition, also represented by George MacDonald and J. R. R. Tolkien, that sought to move from abstract allegories to concrete worlds. Yet like allegories, these imaginative worlds would still communicate something magical and something theological about our own world.

We most clearly see the connection between *Lost* and *The Chronicles of Narnia* when we highlight the central theme of redemption in both imaginative worlds. In Narnia and on *Lost*'s island, characters wrestle with failures and push on toward the possibility of "making things right" through their experiences in the fantasy world. Faith is never easy; it always involves a struggle. Yet in their struggles to find faith, many characters experience crucial moments that become revelatory, that open up new possibilities, even as new questions also arise.

The search for faith is not merely an individual one; if the characters are going to find healing, second chances will come in communion with others. The mythic structures of Narnia and *Lost* open these stories to philosophical and theological discussion and analysis; it is not accidental that there are parallels between these imaginative works and the religious concepts of redemption and community. As we shall see, the Jewish philosophy of Emmanuel Levinas (1906–1995) and the Christian philosophy of H. Richard Niebuhr (1894–1962) will be helpful in illuminating these references.

Myth, Not Allegory

During the first season of *Lost*, many viewers suggested that the mysterious island represented purgatory, the place where Christians who have died (with unconfessed venial sins) go for purification before entering into heaven, according to Catholic teaching. Cuse and Lindelof denied this speculation, in much the same spirit that C. S. Lewis denied that his *Chronicles of Narnia* were allegories, along the lines of *Pilgrim's Progress* or *Piers Plowman*.

Lewis did not want to label his stories "allegories" because he believed that when people read allegories, they focus only on the final message, discarding the process and the means of getting there. In a series of letters to his readers and in the essay "Myth Became Fact," Lewis said he wanted readers to enjoy the fantasy world, the myth, and that any message passed on must stay tied to the "embodiment" of that idea in the fantasy world. We should not, indeed cannot, dissect any meaning from the story itself.

Many consider C. S. Lewis's *The Chronicles of Narnia* his most developed and influential creation. Those who are familiar with Lewis's writings understand that Narnia is a significant realization of Lewis's own philosophical, literary, and theological views. In his essay "Sometimes Fairy Stories May Say Best What's to Be Said," Lewis insisted, though, that he did not start *The Chronicles of Narnia* with a plan to communicate theology to children and shape that theology into this form. Instead, he claimed that the story came from certain images—a faun, a lamppost, a lion—and that he discovered that the fairy tale genre would best communicate those images and that the images only gradually became Christian.

Over time, Lewis discovered that the form also provided a unique teaching opportunity. He believed that one of the biggest obstacles children face in learning about Christianity is a sense of obligation—submitting to what they are to believe about God and feeling that they have to be reverent. Lewis argued that stories presented another possibility: "But supposing that by casting all these things into an imaginary world, stripping them of their stained-glass and Sunday school associations, one could make them for the first time appear in their real potency? Could one not thus steal past those watchful dragons? I thought one could."[2] Lewis noted that adults could be inhibited by obligation just as easily as children are. So the mythic world could also allow adults to have religious encounters that could not occur in a more formal setting.

These encounters in the fantasy world, though, are not inconsequential. They bear on the real world around us. In the essay "On Three Ways of Writing for Children," Lewis defended the genre of the fairy tale against the claim that it is escapist, pulling us from the real world. Lewis wished to praise fantasy stories for their creative side, when they have been discarded by our culture as juvenile. He argued that so-called realistic stories often create self-oriented and unrealistic desires for success and fame, while fantasies frequently open us up to a world that is larger than ourselves. We encounter mysteries and wonders that lead us back to considering the beauty in our own world.

Lewis believed that an appreciation for mystery and wonder is essential in rediscovering a sense of what God is doing in our world. Lewis's vision for Narnia is a Christian one, but he hoped that those who have not adopted a Christian life might also be drawn into the fantasy world. Yet if we see Christian intonations in Narnia, we should remember that Lewis did not wish for us to divorce any message from the stories themselves. Narnia, like theology itself, can be a map to something greater, but the map has a structure and an integrity of its own.

In the last moments of the retrospective that preceded the original broadcast of the final episode of *Lost*, Carlton Cuse expressed that if there is any message that the writers wished to pass on to their viewers, it is imbedded in the series. Cuse, like Lewis, wished to point viewers who were asking for the "meaning" of *Lost* back to the episodes themselves. Although Cuse has shown more sympathies to Lewis's work in public interviews, Damon Lindelof has also said that if he had to pick one book for *Lost* viewers to read in conjunction with their show, he would side with Cuse and choose *The Chronicles of Narnia* for its epic scope and character-driven stories.

Cuse and Lindelof devoted a considerable amount of time to developing the mythos expressed in the stories in *Lost*, and they would not want us to dispense with that world once we thought we knew what the series was all about. Message and purpose are found in the journey and in the discussion, just as they are in Narnia, not in abstract dissection and classification afterward.

Despite this connection between the perspectives of Lewis and Cuse, there is an important difference between *The Chronicles of Narnia* and *Lost*: the former was largely the result of one man's efforts (although Lewis was in conversation with quite a number of important figures in the writing group the Inklings), whereas *Lost* is an ensemble production, a composite of the work of many writers, directors, actors, musicians, and technicians. More perspectives are captured in the stories that are *Lost*.

Even with this caution, we can assert that Cuse and Lindelof have guided the show in accordance with Jewish and Christian themes. They would not want us to divorce these meanings from the narrative. The journey has been too important, the characterization too vivid, the mystery too enticing for us to discard these themes in a discussion of the "meaning" of it all. If we are to discuss the influence of the story, we must also always ground our discussion in the mythic world.

Into the Mythic World

Fantasies typically either originate (and remain) in the mythic world or involve a magical journey from our world into the mythic world. C. S. Lewis's friend J. R. R. Tolkien was strongly on the side of keeping a fantasy world distinct from our own; it should have a separate existence, with its own rules and civilizations. Lewis, however, decided to follow in the footsteps of Lewis Carroll's *Alice in Wonderland* and George MacDonald's *Phantastes* and *Lilith*, works that have characters who start in our world and are then transported in some magical way into a fantasy world.

Those familiar with *The Lion, the Witch, and the Wardrobe* know that the children first enter Narnia through a magic wardrobe. In *Prince Caspian*, the children are sucked into Narnia from a train station, in response to Caspian's blowing of Susan's magical horn in Narnia, and in *The Voyage of the Dawn Treader*, the children pass through a painting of a ship at sea. In *The Magician's Nephew* the characters travel between worlds through the use of magical rings and pools in the "world between worlds." All but one of the books in the series (*The Horse and His Boy*) follow this rule; some magical moment transports various children and an occasional adult into the world of Narnia. Once these characters complete this journey, then they need to relate their former lives to their experiences in Narnia. Their encounters with Aslan, most important, but also with the White Witch and a series of other characters allow the children to grow in ways that they could not have if they had not come into this world. Narnia is crucial to their development.

One of the more vivid examples of this progression comes through Edmund Pevensie's story in *The Lion, the Witch, and the Wardrobe*. Edmund's troubled relationship with Peter, Susan, and Lucy in the "real" world intensifies in Narnia into his betrayal of them, as he sides with the White Witch, only to discover that this pledge was a mistake. Yet in Narnia, Edmund gets a second chance. Aslan's forgiveness and his sacrificial act of taking on Edmund's punishment provide for the final redemption of Edmund, who will eventually serve as a king of Narnia, justly ruling alongside his siblings. Edmund's enlightenment might have happened in the "real" world, but there is something about Narnia itself that has challenged him. And he is not the only one to feel the effects of this magical world. We can trace the changes in Peter, Susan, Lucy, Digory, Polly, Frank, Eustace, Jill, and others. Their experiences in Narnia change their lives.

Lost begins with a plane crash, and some of the most enduring images from the series come from the pilot episode. The characters have violently entered this fantasy world. Later, we learn that others have arrived through various means: Desmond via a sailboat; the Oceanic Six and company via another airplane; the Dharma Initiative via a submarine; Charles Widmore's first group via a freighter and the second group via that Dharma Initiative submarine, and Richard Alpert chained in the hold of the nineteenth-century British trading vessel *Black Rock*.

And what a world it is that these characters enter! The island demands that the survivors face some basic questions about the nature of human existence. The survivors' situation raises metaphysical problems, queries into the nature of reality itself: Why are we here? Where are we? Who are we? Where have we been? Where are we going? *Lost* heightens all of these questions by ripping the characters out of their routines and placing them in circumstances where there are no easily accessible answers to those questions. As Sawyer tells Jack, "I'm in the wild!" ("Tabula Rasa") And as Charlie intones for all the characters, at the end of the first episode: "Guys, where are we?" ("Pilot: Part 2")

Pulled out of a technologically oriented society and placed in the wilderness, these characters find that their decisions have more immediate life-and-death consequences. The environment magnifies their choices. As Desmond observes to Jack, in a little while he is going to be "either very right or very wrong" ("Orientation"). It becomes that much more necessary to try to get to the bottom of crucial existential questions, which people often ignore. As in the Narnia books, the setting forces the characters to commit to something; they must place their faith in something.

The episodes typically revolve around how quickly each of the characters is adjusting to the situation on the island. Characters such as Locke, Rose, and Walt have come to prefer life on the island, but most of the others are preoccupied with escaping the island and returning to civilization. The first major dispute between Jack and Kate centers on this issue, when Jack suggests that the community set up home in the newly discovered caves ("House of the Rising Sun"). All of the characters, though, question whether they will be rescued and whether they should form a new community on the island. In a crucial conversation between Locke and Michael over Walt's activities, Locke argues that as long as they are on the island, Walt should be allowed to reach his potential; Michael, however, adamantly resists Locke's suggestion ("Special").

There is an ongoing struggle with each of the characters to discover what the new community is and what their roles within it are going to be. By the end of "Tabula Rasa," the characters must face the issue of identifying who is the fugitive who was handcuffed on the plane and whether that former title holds any weight in their new situation. This is just one of a number of dramatic examples showing how the characters, at varying speeds, acknowledge that life on the island is different.

When the Oceanic Six finally leave the island, something eventually draws them back. As the Pevensie children are drawn back into Narnia in *Prince Caspian*, so also are the Oceanic Six drawn back to the island in season 5. Carlton Cuse left hints that he patterned his view of this return on *Prince Caspian*: "316" is the number of their flight, but it is also the page number in the HarperCollins collected edition of *The Chronicles of Narnia* where readers find the dedication page for *Prince Caspian*. In addition, the Dharma station, in the basement of a church, where Eloise Hawking reveals to the Oceanic Six how they will find a way back to the island, is called the Lamppost.

The episode "316" opens in a similar fashion as the first episode, with Jack's eye opening as he awakens in a bamboo forest on the island. He has been transported once again into the world of the island, the place where he is tested and where he ultimately finds his destiny. Many of the characters, notably John, Ben, Eloise, Jack, and Hurley, speak about what the island wants; there is something about the island that changes those who land on it.

Tested by Crisis

The fantasy world quickly places characters in the midst of significant conflict, crisis situations where the repercussions of their choices increase significantly. Peter, Susan, Edmund, and Lucy in *The Lion, the Witch, and the Wardrobe* find themselves in the midst of the cruel rule of the White Witch. They find that she is trying to capture them, and their lives are on the line. They see new friends tortured and imprisoned by her, and they learn that there is a war going on between her forces and the forces of Aslan.

When the children return to Narnia in *Prince Caspian*, they stumble into the midst of a civil war within Narnia. *The Voyage of the Dawn Treader* details an arduous passage through a series of treacherous islands, as Prince Caspian and company, with the help of Edmund, Lucy, and Eustace, search for seven missing Narnian lords. *The Silver Chair* presents the hazardous journey that Eustace, Jill, and Puddleglum take in search of Prince Rilian. And *The Last Battle* dramatizes the apocalyptic last days of Narnia.

Each of the Narnia volumes presents its own crises, and the characters in each succeeding story must wrestle with their own troubles and hopefully grow in the process of facing these challenges. Not all characters grow; some remain stubbornly rebellious to the end. Yet most of the central characters, with the controversial exception of Susan in *The Last Battle*, find crisis moments to be opportunities to be heroic. Even if characters happen to fail the tests that they face, Aslan is often there afterward to provide healing and a chance for them to learn from their mistakes.

Episodes of *Lost* also frequently portray characters in crisis moments. On the whole, episodes follow a consistent pattern: one member of the cast is highlighted in a series of flashbacks that are interspersed through an ongoing story about the survivors' struggle on the island. As we put the pieces together, we see distinct connections between the past and the present, typically images of past failures that affect how a character is interacting with new challenges on the island.

Thus, in the first episodes, Kate's past running from a U.S. marshal is juxtaposed against the present challenge of handling the marshal's death; Locke's past struggle against a company supervisor and a walkabout guide who put parameters on what he could do runs against Locke's leading the hunt for a boar; Jack's past perfectionism, his inability to let go, contrasts with his failure to save a drowning woman and his quest to find the vision of his dad in the jungle.

The pattern continues as we learn about the past mistakes of other characters: Charlie's struggle with his brother, Liam, as they both succumbed to the temptations of being a rock star and his feeling sorry for having betrayed Lucy to feed his drug habit; Sawyer's deep-seated hatred toward the confidence man who took advantage of his parents and toward himself for adopting the same lifestyle and for killing the wrong man; Sayid's regret that he allowed himself to be transformed into a torturer and that he cannot get away from that identity, despite vows to the contrary; Claire's struggle to be a single mother and her guilt over contemplating giving the child up for adoption; Jack's remorse over holding his father accountable and for letting his marriage fall apart; Boone's feeling of guilt for being attracted to Shannon and for allowing her to take advantage of him; Shannon's search for self-worth after her stepmother disowns her and cuts her off from her inheritance; Michael's ongoing lament that he allowed Susan to coerce him into giving up custody of Walt; Sun's regret about how her father's influence infected her marriage to Jin and how she sought solace in an adulterous relationship; Jin's struggle to be a man of integrity as he seeks to advance himself socially (involving himself in violence and intimidation at Sun's father's request) for the sake of his wife; Hurley's feelings of insecurity manifested in the curse of the numbers and in the tragic balcony accident and in his hallucinations of Dave; Locke's regret that he was taken in by a father who tricked him out of a kidney and that his obsession with his father spelled the ruin of his relationship with Helen; Ana Lucia's fear of being a victim again; Kate's lament that she became estranged from her mother when she killed her abusive "stepfather" (who was really her biological father) and her regret that her actions led to the death of her friend and high-school sweetheart, Tom; Eko's desire to be a priest to honor his brother Yemi's sacrifice; Bernard's and Rose's separate struggles over her terminal disease; and Desmond's search to reclaim his dignity after a dishonorable discharge from the Royal Scots Regimen and the apparent loss of his love, Penny.

It is a list that lengthens as the series progresses, particularly as seasons introduce new characters, such as those "rescuers" on the freighter in season 4, the Dharma Initiative recruits, Ilana's group in season 5, and the enigmatic characters in season 6. The flashbacks drive home to the viewers at least two major points: that the past haunts each of these characters and that they each hunger for a second chance, some more obviously than others. It is ironic that in "Tabula Rasa," Jack so adamantly argues to Kate that it does not matter what happened before their time on the island, because they all essentially "died" in the plane crash and should each be given a chance to start over. In one sense, they are given new chances in the new environment and will find new roles in the new community, but they do not exactly have clean slates. Although all of the characters feel the weight of the past, most are not lost there; they are actively seeking a new start on the island. We might even say that they are trying to atone for past failures. What is it about the island, though, that might suggest such possibilities for a new start? How does the island create a scenario where these characters would confront their pasts and move on to a new way of life?

"It Has Never Been Easy": The Struggle for Faith and the Quest for Redemption

Faith is not easy to attain in Narnia. Characters often fail when they are tested. Faith, however, is not so elusive as to be a will-o'-the-wisp either. The quest for faith requires characters to be self-disciplined and altruistic. Occasionally, this struggle to find faith involves an encounter with Aslan, who "is not a tame lion." Even the ever-likable Lucy, who has proved to be a reliable witness in the original encounter with Narnia in *The Lion, the Witch, and the Wardrobe* and in the sighting of Aslan in the forest trek in *Prince Caspian*, finds her faith tested in *The Voyage of the Dawn Treader*, when she finds a book of magical spells.

Lucy finds a spell with the power to make her beautiful and is tempted to cast the spell, even though she has a feeling that she should not. A vision of Aslan growling at her finally gets her to turn the page. She then quickly casts a spell that enables her to know what her friends have been thinking about her and then a spell that makes hidden things visible. When Aslan actually appears to her, he scolds her for eavesdropping on her friends, and Lucy regrets it.

In the same book but on another island, Eustace finds a treasure, sleeps next to it one evening, and awakens the next day to discover that he has turned into a dragon. In his encounter with Aslan, he must endure the painful process of having those scales scrubbed away. It is an ordeal to surrender his greed and to recover his humanity.

In *The Silver Chair*, Aslan gives Jill four "signs" to guide her and her friends in their quest to find Prince Rilian, but along their way, Jill, Eustace, and Puddleglum get into trouble by overlooking some of these signs. And in *The Last Battle*, several characters must look past the deceptions of Shift and Puzzle to discern that they do not represent Aslan. Most characters do not just inherently have faith; most of them have to work through doubts, misconceptions, and selfish desires to find Aslan and the path to fulfillment. And many of them must move past failures, as Edmund clearly does in *The Lion, the Witch, and the Wardrobe*, to find redemption in new, heroic roles.

In the world of *Lost*, we find characters struggling to interpret what is going on around them. Are they masters of their own destiny, victims of pure chance, or participants in some divine plan? Many of the heartfelt discussions between characters revolve around what they believe is happening to them on the island. Is there a purpose to their struggles on the island? Is God or fate somehow directing the events of their lives? Or is this just the way life is, according to our choices and to random chance? Are we masters of our lives or not?

This debate over interpretation is no clearer or more passionately expressed than in the conflict between Jack and Locke. Cuse and Lindelof have revealed that they based this relationship at least partially on their own relationship: Cuse is a Catholic who emphasizes taking a leap of faith and Lindelof is a Jew who grounds his understanding of reality in empiricist philosophy.[3] On first look, Jack, the man of science, emphasizes that there is no such thing as fate, that we all stand or fall based on our choices, and Locke, the man of faith, emphasizes that there is a greater purpose, a plan that shapes their lives. Yet on second look, as Lindelof and Cuse admit, Jack at times is a man of faith and Locke becomes more of an empiricist in his crisis of faith.[4] The duality is what interests them as writers, and it is what interests many viewers.

The quarrel between Jack and Locke reaches an important climax early in season 2. While arguing over whether they should continue Desmond's practice of entering the numbers every 108 minutes, Locke asks Jack why he has such a difficult time believing that this is what they are supposed to do. Jack returns the question, asking John why it is so easy for him to believe. Locke's final comment is that it has never been easy. Viewers know that faith has never been easy for Locke; in this very episode, flashbacks tell us of a past time when he struggled with Helen's request that he take a leap of faith ("Orientation").

Viewers will also remember the notable first-season episode "The Moth," which portrays Charlie's wrestling with his drug addiction. Locke, who has already found his own revelatory moment about life on the island, seeks to test Charlie. Holding onto Charlie's heroin, Locke gives Charlie an ultimatum. He will give Charlie three chances: if Charlie requests the drugs three times, then Locke will hand them over. On the second request, Locke turns Charlie's attention to the silk cocoon of a moth. Locke, opening his pocketknife, tells Charlie that he could open the cocoon to help the moth escape, but that it would not be strong enough to survive. It is the digging, the work, that enables the moth to survive. Charlie must fight against his addiction to regain faith in himself, in his place in the new community of survivors, and in the ultimate meaning of his life. Locke has orchestrated events so that Charlie can have his "cocoon" to work through to the other side, to emerge the beautiful moth. The struggle is not easy, however, and Charlie, as we see in season 2, does fall back; he has not fully emerged. The struggle is ongoing, up to his sacrificial death at the end of season 3.

The metaphor applies not only to Charlie's quest, but to the development of each character on the island. Guilt over past failures and the existential questioning brought about by the struggle to survive meet in each character's search to find faith in himself or herself, faith in others, and faith in the fundamental purpose of life. For example, Rose, who along with Eko, offers a Christian spin on faith, says to Charlie, "There is a fine line between denial and faith." ("Whatever the Case May Be")

The moral philosopher and theologian H. Richard Niebuhr reminded us in *Faith on Earth* that we all fundamentally place our faith in something that gives life meaning, something that keeps us going on. We all have some center of value that helps us organize our lives. Yet we must overcome suspicion and "broken faith" in our lives in our ongoing journey of faith. We have all experienced or contributed to promises broken and trusts violated. From the Christian perspective that Niebuhr represents, we live in a state of alienation from God, from one another, and from the world around us. We live with our past failures, and we doubt that we could ever be trustworthy or that we could ever trust others. The characters on *Lost*, as they experience events on the island that recall their pasts, must repeatedly decide whether they are going to live a life of trust or a life of suspicion. (Ana Lucia, who admits that she has "trust issues," is one of the more blatant examples of a life of suspicion.) *Lost* stories often portray a journey from suspicion to trust, speaking in terms of second chances or redemption.

In his second-season commentary on "23rd Psalm," Cuse said that *Lost* is "all about redemption." The series consistently shows characters who have failed in numerous ways in the past attempting to make better lives for themselves on the island; they feel that they have a second chance, that they, in certain ways, can make up for their pasts. The *Lost* writing team has shaped conversations among characters, musical cues, and the structure of most episodes around images of redemption. Redemption is a journey, where we grow in ways to prevent the same mistakes we made in the past. Echoes of, and direct references to, this process appear in many episodes of *Lost*, as characters wrestle with their pasts and struggle for survival on the island.

What brings such a turnaround? How can we move from suspicion to trust and faith? Niebuhr reminded us that faith is often rooted in revelation. Although some readers may find it difficult to relate to the explicit Christian language of Niebuhr's discussion, I think it is appropriate to bring Christian concepts into conversation with the vision within *Lost*, because a number of characters make reference to Christianity and because one of the central writers, Carleton Cuse, has argued that his Catholic faith has shaped his influence on the show.

Niebuhr suggested that the categories of faith and revelation may also say some things about human existence in general. In *The Meaning of Revelation*, Niebuhr argued that revelation provides the context for understanding our experiences: revelation becomes the interpretive key that illumines our understanding of the rest of our lives, including our past. Particularly for Christians, God's love transforms our understanding of what is valuable; revelation demands that we confess our sins. Niebuhr argued that the revelation of Jesus Christ calls us to conversion and permanent revolution. According to Niebuhr, revelation is ongoing, for the reconstruction of our character that it enables is not something easily accomplished. Such growth occurs only in a lifetime of participation in the Christian community. Revelation is a relationship; it is moving, not static, for God continues to reveal Godself. At no point in history will this project be complete; the Christian heart is engaged in a never-ending pilgrimage.

The Christian vision within *Lost* particularly arises when discussing the central figures of faith in the series: Rose, Eko, Desmond, and Locke. Rose and Eko make overt references to having faith that God is directing their lives on the island. Rose prays for healing for Charlie, and Eko carves scripture references into his stick, baptizes (however unorthodoxly) Claire and Aaron, recites (an imperfect) 23rd Psalm over the burning plane wreckage, and starts to build a church before feeling inspired to take Locke's place as pusher of the hatch button. Although some revelatory moments for these characters have already occurred by the time they arrive on the island, the island presents moments for the ongoing revelation that Niebuhr described.

Desmond has had direct contact with the Christian community in a Catholic monastic form (as we see in "Catch 22"), but he also undergoes a revelatory moment at the end of season 2. He feels that he has found his "purpose" in laying down his life for the others, by turning the failsafe key, but his survival and apparent ability to receive visions of the future present new possibilities in season 3. Desmond at this point resembles a first-season John Locke, offering guidance to members of the community, particularly Charlie. Desmond has been affected by a revelatory encounter with the island and has been gifted, much like Rose and Locke, who were healed. In season 6, Desmond resumes this shepherd role as he seeks to guide characters to a realization that they need to let go of the reality in the flash-sideways world. His revelatory moment allows him to guide other characters to their moments of enlightenment.

Locke, in contrast, offers a more ambiguous connection to this Christian concept of revelation, suggesting that the writers themselves may be thinking more in terms of pantheism or transcendentalism or a New Age perspective, influenced by Native American spirituality (as referenced by the sweat lodge)—yet even here, under Cuse's influence, we see in a flashback in "Further Instructions" that Locke offers up a very Christian prayer. Locke finds "beauty" by looking into the "eye" of the island. Locke grounds his revelatory experience in the island: "This place is different." He believes that the other survivors are not willing to talk about the changes brought by the island because they are scared by the possibilities.

The most significant area where Locke could represent a theological commitment, as Cuse has hinted, is in his insistent commitment to the notion that everything happens for a reason.

Revelation grounds faith that our existence contributes to an overall benevolent purpose. It is this message that makes Locke a priest of sorts to a number of others on the island: he guides Jack in "White Rabbit," challenges Charlie in "The Moth," tests Boone in "Hearts and Minds," confronts Michael over Walt in "Special," calls Shannon to a new start in "In Translation," quietly helps Claire with motherhood in "Numbers," diverts Sayid's anger in "The Greater Good," promotes the community's entrance into the hatch in "Exodus," and assumes the hatch duties in "Orientation."

Locke, more than any other character, embodies the transformative power of revelation. Thus, it is that much more important when he has his crises of faith: in season 1, concerning Boone's death, and in season 2, following the discovery of the Pearl hatch. Locke is not without setbacks, as we see in season 3 when he encourages Sawyer's killing instinct ("The Brig"). Sawyer had earlier made quite a bit of progress in becoming part of the community under Hurley's tutelage, but Locke contributes to the devolution of Sawyer's character ("Left Behind"). Locke is still struggling on his journey as well, as we see in his third-season destructiveness and in his wrestling with Ben and company. Revelation-inspired transformation is an ongoing process. His faith has a distinct influence on Jack, of course. Locke's suicide note to Jack is simple: "I wish you had believed me." And because Locke was such a courageous character, it is all that much more shocking when the Man in Black takes his identity.

Finally, though, Jack himself takes a journey from his earlier skepticism to being a figure of faith in the end, too. In the earlier seasons, he is so focused on getting off the island, but when he finally does escape and return to the mainland, his life becomes a wreck. A burden of guilt weighs him down. Viewers start to see a change in his character when Ben and Eloise and others convince him to return to the island. He resists all along the way. He wishes to set off the nuclear bomb in season 5 so that he can erase their ever coming to the island. And in season 6, when Hurley shows Jack the location of Jacob's lighthouse, Jack smashes the mirrors. Yet after taking some time to reflect and listening to Hurley's (and, indirectly, Jacob's) encouragement, Jack does start to demonstrate a faith of his own that there is a purpose to their being on the island and particularly to his being on the island. Jack's final moments on the island parallel Desmond's own sacrificial deed and reveal an act of faithful self-sacrifice.

The White Witch vs. Aslan and the Man in Black vs. Jacob

In both Narnia and *Lost*, as characters struggle with their own weaknesses in a world that magnifies their choices, as they look for ways to redeem themselves, they encounter forces that foster vice, as well as those that encourage virtue. Both fantasy worlds offer vivid pictures of good and evil. We need to remember at this point that Lewis wrote the Narnia books for children, so the lines between good and evil are much more sharply drawn.

Aslan is presented as a possible alternative incarnation for Christ, if he were to appear in Narnia. There are obvious connections between Aslan and Jesus: Aslan lays down his life but comes back in a resurrection in *The Lion, the Witch, and the Wardrobe*. Aslan sings Narnia into existence in *The Magician's Nephew* and is there to close the book on Narnia and usher the children into heaven in *The Last Battle*.

Although Aslan is not exactly like Jesus, Lewis hoped that children who liked Aslan would grow up and find a parallel in Jesus. Aslan prefers to be gentle and loving but will not hesitate to show his power when it is necessary to discipline a character. Aslan's influence colors all of Narnia; even when he appears to be absent, characters later learn that he has shaped events in a certain way (as seen in *The Horse and His Boy*).

On the other side, we have a series of evil characters. The most enduring is the White Witch of *The Lion, the Witch, and the Wardrobe*, largely because she is the one who negotiates with Aslan over the fate of Edmund and orchestrates the death of Aslan. In *The Magician's Nephew*, we learn of her escape from the world of Charn and her arrival into Narnia when Aslan is singing it into existence. Although Aslan takes her life at the end of *The Lion, the Witch, and the Wardrobe*, Lewis suggests her influence in *Prince Caspian* as various characters try through dark magic to bring her back. Lewis also presents a similar version of her in the witch in *The Silver Chair*.

In his portrait of the White Witch, Lewis is heavily influenced by George MacDonald's *Lilith*, which also casts evil in the form of a dangerously seductive woman. The witch's most powerful weapon is persuasion. Lewis would have us think about the story of the serpent's tempting of Eve in Genesis or about John Milton's version in *Paradise Lost*. Adam and Eve bring sin into the world because they listen to and begin to believe the lies of the serpent.

The White Witch twists the truth in her manipulation of Edmund and in her serpentlike tempting of Digory (when he is attempting to bring a golden fruit back to Aslan). In *The Silver Chair*, another witch, the Lady of the Green Kirtle, holds Eustace, Jill, Rilian, and Puddleglum in her spell, as she seeks to persuade them that Aslan does not exist. Persuasion through misdirection and deception is the central tool of those who are evil. We see this in other evil characters in Narnia: King Miraz, Shift, and Puzzle.

Lost, pitched more toward adults and written half a century later, blurs the line between good and evil characters. The plot complications often leave us guessing about whether we should be supporting Benjamin Linus or Charles Widmore, whether we should be glad that the freighter has arrived or terrified of who has come to the island, whether the Others are the "good guys" after all the time we have seen them as a threat to the survivors of Oceanic flight 815, whether we should pity the Man in Black or Jacob (who is the most deluded?).

Despite this ambiguity, there are also images that distinguish good and evil. Locke plays a game of backgammon, holding up white and black pieces. A similar game appears later in "Across the Sea"; Jacob's brother, who has no name but becomes the Man in Black, is fascinated with the game and the rules that govern it. He tells Jacob that he has to follow the rules, although there may come a day when Jacob can make up his own game and rules. Jacob and his brother have a game that they play, wagering on the outcome of each person's journey on the island, exchanging white and black rocks.

Cuse and Lindelof introduced readers slowly to Jacob through the expectations of other characters, just as Lewis did with Aslan. We hear about Jacob from various characters before we are allowed to see him, and our impressions are distorted by the Man in Black pretending to be Jacob (in the cabin scenes in the jungle).

In the finale of season 5, Cuse and Lindelof presented Jacob as being like a majestic lion, only to magnify this portrait in the season 6 episode "The Lighthouse." Jacob has been observing Jack, Kate, Sawyer, Locke, Hurley, and others for quite some time, actually going to the mainland and touching them at pivotal points in their lives. He has brought them to the island, as we learn in "What They Died For," because they are broken and searching.

In "Across the Sea," however, we learn that Jacob, too, is a human being, who has made his own major mistakes, who has his own sins to confess and for which to atone. We now understand why he told Richard Alpert in "Ab Aeterno" that he could not offer absolution for Richard's sins. Yet this plot turn also blurs Jacob's "goodness"; he seems to be most persuaded by the false vision of his adopted mother (who killed his real mother). Jacob is too flawed to be the island's Aslan, but despite his own shortcomings, he still serves as an example of virtue for the other characters.

In Jacob's final scene, brought about by the burning of his ashes, in only a temporary resurrection sequence, he states that he has drawn the others to the island because they are flawed, as he is, looking for ways to atone for past failures. Jacob says that he has faith in them; he offers them a choice, and Jack volunteers to be his successor. There is a legacy of goodness. Jacob does not resist Ben, because he feels that he deserves death. Jack takes up Jacob's mantle and lays down his life to save the island from the Man in Black's attack.

The characters who show signs of being villainous most often are characters who know how to lie. In "Across the Sea," the surrogate mother observes that Jacob does not know how to lie, unlike the unnamed boy in black. When he grows up and undergoes the transformation into the Smoke Monster, the Man in Black frequently assumes the forms of those who have died. He uses this deception to manipulate the survivors, taking the form of Jack's father to manipulate not only Jack, but also Locke and later Claire. The ultimate manipulation comes in his assumption of the form of Locke and his persuading Ben to kill Jacob.

Yet it is not surprising to see Ben take on this ignominious role. He is another great liar. Remember, we are first introduced to him as Henry Gale; he, too, has assumed the identity of another (not to the eerie extent of the Smoke Monster, but enough to confuse the flight 815 survivors). Because Ben's machinations are so complex throughout the series, we are never entirely sure how to take anything he says. He is equally matched in the figure of Charles Widmore, another manipulator who reveals information only to promote his own purposes.

Beyond these corrupted characters, we have central characters wondering about their own lies. Sawyer is the best con man among the survivors, running a long con on them to get control of the guns. At times he feels guilty about the deceit, but he also feels that it is necessary for survival. Other characters, such as Sun, wonder whether they are being punished on the island for their lies ("Exodus"). Sun, after all, was keeping the truth about her affair from Jin.

The Oceanic Six, and Michael before them, are eaten up with guilt about the lie they felt they had to tell to protect those who remained on the island. In "The Lie," Hurley feels that he has dropped a great burden when he finally confesses this lie to his mother. Many episodes that show characters slipping into old (sinful) ways naturally center on their misdirection and deception. Lies destroy trust; they make suspicion and broken faith the norms, blocking the path to redemption and community.

"Live Together, Die Alone": Redemption and New Community

The paths of redemption in the fantasy worlds of *Narnia* and *Lost* lead to the building of a new community, new relationships. In Narnia, the children live for years, growing older with friends (only to discover when they return to our world that mere minutes have passed and that they are children again). Their stories are intertwined with their new friends. Lucy depends on Mr. Tumnus. Eustace, though first irritated by the chivalrous mouse Reepicheep, later learns to value his friendship. Eustace and Jill owe their lives to Puddleglum, who helps deliver them from the seductive voice of the witch. It is Aslan's followers, the Old Narnians, who make a last desperate stand against King Miraz's troops. The children who come into Narnia, who face all sorts of challenges, draw strength from their new friends. Above all, in Narnia, it is the presence, guidance, and love of Aslan that inspires and sustains his followers and allows them to develop a community, where they depend on one another in common service to their king.

Lost presents a more troubled and complicated quest for community, but this quest is still a central theme. Once characters have faced their past failures, asked the crucial existential questions, engaged the struggle to faith, and found some revelatory experience on the island, they may find redemption, but this opportunity for a new start, for a second chance, arrives primarily in their becoming a part of the community of survivors. The story of *Lost* reminds us that our identities largely arise in our relationships with those around us. The survivors on the island define themselves according to a common experience: surviving a plane crash and an island full of mysterious dangers.

The moral philosopher Emmanuel Levinas reminded us in *Totality and Infinity* of the primacy of relationship; we do not live as discrete individuals but as beings in relationship to "others." When we encounter another face-to-face, we are bound to the other in a relationship of responsibility. In *Otherwise than Being*, Levinas argued that we understand ourselves only in transcending ourselves in encounters with others. These encounters occur through the use of language and through the proximity of our bodies. We find ourselves in situations that we did not create, in connection with other beings; we have a responsibility toward those others.

Niebuhr, once again in *The Meaning of Revelation*, also called us to see revelation as a social event, rooted in relationships, rather than in ideas. True knowledge is not simply the acquisition of a concept; it is a give-and-take between people. We come to knowledge of others as others come to knowledge of us. Thus, overall, the Christian life consists of becoming a person in relationship with Jesus Christ and his followers, rather than solely in accepting certain laws and beliefs. Revelation alone does not accomplish conversion; there must also be a reasoning heart, a participating self, no longer oriented around itself.

Niebuhr further reminded us that our identities arise in communities, that our "knowledge" of the world is always in dialogue with the "knowledge" of those around us. All of our knowledge fundamentally rests on the trust we place in certain persons within that social setting. We seldom seek to verify the language we inherit from our society and are not usually aware of our language's effect on our knowledge until we are challenged by another set of beliefs. In addition, knowledge from direct experience can move toward certainty when it is "verified" by observations from others, particularly those with social authority. Faith is communal.

Those who find faith are community builders. Locke, who at first seems to be an outsider, leads a number of the survivors through their struggles, allowing them to become part of the developing community. Jack becomes their early leader, in many ways because his profession of physician is clearly oriented around the community. He struggles with this calling but assumes the mantle adeptly when he proclaims to the community that they cannot function on "every man for himself," that they need to organize to survive. If they cannot "live together," then they will "die alone" ("White Rabbit").

There are many signs of the new community. Hurley builds a golf course to help relieve the tension the survivors suffer. In the send-off at the end of season 1 for Walt, Michael, Jin, and Sawyer, a bottle of letters carries everyone's hopes. The community develops with the ongoing story, and each survivor represents a different level of commitment to it. Not everyone warmly embraces the community. Charlie, Michael, and Sawyer obviously, to different degrees, rebel against it. Charlie struggles with his place in the community in season 2, joining Sawyer in the con to get the guns, but by the time of his sacrificial death in season 3, he has worked to redeem himself. Michael betrays the community in an effort to free his son, Walt, from the Others, killing Ana Lucia and Libby in the process, but seeks to redeem himself in his death on the freighter and in his apology to Hurley in the final season.

Although Sawyer rebels against community, even he longs for it. Quoting from *Of Mice and Men*, Ben argues that Sawyer needs companionship: "A guy goes nuts if he ain't got nobody. It don't make no difference who the guy is, long as he's with you. I tell you, I tell you a guy gets too lonely and he gets sick." ("Every Man for Himself") Sawyer is capable of sacrificial acts, too, as we see him jump from the helicopter in season 4. He, of course, finally finds someone in Juliet. The love he learns from her infuses his character and enables him to become a team player. When she dies, he goes through a period of nihilism but emerges a hero, helping other characters survive in their encounters with the Man in Black and, in the final moments of the series, delivering Claire and Kate to the escaping airplane in the nick of time.

Lost ends with Jack's sacrifice to save the island and with a purgatorylike moment when he realizes the significance of his life on the island and learns to let go of this world in order to take the journey into the next. We might remember Ben's comments about the apostle Thomas in "316": eventually, we are all convinced. It is ironic that Ben makes this observation, because he is sitting outside the church as the series ends. Apparently, he was not yet convinced—but Jack was. He began his journey as a skeptic, presenting adamant opposition to Locke's "steps of faith." In many ways, Jack's journey from skepticism to faith models that of C. S. Lewis, who was known as "Jack" among friends and family. An atheist as a teen, Lewis came to faith as an adult only after a long, complex journey.

This personal journey distinctly informs Lewis's vision in Narnia, and it is not as narrow-minded as some might think. The ending of *The Last Battle* illustrates a more generous portrait of how characters can find Aslan and redemption. Aslan allows one of the Calormen, who serve the god Tash, into heaven. The controversial explanation is that although the man thought he was serving Tash, he was actually serving Aslan. *Lost*'s interfaith stained glass in the background of Jack's final scene with his father is equally controversial, despite the prominent glimpses of the statue of Jesus in front of the church. Lewis, however, as well as Cuse and Lindelof, wrote in the spirit of invitation, noting parallels with other faiths, while expressing their own cherished beliefs. They wished to build community and dialogue. The many warm embraces in the final moments of "The End" crystallize the point: relationships are the key. Jack's sacrifice affirms the relationships he has built on the island, and his journey could not have happened without them.

The island on *Lost* is a place of transformation, just like the lands of Narnia. Those who travel through find themselves in new relationships, with new responsibilities and new challenges. They are a multicultural mix, a microcosm of the world, and the encounters among them bring both violence and healing. They face existential questions; they wrestle with faith; they learn to trust one another. Following the example of C. S. Lewis, Cuse and Lindelof intentionally shaped the mythic structure of *Lost* to reflect Jewish and Christian traditions. Yet they have also shown that the mythic structure has a wider appeal, as we all are drawn into a discussion about these stories of failure and redemption. We, too, have been changed by our visits to Narnia and to that ever mysterious island.

NOTES

1. "The Best of 2005," *Entertainment Weekly*, January 6, 2006.
2. C. S. Lewis, *On Stories* (New York: Harcourt, 1982), p. 47.
3. "The Best of 2005," *Entertainment Weekly*, January 6, 2006.
4. Lindelof's and Cuse's commentary on "Man of Science, Man of Faith," *Lost* DVD set, season 2.

I ONCE WAS LOST

Aquinas on Finding Goodness and Truth

Daniel B. Gallagher

From one episode to the next, *Lost* fans repeatedly searched for some central point that might finally turn out to be the key to unlocking the island's secrets. The hatch, the Others' camp, the communications center, the underwater station, the freighter, the frozen chamber, the Orchid station: all emerged as candidates over time. Perhaps one of the most fascinating possibilities was the cabin, a remote place inhabited by the elusive and seemingly omnipotent and omniscient Jacob. It was there that Ben allegedly took counsel, Locke had a conversion, and Hurley got majorly spooked out—dude. We find these three characters trudging toward the remote hideaway in "Cabin Fever," an episode that culminates in the "one question that matters" for John Locke: "How do I save the island?" The character thought to be Jacob eventually turns out to be Jacob's rival, but the former's preternatural powers continue to work in the lives of the characters nonetheless. The image of the empty rocking chair remained etched in the minds of many Losties as a sure sign that the bizarre events occurring on the island were at least partly due to some authority figure gifted with supernatural powers. Indeed, the name Jacob evoked the Old Testament patriarch who dreamed of a ladder stretching up to heaven on which angels ascended and descended (Genesis 28:12); the one who wrestled throughout the night and prevailed against God and men (Genesis 32:28).

The ability to see and hear Jacob, a major point of contention between Ben and Locke, was closely tied to the theme of who each thought Jacob was and which of them had been chosen by Jacob as leader. The reception of a special message and the placing of one's faith in the messenger are typical of Judaism, Islam, and Christianity, among other religions. Both the Old and the New Testaments contain stories of divine manifestations that strengthen the faith of some but cause others to doubt. Jesus of Nazareth himself was reportedly received by some while rejected by others. Bitter divisions broke out about which criteria to employ in testing Jesus' claim to be the Christ and how to authenticate his prophetic status.

Similar issues of criteria and authentication were on the minds of Ben, Locke, and Hurley, with regard to not only Jacob's authority, but Jacob's very *existence*. Thomas Aquinas (1225–1274), one of the most brilliant minds of the medieval era, also touched on these issues with regard to the existence of God. He asked whether the proposition "God exists" was self-evident. Just as Ben, Locke, and Hurley make their way through the woods to a place they know and don't know, so Aquinas compared faith to someone approaching you from afar: you recognize a human being but do not recognize *who* the human being is. He wrote,

> To know that God exists in a general and confused way is implanted in us by nature, inasmuch as God is man's beatitude. For man naturally desires happiness, and what is naturally desired by man must be

naturally known to him. This, however, is not to know absolutely that God exists; just as to know that someone is approaching is not the same as to know that Peter is approaching, even though it is Peter who is approaching; for many there are who imagine that man's perfect good which is happiness, consists in riches, and others in pleasures, and others in something else.[1]

In Aquinas's estimation, those who mistake some finite good for the ultimate good are like the *Lost* characters encountering the Smoke Monster in the woods. When Locke first encounters it, we the viewers are not given a chance to look at it. Finally, when Mr. Eko stares it down "face-to-face" during his hike with Charlie, we are offered a good, long look. We see that it is composed of dark black smoke, and that it seems to contain vague flashing images within, but we still do not know what it really is. For Aquinas, this is like the experience of people who encounter goodness but never take the time or trouble to find out what it is or where it comes from.

"I *Know* There's Someone There"

Building its theme of faith, *Lost* portrays many "approaching Peter" scenes with different twists. When Daniel Faraday meets Desmond in "The Constant," Desmond recognizes Daniel immediately, even though Daniel has never seen Desmond before. In "Catch-22," Desmond is certain that the woman who just parachuted onto the island is Penny, before he removes her helmet and discovers that it is Naomi. And there are countless times when one of the castaways sees or hears "a stranger" approaching in the woods, hides behind a tree, and cocks a gun, only to discover that the "stranger" was actually someone whom he or she knew the whole time.

Aquinas drew on this common experience to illustrate what he meant by things known "in themselves": that is, things the knowledge of which is naturally implanted within us. John Damascene (c. 676–760), who exerted a considerable influence on Aquinas, taught that knowledge of God is "self-evident." Aquinas agreed with Damascene to a certain extent. Aquinas was convinced that *everyone* has a confused, imperfect knowledge that God exists, insofar as God is the end of human happiness. Yet Aquinas also taught that our knowledge of what happiness is and our desire to attain happiness do not equal knowledge of God "simply" (*simpliciter*). Aquinas's approaching Peter image, though commonplace, is startlingly enlightening. I see a man coming toward me. I do not recognize him as Peter, even though he really *is* Peter. So it is with those who see in some small way the "perfect good" but nevertheless mistake it for riches, pleasure, or something else. Thus, finite goodness gives us a basis for faith in God, the perfect good.

"Welcome to the Wonderful World of Not Knowing the Hell What's Going On"

Simply put, Aquinas capitalized on the contrast between our uncertainty about God's existence and our certainty about our desire for happiness. He thus began to address the question of whether God exists by first pointing to our incontrovertible desire for happiness. He then continued by saying that we will look for a good outside ourselves to achieve this happiness, and that we consider this good the supreme good (the *bonum perfectum*).

To return to his example, if I see Peter coming toward me but have not recognized him as Peter, this does not change the fact that the person coming toward me really *is* Peter (rather than Paul). The other side of the analogy, however—that is, our search for happiness—presents a very different case, because whenever I go out to search for happiness and choose riches as the supreme good, riches are *not* the same "thing" as God. Riches and God are two entirely different entities (even though both are "goods"). I have taken riches as the perfect good, when in fact the perfect good is not riches at all, but something else entirely: namely, God.

Alternatively, Aquinas suggested that our knowledge of the good essentially involves knowledge and love of God. He explained that because nothing is good except insofar as it is a likeness of, and participation in, the highest good, the highest good itself is in some way desired in every particular good. In this way, Aquinas believed that we can legitimately say that there is one good that all things desire. Aquinas also explained that every movement of the will can be "reduced" to God as the first object of the appetite and the first agent of willing.

Whether or not I recognize the man walking toward me as Peter, he is nonetheless Peter. Just as the man whom I do not recognize and the man I recognize are the same man, so the good that I desire is in some way identified with the ultimate good. On recognizing the man walking toward me, I say "Ah!—the man I was seeing this whole time was actually *Peter*." Similarly, after having recognized the ultimate good to be God, I say, "Ah! The *good* I was desiring this whole time was actually *God*!" Augustine of Hippo (354–430) crystallized the point when he prayed, "You made us for yourself and our hearts find no peace until they rest in you."[2]

Human beings often take partial goods as the ultimate good. This leads the characters on *Lost* to place their hopes in some limited good that ultimately fails to satisfy. In his life prior to the air crash, Jack placed his ultimate hope in his ability to cure people ("Man of Science, Man of Faith" and "The Hunting Party"). Kate placed her hope in her ability to deceive people ("Born to Run" and "Tabula Rasa"). Jin placed his hope in the employment offered to him by his father-in-law (". . . In Translation" and "Exodus"). Charlie placed his hope in his big brother, Liam ("The Moth" and "Fire + Water"); Claire in the psychic Mr. Malkin ("Raised by Another"); and Locke in his biological father, Anthony Cooper ("Deus ex Machina"). The Virgin Mary statues containing contraband become a potent and multilayered symbol of the human tendency to place ultimate hope in something nondivine, even when that something—or someone—should ultimately lead us to the divine ("House of the Rising Sun," "Exodus," and "The 23rd Psalm"). Because the "ultimate good" that so many of the characters were searching for was lost even before they found themselves on the island, they wander around carrying a heavy load of betrayal and regret during their plight, while bumping into various opportunities to redeem themselves once more.

"We're Going to Have a Rational Conversation Regarding Our Next Move"

Aquinas took the desire for the ultimate good as something grounded in human reason, rather than as an expression of sheer will or blind faith. He therefore would have admired the faith of Rose Henderson, but he would have cautioned her against allowing her faith to trump the role of her natural ability to reason. Aquinas often referred to a passage from the First Letter of Peter expressing his conviction that faith cannot stand without solid reasons to buttress it: "Always be ready to give an explanation to anyone who asks you for a reason for your hope." (1 Peter 3:15)

As we saw in the passage about the approaching Peter, the locus of this general and confused knowledge is neither in scientific truth nor in one's moral sense nor in the world's natural beauty. Aquinas rather connected it to human happiness. He argued that human beings naturally desire happiness, and that whatever is desired naturally must in some way already be known by the desirer. In other words, although we may ignore scientific truth and refuse to do what is right, it is impossible for us not to desire happiness, and this itself is already a type of knowledge. I can be mistaken about what will truly make me happy, but I cannot doubt that what I really want is to be happy.

In fact, happiness is a sort of argumentative impasse when it comes to justifying our choices and actions. All of the *Lost* characters realize this when they compare their lives before, during, and after the crash on the island. So it is with all of us. While searching for a job, I look for a position that will allow me to earn a decent wage. I desire money because it will enable me to buy a house. I desire a house because it will offer me shelter, security, and comfort. At each of these steps, my implicit motive for choosing x over y is that I believe x will make me happier than y. Indeed, people sometimes choose a lower-paying job precisely because they know it will bring them greater satisfaction, be it due to more pleasant coworkers, a less stressful environment, or more time to spend with the family. The various factors that feed into the equation produce the desired sum of greater happiness, which Aquinas identified as the ultimate human good. Of course, it is senseless to ask, "Why do x if it makes you happier?" Asking such a question merely reveals that one has not understood the nature of reasoning and the meaning of happiness. I perform the action x precisely because I think that doing x will make me happier.

The tension between what the *Lost* characters think will make them happy and what will really make them happy is a key element of the drama. This is especially apparent in the difference between deliberations made in earlier episodes about whether it was better to leave the island or stay on it and deliberations in later episodes about whether to go back to the island or stay away from it. To persuade Claire to take the injection she needs to deal with her pregnancy, Juliet tells her, "You want to get off this island more than anything else in the world." ("One of Us") Contrast this with Jack's earnest plea to Kate that they must get back to the island ("Through the Looking Glass"). Each deliberation involves considerations of friendship, loyalty, and what is truly the "right thing to do."

The Oceanic Six have a particularly tough time wrestling with these questions, as they continually discover new things about what they have left behind that will influence their ultimate decision. In the end, however, each decides based on the conviction that he or she will be happier "there," rather than "here."

"I'm a Coward"

Desmond is a particularly interesting example of how confusion with regard to happiness can severely stunt one's ability to choose. Desmond is afraid to go through with his engagement to Ruth—a mistake he regrettably repeats with Penny. His decision to enter the monastery ("Catch 22") was inspired by the charitable care he had received from Brother Campbell, leading him to think that he, too, would be happier if he took religious vows. He passes the "test" of silence—a test the abbot did not think he would pass—but it soon becomes evident that although Desmond thought he would be happier leading a life of contemplation, his real motivation is to escape the shame of having left Ruth in the lurch at the altar. In a fit of misery, he breaks into the wine cellar and gets drunk on the monastery wine. The abbot catches him and dismisses him from the order, upbraiding him for spending too much time running away from things to realize what he might be running toward. Not knowing where to go, Desmond, whose last name is appropriately Hume, feels consigned to do "whatever comes next": a sort of indeterminism quite compatible with the philosophy of his namesake. At the same time, Desmond's irresoluteness forces him to confront the question of faith that the label on the monastery wine cleverly alludes to: "Moriah," a name taken from the mountain on which God asked Abraham to sacrifice his son Isaac.

Desmond's simultaneous attraction to faith but incapacity to act decisively on it illustrates what Aquinas identified as the greatest sin against faith. Aquinas called it *acedia*, often translated as "sloth," although the meaning of this technical term is actually much broader. *Acedia* designates a type of torpor that prevents a person from enjoying the things that are genuinely good. It is a kind of spiritual paralysis that stymies the ability to look beyond the worst-case scenario. Aquinas described acedia as viewing "some worthwhile good as impossible to achieve, whether alone or with the help of others," and said that it could "sometimes dominate one's affections to the point that he begins to think he can never again be given aspirations towards the good."[3] In Desmond's case, the "good" in question is Penny. He despairs of being unworthy of her and incapable of supporting her.

Earlier in the show, Charlie Pace also showed clear signs of acedia. During the first season, Charlie and Rose were standing on opposite ends of the spectrum spanning from hope to despair, from faith to acedia. Charlie was once religious, faithful, and repentant. He sought reconciliation for the sins he'd committed during the wild, early days of Drive Shaft, only to be lured back into heroin addiction by none other than his big brother Liam—the handsome lead singer ("The Moth"). Charlie has been so deeply hurt through relationships with his father ("Fire + Water"), his brother, and Lucy—the one person whose trust he won, only to abuse ("Homecoming")—that he is all but completely incapable of entrusting himself to anybody or anything. Although he remembers how he was once a religious man, he now thinks he can "never again be given aspirations towards the good." Just at the moment when it seems as if Charlie will never dig himself out of his deep acedia, Rose reminds him that faith is never impossible ("Whatever the Case May Be"). "It's a fine line between denial and faith," she says to him, as they sit together in the dark on the beach. "It's much better on my side." She then reminds Charlie of what he once knew but finds impossible to do anymore: "You need to ask for help." At this, Charlie breaks down and sobs, which prepares him for the grueling road to recovery from addiction, with Locke's help.

"So Much for Fate"

For Aquinas, faith did ultimately depend on God's initiative; we ourselves must pave the way to faith by seriously engaging our natural desire for happiness. The sincere and persistent attempt to reason about the nature of the source of that desire opens the mind to grasp a *truth* that satisfies our yearning to understand but simultaneously surpasses our ability to grasp it fully. Even though the incontrovertible naturalness of our desire for happiness suggests that there is some implicit knowledge within us of the object that will ultimately fulfill our desire, this does not mean that we explicitly and absolutely know that God exists. To return to Aquinas's analogy, we know *that* someone is approaching, even though we do not know *who* is approaching, despite the fact that it really is *Peter* approaching.

Aquinas did not believe that it was the essence of faith to fly in the face of reason. Unaided human reason can in fact arrive at knowledge of God's existence, but it is unable to know the full nature of that divine being without the divine being's aid. We may nevertheless prepare to receive faith through what Aquinas called the *praeambula ad articulos*, or the "preambles to the articles of faith."[4] Philosophy is able to assert that God exists, that God is one, that God is the "first truth," and other such things because the human mind is able to deduce truths regarding supersensible realities based on its direct experience of sensible realities. Yet left unaided, human reason can never know, for example, that God exists as a Trinity of persons or that the second person of the Trinity took on human flesh, if it were not for the self-revelation of God and the gift of faith.

This is why the certainty of faith is quite different from the certainty of science, and ultimately why Aquinas grounded our natural knowledge of God in the natural desire for happiness, rather than for truth. This initial grounding of knowledge of God in human happiness avoids an artificial two-tiered approach to knowledge of God. In the closely knit fabric of

Aquinas's philosophical-theological thinking, it is not that we first have "head knowledge" of God and later "heart knowledge." Although Aquinas is often interpreted in this way, such a division is incompatible with his anthropology.

Indeed, Aquinas's anthropology faced the stark fact that happiness does not equal happy-go-luckiness. Faith is just as often the *cause* of suffering as it is a *remedy*. Eko, the Nigerian priest who gradually realizes that his faith in God involves something much deeper than mere intellectual satisfaction or certainty, is a fine example of this. His courage in the face of imminent danger and steadfastness in the face of opposition are an inspiration to Locke, who apologizes to Eko as the latter lies dying: "Sorry I ever doubted you. Sorry I gave up on my faith in the island." Drawing his last breath, Eko replies, "You can still save them." ("Further Instructions") In the "Cost of Living," Eko is haunted by the voices of those who insist that "it is time to confess." Eko is ashamed to be a priest who has killed someone and, by killing, has set a deplorable example for the young. Ultimately, however, he concludes that God alone knows whether he is a bad man. He then bursts out, "I ask for no forgiveness, for I have not sinned. I killed a man to save my brother's life. I am proud of this." ("Cost of Living")

Eko's character shows how faith teeters on the edge of the fullness of life's meaning and the elusiveness of life's mystery. After Eko's death, Locke follows his example and trusts that it is acceptable for him to have faith, even though he does not know where it will lead him. Placing Eko's cross in his own pocket, he says to Sayid, "I believe Eko died for a reason; I just don't know what it is yet." ("I Do")

"You're More Lost Than You Ever Were"

Yet is that kind of knowledge enough? How is knowledge in general any different from opinion? And how is it related to faith?

Humans, of course, did not have to wait until the crash of Oceanic flight 815 to begin to ask such questions. They have been around as long as philosophy itself. Socrates (c. 470–399 B.C.E.), in fact, could not help but wonder whether *all* of our "knowledge" might not be anything more than mere "opinion." Socrates' star pupil, Plato (c. 428–347 B.C.E.), in his *Republic*, discusses these two types of cognition. Knowledge (*epistēm* in Greek) is the type of certitude we have only after all of the sensible, changeable characteristics of things are somehow left aside. Consequently, knowledge of a thing is had only when we fully possess the "idea" or pure "form" (*eidos*) of a thing. Opinion (*doxa*) refers to the imperfect, but by no means false, knowledge that we have of things through our senses.

So, is faith one of these? Is it something like "knowledge" or "opinion"? During the first season, when Rose claims that she knows her husband is still alive, does she mean that her certitude even surpasses the concrete, sensible experience she had of him when they shook hands for the first time on that blistery winter night in Brooklyn ("S.O.S.")? If so, then perhaps faith is something like epistemē. Or does she mean that she is quite satisfied with accepting even the fuzziest of premonitions as if they were cold hard facts? If so, then maybe faith is something like doxa. Aquinas, following the lines of a highly influential definition of faith proposed by Hugh of St. Victor in the twelfth century, asserted that faith is actually "midway between knowledge and opinion."[5] He believed that faith shares in the certainty we associate with knowledge, as well as in the imperfection that characterizes opinion. In fact, Eko is really echoing Aquinas, who wrote that "to be imperfect as knowledge is the very essence of faith."[6]

The saga of *Lost* has taught us that we can begin to penetrate this paradox only after we have clarified the object of faith. We must ask ourselves what, or whom, we ultimately place our faith in. Aquinas, who was a master at making distinctions, began by distinguishing between the "formal" object of faith and the "material" object of faith. Though the material object of faith is God, the formal object—that is, the aspect under which the believer views God as the object of his or her belief—is the "first truth."[7]

Aquinas was making what philosophers call a "conceptual distinction," a distinction based on the variety of ways we can conceive a single identical object. A single piece of wood, for example, can be "conceived" either as a branch (when it is attached to a tree), a stick (when it is lying on the ground), or a walking staff (when I pick it up and use it during my hike). Similarly, "God" and "first truth" refer to the same object (namely, the divine being), but through different conceptual lenses. "God" refers to the omnipotent, omniscient being that is the source of everything. "First truth" refers to that same being, but with reference to the fact that such a being is the ground of all other truths. We could say that "God" refers to the divine being in a descending way (that is, all things pro-ceed "downward" from God), whereas "first truth" refers to God in an ascending way (that is, all truths lead "upward" to God). Someday, when we behold God face-to-face, we will perfectly and directly know the divinity simply as "truth." In the meantime, because our knowledge of the divinity is merely imperfect and indirect, we are able to conceive God only as the "first truth" among many truths. We reason to the existence of a "first truth" because other truths appear to us as contin-gent and dependent. Rose falls into the trap of equating the power of the "first truth" with all contingent truths. Her faith in a higher power tends to trump the uncertain and imperfect contingencies in the finite world. She claims to "know" things that she really only "believes."

"I Believe in What I Can See"

Consequently, Rose misdirects her faith. Although she seems to rise above the fickle fortunes that distress everyone else, she is not immune from the temptation to mistake what Aquinas called the "first truth" for the truth itself. In other words, she claims to *know* what in reality she only *believes*. To understand the temptation, we have to take a closer look at what Aquinas taught about the relationship between faith and reason.

Reason, Aquinas wrote, is the faculty by which human beings attain knowledge of what is real. Any such knowledge, Aquinas held, must be acquired through the senses. "Nothing comes to exist in the intellect which does not first exist in the senses."[8] In this way, Aquinas distinguished himself from the Platonic tradition we considered earlier. Although it is true that sensible realities are always in a state of flux and instability, our intellect is able to abstract a stable nature from reality that allows us to call it x.

Yet if all of our knowledge comes through the senses, how can we ever attain knowledge of supersensible things? God, having no sensible qualities that can be seen, heard, or touched, would be included among such things. Aquinas argued that although we can have no direct, sensible experience of God, we can come to know God's existence by exercising our natural power to reason. Using Aquinas's own terminology, the existence of God must be shown by way of demonstration.[9] Among the most famous of Aquinas's demonstrations were his "five ways" by which he "proved" that God exists: by motion, efficient cause, possibility and necessity, the hierarchy of beings, and the government of things.[10]

The first two of these five proofs most manifestly began with sensible realities and proceeded to demonstrate that all finite things are dependent on a first efficient cause. In philosophical lingo, an "efficient cause" is a maker or producer. "Looking at the world we can trace a chain of efficient causes backward, but the chain cannot go backward forever. The first of these efficient causes, at the beginning of the chain," Aquinas concluded, "is what all call God." Philosophers continue to argue over whether the five ways can maintain their persuasive power if detached from the monotheistic Christian context in which they were formed, but Aquinas clearly believed that there is a reasonable, logical basis for the assertion "God exists." *That* God exists is wholly within the grasp of natural reason; *what* or *who* God is can be partially penetrated by natural reason, but comes to fuller light only through revelation and faith.

"I Have Made My Peace"

Accepting God's revelation is not such an easy thing to do, and faith is an all-or-nothing proposition. Rose shows clear signs that she has given everything to this divine proposition. This becomes more evident through her relationship with Bernard and the contrast between their attitudes of acceptance and nonacceptance. It begins the moment that Bernard makes his all-or-nothing marriage proposal to Rose at Niagara Falls ("S.O.S."). Only then does Rose return his proposition by informing him of what he must accept if she says yes: a wife who is terminally ill. This, so to speak, is the return proposition to him. He also accepts.

We soon learn that there are two different worldviews at work in Rose and Bernard's relationship. Rose is at peace with the fact that she is dying. Bernard, though he initially accepted her, cancer and all, believes it's worth taking every conceivable measure to stop her from dying. Hence the trip to Australia to visit the faith healer Isaac of Uluru ("S.O.S."). Although it seems at first that Bernard's efforts to find a cure for Rose are magnanimous, we discover a hint of selfishness in his motivations. In answer to her protestations against going through with the faith-healing ritual, Bernard begs her, "Will you try, Rose? For *me*?" Bernard cannot help but put his faith into each and every worldly means that might lead to Rose's recovery. Rose, in contrast, has put all of her faith in divine providence. "I have made my peace with what is happening to me." She has accepted the all-or-nothing proposition of trust.

Aquinas taught that the only thing that can elicit such a complete act of trust from us is a wholly perfect being—the first truth. Because this is a being that can neither deceive nor be deceived, it is the only being worthy of our absolute trust. Aquinas quickly added that this perfect being in no way undermines our freedom. Yet whatever trust we place in God is based wholly on God's own credibility. The act of faith is an act that transcends reason but is by no means unreasonable.

Rose's complete trust in this perfect being makes it impossible for her to receive aid from any other source outside of this being. Despite Isaac's efforts to harness the geological energy that resulted in the miraculous healing of so many hopeless cases before Rose, he tells her, "There is nothing I can do for you" ("S.O.S.").

Although Rose calmly accepts these words, she makes a stunning decision: she will tell Bernard that she has been healed. She will lie to him. This is a critical turning point in Rose's journey of faith. Her faith begins to trump everything else—even the moral rectitude of telling the truth. There is a strong allusion during the scene with Isaac that the "place" where Rose might find a home may not be the divine "heaven" she has hoped for.

The contrast between the respective theological and secular worldviews of Rose and Bernard comes to a climactic point only after they are reunited on the island after the crash. While Bernard drums up support for his plan to construct a large S.O.S. sign, Rose seems to have found a home on the island ("S.O.S."). Just as Bernard once searched frantically for a way to save Rose from imminent death, he now works furiously to save everyone from being perpetually lost. And this drives Rose crazy. "Why can't you just let things be?" she asks him in exasperation.

Whereas at Isaac of Uluru's house it was Bernard who was partly selfish, now it is Rose. What Isaac was unable to do for her, the island now has done for her. She knows that she has been cured of her cancer. Bernard feels as if he must do everything he can to help their desperate situation and get them off the island. Rose has found that the island has already saved her from a desperate situation. Whereas Desmond and Charlie were guilty of acedia, Rose is guilty of an opposite sin that Aquinas called *praesumptio* (presumption). Aquinas defined *presumption* as "a certain type of immoderate hope."[11] The presumptuous person, though a person of faith, directs her hope (often unconsciously) toward one of God's powers, rather than toward God alone. Rose believes that this mysterious island has become an instrument through which God has worked a miracle in her life. Indeed, she even suggests that the island itself is the source of the cure. It has become the "place" of which Isaac spoke.

"The Universe Has a Way of Cross-Connecting"

The tension between two different ultimate horizons—the secular and the supernatural—was symbolized by the simultaneous construction projects of Eko's church and Bernard's large S.O.S. signal ("S.O.S."). The church is a sign that the immediate, visible world is not the ultimate horizon. The letters in the sand are a sign that human beings must do everything within their power to save themselves. When Bernard insists that he is only trying to save everyone, Eko confidently remarks, "People are saved in different ways."

Aquinas taught that it is entirely possible to come to certain knowledge of some basic realities—including God—that we tend to relegate exclusively to the realm of faith. The certain knowledge of those things, however, can attain its true goal only if one further assents to that which is revealed by God. Faith and reason are in harmony with each other, not in opposition. Faith does not abrogate the role of reason, but neither can reason wholly take the place of faith.

Rose is an inspiration to her companions because she is a woman of faith. Yet her faith has left little room for the role of natural knowledge. What she claims to "know," she actually "believes"—not in the sense of doxa or opinion, but in the sense that the things she holds by faith pertain to a transcendent essence so as to be uniquely distinguished from the things she knows by the light of natural reason. The knowledge involved in faith is radically different from the knowledge involved in natural cognition. The latter begins in the senses, whereas the former is beyond the senses. According to Aquinas, the respective objects of natural knowledge and supernatural faith grant them each a legitimate autonomy. Rose is guilty of a confusion of idioms. She mistakenly believes that the type of knowledge distinctive of faith is interchangeable with the type of knowledge distinctive of natural reason.

Aquinas thought differently. "One should not presume that the object of faith is scientifically demonstrable, lest presuming to demonstrate what is of faith, one should produce inconclusive reasons and offer occasion for unbelievers to scoff at a faith based on such ground."[12] Rose doesn't necessarily presume that she can "scientifically" demonstrate her faith, but her experience of being cured elevates all of the things she once held by faith to the level of certain knowledge—epistemē, to be precise. Rose knows, but Rose also believes. Aquinas would admonish her, and us, to know the difference between the two. At the same time, he urged people to probe what we believe with our minds and to allow our minds to lead us to belief.

"Free Will Is All We Really Got, Right?"

Not all philosophers agree about how to interpret Aquinas's brilliant synthesis of goodness, truth, and God's existence.

In his highly influential work *God without Being*, the contemporary French philosopher Jean-Luc Marion dismisses Aquinas's notion of God as "being itself" (*ipsum esse*), in favor of Aquinas's suggestion that God is without or beyond being, insofar as there is an enormous gap between divine being and the being of creatures. Marion claims that God's being should be understood as lying outside the being studied by metaphysics, as we can see from Aquinas's multiple affirmations that God is indeed unknowable.

Yet such a claim must always be scrutinized in light of Aquinas's repeated assertions that indeed we *can* and *do* know God. As we have seen, Aquinas taught that our first taste of God is had in our desire for happiness. Unfortunately, whereas Aquinas found a key to the mystery of life in the desire for happiness, we were all left wanting for a key to unlock the secrets of the island. Yet for all of *Lost*'s weaknesses, the series was nonetheless a powerful reminder that we cannot help but desire happiness, and that both the source of our happiness and its apex ultimately lie somewhere outside ourselves. Many loose ends remained untied at the end of the series, but perhaps that is precisely the point. To mistake any finite truth for the "first truth"—to desire any finite good above the "ultimate good"—only carries us to *Lost*'s and life's next episode. Yet if we follow Aquinas's lead in allowing any finite truth to open our minds to the first truth—any finite good to open our hearts to the ultimate good—then we will surely be carried well beyond "The End."

NOTES

1. *Summa Theologica: Complete English Edition in Five Volumes* (Westminster, UK: Christian Classics, 1981), vol. 1, p. 48 (I-I, q. 1, a. 2).

2. Augustine, *Confessions*, trans. R. S. Pine-Coffin (New York: Penguin Books, 1961), p. 21.

3. *Summa Theologica*, vol. 3, p. 1256 (II-II, q. 20, a. 4).

4. Ibid., vol. 1, p. 12 (I, q. 2, a. 2).

5. Ibid., vol. 2, pp. 873–874 (I-II, q. 67, a. 3).

6. Ibid.

7. Ibid., vol. 3, pp. 1185, 1191, 1193 (II-II, q. 4, a. 1; q. 5, a. 1, q. 5, a. 3). See also *The Disputed Questions on Truth*, trans. Robert W. Mulligan (Chicago: Henry Regnery Company, 1952), vol. 2, pp. 204–206 (*Quaestiones disputatae de veritate*, q. 14, a. 1).

8. Ibid., vol. 4, pp. 1896–1897 (II-II, q. 173, a. 2), and vol. 3, pp. 278–279 (I, q. 55, a. 2).

9. Ibid., vol. 1, pp. 11–12 (I, q. 2, a. 1).

10. Ibid., vol. 1, pp. 13–14 (I, q. 2, a. 3).

11. Ibid., vol. 3, p. 1256 (II-II, q. 21, a. 1).

12. Ibid., vol. 3, p. 1166 (II-II, q. 1, a. 5).

THE TAO OF JOHN LOCKE

Shai Biderman and William J. Devlin

John Locke stands out among the survivors as someone who wants to move from "being lost" to "being found." He helps Jack deal with his role as leader, Charlie overcome addiction, Michael be a good father, and so on. In short, Locke is the central figure who uses philosophy to make sense of what is going on and to help others. He seeks explanations to help him understand their situation so that he can restore a sense of order and purpose. As Charlie puts it, "If there was one person on this island that I would put my absolute faith in to save us all, it would be John Locke." This point foreshadows Locke's future role as the leader of the Others, because he goes as far as making himself a sacrifice by leaving the island to help end the erratic time traveling that the people on the island go through.

"I'm Good at Putting Bits and Pieces Together"

As with the other characters, at first we know nothing about "Mr. Locke." Yet we are slowly introduced to his character through his behavior and mannerisms early in the first season. We get our first real introduction to Locke in "Walkabout." When the survivors run out of food from the plane and a mild panic sets in, Locke takes the initiative to hunt the wild boars on the island. With his suitcase full of hunting knives, he explains to his fellow survivors that the boars they saw were piglets, and he lays out a plan to capture one by distracting the mother. Our first impressions of Locke thus tell us that he is someone who knows his way around nature—he can hunt, he can track, and so on.

At the same time, we can see that Locke has a close relation to his philosophical namesake. The philosopher John Locke (1632–1704) maintained that at birth, the human mind is empty—it is a sheet of "white paper, void of all characters, without any ideas" and without any furnishings. That is, at birth, the human mind is a tabula rasa, or a "blank slate." The human being has no innate ideas, whether it is the idea of God, the idea that 2 + 2 = 4, or anything else. If we are born without any ideas or concepts, though, where do we get them: how do our minds "come to be furnished"? The answer, for Locke, is experience—the mind begins to accumulate ideas and concepts through our interactions with the world around us. We thus come to know and understand the world through our perceptions. Intuition and divine revelation are simply not reliable sources for deriving knowledge and understanding of the world. We call this philosophical position *empiricism*—the view that knowledge and understanding are derived primarily through experience, sensations, and perceptions.

The scientific method is essentially an empirical method, because it uses observation and sensations to explain the world around us. This can be seen through the steps of the scientific method, where the scientist observes and describes phenomena in the world, formulates a hypothesis to explain the phenomena, uses that hypothesis to predict the behavior of the phenomena, and tests the hypothesis with experiments.

Scientists thus come to understand and explain the world by formulating and testing scientific hypotheses through observation and experience.

Locke's process of explaining and understanding his world around him employs the scientific and empirical method. His knowledge concerning knives, hunting, tracking, hiking, and even weather forecasting comes from experience. Locke's depth of knowledge in these fields is derived from empirical observation and action and the scientific rules of hypothesis, testing, and deduction. Thus, whether he is hunting boars or tracking people on the island, Locke's emphasis on observing nature and testing hypotheses to learn about the island through his perceptual experiences employs the scientific and empirical method.

"This Is Destiny. This Is My Destiny."

Although John often applies Lockean empirical methods of scientific investigation, we must remember that his life on the island begins with a phenomenon most foreign to science: a miracle. After the crash, Locke, who was in a wheelchair for the previous four years due to his father throwing him out of a window, finds that he now has full control of his legs and feet. Locke doesn't try to (or is unable to successfully) explain this occurrence through empirical methods. One reason Locke dismisses the Lockean method of explanation for such an event is because this method, as the scientific method, addresses *how* something occurred. That is, scientific explanation reveals the mechanism behind the events that occur, allowing us to understand the causal steps that led to the event. Yet the scientific method can never tell us *why* something occurred—it doesn't explain the purpose or the meaning of the event. So, when Locke discovers that his legs are now healed, he is not concerned with how this recuperation came to be, but he *is* concerned with why it came to be. Thus, he confides to Walt his "secret" that a "miracle happened on the island" ("Pilot: Part 2").

In order to understand this miracle, as well as other miracles (such as the castaways' survival of the plane crash), Locke uses another method of explanation. When Locke encourages Jack to become the leader of the camp, Jack reveals that he has been seeing someone who's "not there." Locke's initial explanation is empirical: it is "a hallucination. The result of dehydration, posttraumatic stress, not getting more than two hours of sleep a night for the past week—all the above." When the empirical explanation fails to satisfy, however, Locke provides another method for explaining this hallucination and other strange occurrences on the island:

> I'm an ordinary man, Jack. Meat and potatoes. I live in the real world. I'm not a big believer in . . . magic. But this place is different. It's special. The others don't want to talk about it because it scares them. But we all know it, and we all feel it. Is your White Rabbit a hallucination? Probably. But what if everything that happened here happened for a reason? What if this person that you're chasing is really here? ["White Rabbit"]

Locke originally believes he is a "meat and potatoes" guy who "lives in the real world" and so adopts the scientific method. Yet then he comes to believe there are "special" powers on the island that explain Jack's hallucination, Locke's own physical recovery, his ability to hear the voice of Jacob in the cabin, his vision of Walt as he lay dying after being shot by Ben, and so on. These phenomena cannot be fully explained by science. In other words, Locke slowly discovers that he is not an ordinary man; he is, in fact, a special man, a candidate chosen by Jacob, who touched him after his fall to an almost-certain death. Locke has been thrown down the rabbit hole and has entered the wonderland of the island, a reality that defies the empirical expectations of both Locke the philosopher and Locke the character. Realizing that he isn't in Kansas anymore, as it were, Locke, the character, adopts a different method—one that allows for, and even invites, miracles, special powers, and occurrences that are meant to be. As he tells Jack, "I've looked into the eye of this island, and what I saw . . . was beautiful."

Locke's new method to explain the phenomena on the island follows the Eastern philosophy of Taoism (pronounced "dow-ism," as in the Dow Jones Industrial Average). This religious and philosophical view, which stems from Lao Tzu's *Tao Te Ching*, holds that there is a special force, or power, in nature called the "Tao." The Tao is said to be "unnamable"—"The Tao that is named is not the real Tao."[1] In other words, the Tao is beyond names and conceptual distinctions. The Tao is the origin of all things, both natural and "supernatural." As the unnamable, the Tao can be represented by the "yin-yang" symbol—a circular symbol that unites one light side (the yang) and one dark side (the yin). The yang represents specific attributes of the universe, such as light, activity, and the masculine, while the yin represents the polar opposites: darkness, passivity, and the feminine. Even though these two sides are said to be opposites, the yin-yang symbol presents them as being complementary. Neither side can exist without the other. The two are interdependent and so not only need each other, but exist within each other. This interdependence captures the holistic aspect of the Tao, as what may appear to be opposites are united.

As fans of the show will recognize, the black and the white in the yin-yang symbol is a prominent visual element in *Lost*. Consider the backgammon pieces and Sawyer's glasses. Think of Claire's dream, in which Locke appears with one eye black and one eye white, signifying not only that this dichotomy is in Locke's eyes, but also that Locke sees the world through such a complementary disjunction. Later in the series, Jacob and his arch nemesis embody the black-and-white polarity, not only in clothing but also in their use of the stones in the game they're playing together.

The word *Tao* can be translated as "way," and the *Tao Te Ching* is concerned with the way of nature. The world is made up of many different objects, and these objects are dynamic—they are moving, they are changing, and they are interacting with one another. According to Taoism, all objects in nature follow the Tao as the path or "way," so that nature flows as the Tao directs it. This claim that nature is flowing with the Tao thus enables the Taoist to explain why events in nature occur. Because the direction of the dynamic motions of nature follows the Tao, the Tao is the purpose, the "why" behind events that occur.

Since humans are part of nature, the Tao provides proper direction for human beings. When we confront the world—facing challenges, events, decisions, and questions—we should apply the holistic picture of the Tao to help us understand what we should do. Once we realize that nature flows with the Tao, and that the Tao helps explain why events unfolded they way they did, we can then use this understanding to direct ourselves. That is, Taoism maintains that we should follow the flow of nature, as it is the same as following the Tao. Our lives, then, too, should also follow the path of the Tao.

When Locke looks into the "eye of the island" and sees its beauty, he takes the first step in becoming aware of the Tao. Locke recognizes a beauty that he cannot explain—something inexpressible—in the island. That is, he becomes aware of the Tao as the "unnamable." This awareness allows Locke to begin to shift his method of explaining the events that occur on the island. Everything that takes place on the island—all of the events of nature—follows the Way of the Tao. Locke accordingly begins to suppose that "everything that happened here happened for a reason." From Locke's miracle to the group surviving the crash, to the splitting and reuniting of the two tribes (as well as the uniting of the two parts of the

Dharma Initiative film), to the various "hallucinations" and dreams of the castaways—everything that occurs on the island is happening for a reason. That is, there is a reason why these events have unfolded the specific way they've unfolded. For Locke, the explanation lies in the "Way" of the island. As he tells Jack, "Do you really think all this is an accident? That we, a group of strangers, survived, merely with superficial injuries? Do you think we crashed on this place by coincidence? Especially this place? We were brought here! For a purpose! For a reason! All of us! *Each one of us was brought here for a reason.*" ("Exodus: Part 2") For Locke, what brought everyone here is "the island," or the Tao.

Locke's appeal to the Tao as a way of explaining what occurs on the island and his application of this understanding as a guide for how human beings should act can be seen in his sagelike advice to his fellow castaways. For example, Locke uses a moth that must break out of its cocoon as an analogy to Charlie overcoming his addiction to heroine ("The Moth"). The moth's struggle to become free and survive in the natural world is an example of nature following the Tao. Locke—who sees that it is best for human beings to follow the Tao—believes that Charlie should struggle to free himself using his own will power. Likewise, when Locke teaches Walt how to throw knives, he advises him to picture the knife hitting the mark in "his mind's eye," where he can "visualize the path" ("Special"). Locke is thus helping Walt see where the knife should be—its proper place as a result of its proper path and motion—in order to succeed. Such visualizing is a process of seeing and following the path of the Tao. Furthermore, when Sun loses her wedding ring and is frantic about finding it, Locke explains how he found what he was looking for: "By finding it the way everything gets found . . . I stopped looking." (". . . And Found") Later, Locke develops his faith in the island through his encounters with Jacob, as he comes to see that he was destined, if only temporarily, to lead the Others. Locke has realized that he should not struggle *against* the flow of the Tao. Instead, he allows nature and the Tao to take its course. As one follows this flow, what once was lost will soon be found.

In short, although the character never specifically mentions the Tao, he clearly adopts Taoism as a way to understand *why* the events in both nature and human beings occur the way they do. Locke has a growing *faith* in the Tao as he is on the island, and he uses that faith to understand his "destiny" and the destiny of those around him.

Man of Science, Man of Faith

In addition to the implicit Taoism I have just traced, *Lost* makes an explicit allusion to Eastern philosophy with the Dharma Initiative. In Hinduism and Buddhism, dharma is the cosmic "law of nature" or "reality," which one should follow to free oneself from the chains of reincarnation.

Locke's Eastern consciousness slowly develops during the first season of *Lost*. In particular, however, the discovery of the hatch pushes Locke away from empiricism and toward Taoism ("All the Best Cowboys Have Daddy Issues"). When Locke and Boone discover the hatch, their top priority is to figure out how to open it. Boone becomes skeptical of Locke's "obsession," reminding Locke that their role in the tribe is to hunt boars. Locke, however, dismisses this role, which, as we saw, was linked to Lockean empiricism: "There's plenty of fruit and fish to go around. . . . What we're doing here is far more important. . . . Right now, this is our priority." Locke thus begins to change priorities from a role that has an empirical basis (hunter) to a role that has a spiritual basis (hatch guru). The reality of the island forces him to confront and acknowledge the limits of science, so that he turns to Taoism to complete his understanding of what is really going on. The hatch is Locke's "calling," as it were: "We didn't find this by accident. We're supposed to."

Guided by the spiritual power of the island, Locke redirects his attention to opening the hatch. To accomplish this new challenge, however, he returns to what he knows best: the scientific method of trial and error. As if he were an "engineer," he constructs a trebuchet, with the hope that it will provide enough force to break the glass of the hatch. Like a true empiricist, when this experiment fails, he suggests to Boone that they should "build another one . . . and hope it works this time." Yet the Lockean approach to determining how to open the hatch only goes so far. When Boone questions what will happen if the next experiment fails, Locke turns to the Taoist approach and an appeal to the powers of the island: "The island will tell us what to do. . . . The island will send us a sign." Locke thus chooses the spiritual method to explain and understand their role of opening the hatch. Their discovery of the hatch is accounted for by the power of the Tao. Locke and Boone were meant to find and open the hatch, because the Tao was directing them toward this role. Likewise, when they initially fail to open the hatch, Locke doesn't appeal to scientific reasons for their failure; rather, he appeals to the Tao: "All that's happening now is our faith is being tested—our commitment. But we will open it. The island will show us how."

Just as Locke's advice to Charlie, Walt, and Sun is successful in producing the desired results, so, too, Locke's decision to "ask for a sign" from the island is fruitful, as he has "a dream [that] was the most real thing he's ever experienced" that lets him "know where to go now." The dream points him to find the Beechcraft 18 that crashed years ago on the island. This triggers a sequence of events—the discovery of the plane, the death of Boone, the revelation of the hatch to Sayid and Jack—which ultimately ends with the explosive destruction of the hatch. In short, through his appeal to the Taoist method of listening to and following the path of the Tao, Locke is able to fulfill his destiny.

Locke's adoption of the Taoist method over the Lockean method, and so his full transformation, continues when Locke realizes what is in the hatch. During the chaotic events that surround his meeting Desmond, Locke learns that the purpose of the bunker sealed by the hatch is to type a specific series of numbers into a computer every 108 minutes to prevent "the end of the world" from occurring. Locke decides that even when Desmond leaves, the numbers still need to be entered. He employs the scientific method to figure out how to succeed in "entering the numbers" properly as he follows the rules of "executing" the numbers at the appropriate time, which is indicated by the empirical movement of a flip-card timer and the sound of an alarm. He will know that he is successful when the timer returns to 108. Yet although Locke employs the scientific method to determine how to succeed, the question of *how* to do it is secondary to *why* Locke is pushing the button. The "why" question is the ultimate question for Locke, and it is answered by the Taoist method. Locke comes to understand that this is not only the purpose of the hatch, but it is *his* purpose. It is his destiny to make sure that the numbers are entered on time.

Even after Locke seems to lose faith in entering the numbers, he quickly finds that this denial of faith was a mistake, as he confesses to Eko ("Live Together, Die Alone: Part 2"). Soon after the explosion of the hatch, Locke rekindles his faith by experiencing a vision quest through a sweat lodge, as he learns from his vision with Boone that he has a new direction: namely, to "clean up his own mess" ("Further Instructions"). Gradually, by following the Tao, Locke finds himself joining the Others. Here, it appears as though Locke has found his true calling, because he tells Kate he has no intentions of going home ("Left Behind") and even goes as far as blowing up the submarine to help ensure his place on the island. Later, Locke delivers the corpse of his father so that he has the opportunity to meet Jacob. This meeting helps set up Locke's future, because he becomes the leader of the Others, replacing Ben, who finds himself banished from the island. Locke thus finds his purpose by listening to the island. As the leader of the Others and those stranded on the island after the Oceanic Six are rescued, Locke ironically follows his path to the point where he chooses to go home, as it were, to sacrifice himself, in order to save everyone from the rapid time-traveling motions of the island. In other words, just as Locke once told Jack that "Boone was a sacrifice that the island demanded" ("Exodus: Part 3"), so, too, Locke made himself a sacrifice for the island, which led to his ultimate death. Thus, Locke follows the Way of the Tao: all prior events in Locke's life on the island—events that are guided by the Tao—have led him to this final sacrifice.

Locke completes his transformation by taking the leap of faith to the Tao, listening to the island. This completion is foreshadowed when Locke discusses the number-entering with Jack. Locke encourages Jack to make that leap of faith and believe that they were brought here to enter the numbers. Although Jack is skeptical and accuses Locke of falling into faith too easily, Locke protests that it has not been easy. Locke has slowly moved from being a strict "man of science" to become a "man of faith." As he explains to Jack, "That's why we sometimes don't see eye to eye, you and me. You're a man of science and I'm a man of faith." ("Orientation") Through faith in the Tao, Locke now understands why things occur the way they do.

"I Was Looking for Something . . . It Found Me"

Locke's spiritual transformation has completed him. As he tells Boone, "This island . . . it changed me. It made me whole." ("Deus ex Machina") In adopting Taoism, Locke has not, however, completely abandoned empiricism. And this itself is very Taoist. In the yin-yang symbol, we find a dot of black in the white half and a dot of white in the black. As yin and yang are complementary and interdependent, so, too, are Taoism and empiricism.

Most important, through his spiritual and empirical journey on the island, Locke is no longer lost. The completion of his journey is made clear as Locke gives his compass to Sayid, saying that he doesn't "need it anymore." ("Hearts and Minds") That is, empirically, Locke no longer has a need for this "scientific instrument" because he knows how to move around the island—he has found the direction he sought. Likewise, giving up the compass has a spiritual significance, indicating that Locke now knows who he is, where he should be, and why he is going where he is going. In short, through both the Taoist and the empirical methods, Locke is now found.

NOTE

1. See Lao Tzu, *The Tao Te Ching*, trans. J. C. H. Wu (Boston: Shambhala, 1991), chap. 1.

LOST METAPHYSICS

Keeping the Needle on the Record

Donavan S. Muir

Every narrative has a world, and every world has a reality. As a reality, a narrative world must have a metaphysics. That is, every narrative world must have a corresponding set of rules that allows us to comprehend that reality. In most cases, narratives are built on the metaphysical structure of our world. In other cases, particularly in science fiction, a new metaphysics is constructed based on the imagined narrative of the author.

For instance, when we encounter Charlotte Brontë's famous novel *Jane Eyre*, we understand that it "takes place" in a world. Even though the narrative is a fiction, that world is not fundamentally different from our own. Thus, we understand "Jane" within the context of our world, one where causal relationships work in the same way that we ordinarily understand them. The metaphysics of *Jane Eyre* is our metaphysics, and the narrative takes place in our world, albeit in a different time and place.

In contrast, some narratives are set in worlds that are so foreign to our ordinary, everyday understanding of reality that they require their own metaphysics. The viewer subconsciously demands a metaphysical justification for a fictional world, and that justification has to work, or the viewer will disengage. With *Star Wars*, for example, George Lucas not only created a story, but constructed a world (perhaps a complete universe) where that story could take place. The *Star Wars* narrative, though a fiction, operated according to a consistent set of rules and therefore succeeded in captivating our imagination.

Is *Lost* more like *Jane Eyre* or *Star Wars*? Although the series began in our world, it soon wandered into another, which led us to question how this new world worked. In other words, we began to question *Lost*'s metaphysics.

Metaphysics, in its most general sense, is an inquiry into the nature of reality. Metaphysical investigations usually begin by extrapolating aspects of a world that are responsible for, and necessary for, that world's existence. For example, causality is a metaphysical attribute of our world. Although we typically think of causation as a matter of science, it is metaphysics that asks the "why" questions, such as Why there is causation in the first place? And, in order to understand the why of causality, metaphysicians must investigate what causation is.

For us to learn about *Lost*'s metaphysics, we must first be clear on its metanarrative. A metanarrative is the overarching story we tell ourselves in order to make sense of reality and the world we inhabit. The practice of philosophy usually involves the identification and evaluation of metanarratives. So, for example, the view that there is a God who's responsible for, and gives meaning to, any and all events within our universe is a metanarrative. It may very well be the case, however, that this metanarrative simply isn't true and actually distracts us from understanding reality. Hence, philosophers are preoccupied with arguments for and against the existence of God in the attempt to either support or deny the metaphysics that provides the foundation for theocentric metanarratives.

A metanarrative is logically dependent on its metaphysics. In other words, a metanarrative can provide a viable framework for understanding reality only when it is built on a solid foundation. For example, a metanarrative about a God that is responsible for order in the universe requires a metaphysical justification for belief in God's existence at the outset. Otherwise, the metanarrative becomes myth, simply "a story" and nothing more.

We expect fiction to provide us with a justification for believing in a narrative, and we expect it to construct its framework on a solid foundation. Our question is, does *Lost* succeed in this endeavor?

Lost's Narrative Structure

The genius of *Lost* was in keeping its metanarrative incomplete. Throughout the series, increasingly strange events on and off the island occurred within the context of the unknown, leaving viewers perpetually pondering. Without a framework for interpreting events, viewers had to think differently and outside of conventional narrative patterns. This means that not only did we actually have to think, but we had to think in very critical, creative, and innovative ways. Just visit Lostpedia's theory pages or peruse any of the many *Lost* blogs for evidence of the kinds of mental acrobatics *Lost* viewers engage in.

Most contemporary television programs simply deliver their metanarrative prepackaged, like fast food, at the outset. Consider, for example, the ABC television show *FlashForward*. The viewer learns that a mysterious event has caused nearly everyone on the planet to simultaneously lose consciousness for 137 seconds. During this period, people see what appear to be visions of their lives approximately six months in the future. Viewers know what happened but not how it happened. As the series unfolds, the audience's task is simply to follow the events that slowly unravel the mystery. For *FlashForward*, the metanarrative is the loss of consciousness and the events unraveling the mystery surrounding it.

Lost, on the other hand, inverts this narrative structure. We know how the castaways got to the island, but we do not know what the island is. *Lost* postpones and never really completes its metanarrative, requiring the viewer to *participate*, rather than simply *follow*. We must *actively do*, rather than just *passively watch*, and what we must do is construct the show's metanarrative.

Although *Lost*'s metanarrative was absent at the outset, and although it is never completely delivered at the end, this does not mean that *Lost* doesn't have one. Rather, it means that it is up to the viewers, armed with their particular *Lost* experience, to put the pieces together as best they can.

Lost Metaphysics

The characters on *Lost* increasingly seem to be playing some sort of game. Every game has rules that are designated either by the players or by the creator of the game, and the rules are meant to establish the "order" of the game. Logically, if there are rules, then there is an implied order through which the rules derive their meaning. In "The Shape of Things to Come," we learn that the island has rules, and these rules actually provide insight into the foundations of *Lost*'s metaphysics.

The island is grounded in an order of binary oppositions. Some of the most notable oppositions are known/unknown, free will/determinism, accidental/purposive (intentional) action, science/faith, nature/technology, rational/intuitive decision-making, absolute/relative, paradise/hell, and, of course, *Xanadu/Devil's Doom*. Although it is difficult to uncover the important roles some of these dualities play in *Lost*'s narrative because they are subtly represented, some are given to us directly.

For example, the beach scene in the final episode of season 5, where Jacob and the Man in Black confront each other, is quite obviously an important and direct representation of the supreme duality in *Lost*. When we interpret this duality within the traditional Western framework of good and evil—where the divide between opposites is clear and wide—we conceive each component as distinct and independent. *Lost*, however, challenges this conception with interdependency.

Each opposite contains seeds or *traces* of the other opposite. Not only does one pole reflect the other (for example, good must perform evil acts to "be" good), but the identity of the poles in each binary opposition occasionally converts into the other. For example, Jack, once a man of science, becomes a full-hearted man of faith. Moreover, Sawyer, once a con man extraordinaire, becomes a devoted and honest protector of his people.

The Taoist yin-yang symbol illustrates this point succinctly. Although most everyone has seen this symbol (figure 1), what is not well-known is the fact that it is adequately represented only when it is in motion. That is, the meaning of the yin-yang is fully understood only when it is spinning (figure 2).

Figure 1   Figure 2

When the yin-yang is spinning, its character changes radically.

First, the binary oppositions that compose the spinning yin-yang are no longer perceivable as independent entities. When active, the opposing natures interdependently support each other.

Second, and more important, the spinning of the yin-yang represents how combined opposites *create a world*, which is "the Tao." The Tao is a perpetually balanced ontological flow, responsible for how opposites simultaneously wax and wane in and out of being. The balance of opposites is the order that makes existence possible and imparts its character. The interactive flow from one binary opposite into another (and vice versa) regulates the balanced order of existence. Without this balance of opposites, one pole dominates and determines the course of reality, if not annihilating the possibility of existence altogether. Once balance is destroyed, order disappears, and thus existence ceases to be.

The fundamental metaphysics of *Lost* is the order of balanced oppositions. Without this balance, existence would fall into an asymmetry and, as a consequence, the *Lost* world as we know it would end. The more divergent the oppositions become—the more they are conceived as independent and distinct—the more likely the balance is threatened by an asymmetry. Thus, the rules, in one fashion or another, are meant to establish and maintain balance and to assist in the reunification of opposites. They return Jacob and the Man in Black to their "source" or original, convergent position. This position is where oppositions unify, rather than diverge and independently dominate.

We can see countless representations of this dynamic interchange between oppositions during every season of *Lost*. Two representations, however, are particularly relevant for our purposes here.

The first representation is the scale. There are two moments when we see the scale: in a painting behind Widmore's desk ("Happily Ever After") and in the cave ("The Substitute"). In both cases, we see the scale equally balancing light and dark rocks, indicating that balance is the original or intended state of the scale. In other words, balance is the state in which the scale is "supposed to be." In "The Substitute," Locke challenges this original state by throwing the light rock out of the cave, leaving the black rock on the scale. This imagery implies that Locke annihilated the balance by removing his opposite.

The second representation is in the episode "Across the Sea," where we see that the two important oppositions, Jacob and the Man in Black, are twins. Once unified in their mother, Claudia, these twins diverge at birth. Their divergence is accentuated by their "independent" conceptions of being-in-the-world. Jacob senses that he belongs on the island, and the Man in Black asserts the opposite, that he doesn't belong:

> Jacob: "I don't want to leave this island, it's my home."
> Man in Black: "Well, it's not mine."

These positions represent the Buddhist conception of the oppositions "Being" and "Nonbeing," both of which are simultaneously affirmed and denied by the Middle Way—which is to say, "balanced."

Annihilation of Oppositions

Like Taoists, Buddhists hold that opposites are interdependent. Yet Buddhists, particularly those of the Mahayana tradition, hold the view that part of the path toward enlightenment requires the realization that oppositions, ultimately, do not exist. That is, because all things inter-depend, there are no "true" oppositions. This is a necessary feature of Buddhist enlightenment, to "let go" of thinking in terms of rigid oppositions. Enlightenment, then, occurs only after we come to understand that interdependency "double negates" the possibility for independent entities to dialectically oppose each other. This can be represented by the scale naturally resting in balance without light and dark rocks. Appropriately enough, this is also where we end up in "The End," when both Jacob and the Man in Black cease to exist. It is not until both sides of this ultimate opposition are annihilated that Jack and the other castaways are finally set free.

Keep the Needle on the Record

Although *Lost*'s metanarrative is only a partial framework meant to be filled in by the viewer, it is built on a metaphysical foundation of balanced oppositions. Expressed metaphorically, in order to keep the music—the life—of *Lost* alive, the characters must keep the needle securely placed on the *spinning* record. Without this balance, the record will not spin and the music will cease to exist.

In understanding *Lost*'s metaphysics, we look at our own metaphysics with new eyes, realizing that ultimately, there are no absolute, independent entities. Acknowledging this fact allows us to rid ourselves of the delusion that reality is binary and enter into enlightenment, much as our castaways did.

APPENDIX

Who are Locke, Hume, and Rousseau? The Losties'
Guide to Philosophers

Scott F. Parker

One of the pleasures of watching *Lost*—and one of the games the show invites us to play—is to identify connections within and beyond the show. Cultural allusions abound: literary, religious, and musical, among them. Yet it is the philosophical references that are most prominent. Well-known philosophical works are scattered around the island; characters occasionally mention philosophers; and, of course, several characters share their names with philosophers.

In an effort to chronicle and understand the philosophers named on *Lost*, the following guide summarizes the lives and the major works of John Locke, David Hume, Jean-Jacques Rousseau, and others. Of course, with a show as complicated as *Lost*, it's hard to decide exactly who to include in such a guide. First, there's the question of what counts as an allusion. And second, there's the question of who counts as a philosopher. I've tried to err on the side of exclusion in the former case and inclusion in the latter, thinking it more fruitful to consider the philosophical implications of characters explicitly named after philosophers than to hunt for links to philosophers who aren't obviously intended to be part of the show. So the homonyms (such as the semiotician Umberto Eco for Mr. Eko, and Vladimir Lenin for Lennon) are out. And the identical names (such as the physicist Michael Faraday for Daniel Faraday and John Lennon for Lennon) are in, even if they're not strictly speaking philosophers. *Lost* is so complex and layered that I had to draw a line, or this guide would be as long as the rest of the book.

Yet the line is really a guideline, which is to say I don't follow my own rules all that well. I make exceptions to include the literary theorist Edward Said and the feminist, anarchist Kate Austin. Said for Sayid, because the connection between them is strong and has implications for the whole show; Kate Austin for Kate Austen, because the names are so close, and the latter has some undeniable feminist and anarchist leanings of her own. I resisted a strong urge to exclude Thomas Carlyle and Samuel Rutherford. It's not obvious that they're the source of Boone's and Shannon's respective last names, and the characters and the philosophers aren't crucial to the show.[1] Another inclusion that deserves comment is Søren Kierkegaard, who does not share a name with any of *Lost*'s characters, but whose book *Fear and Trembling* Hurley finds beneath the Temple in "LA X: Part 1." Of all the books that make conspicuous appearances on *Lost*, Kierkegaard is the only author I include, and I do so because of the explicit philosophical content of the book and its relevance to many of *Lost*'s themes.

I assume the reader is familiar with the characters from *Lost*, so I focus this guide primarily on the philosophers, highlighting aspects of their lives and works that may be of interest to fans of the show. I also suggest some links between the characters and the philosophers, but I certainly don't claim to be exhaustive in this regard. For one thing, some of the common names may be accidental or intentional misdirections. For another, the nature of this kind of reading is speculative, and the degree to which one is open to making connections informs the number and kind of connections one finds. So by all means, look for other connections—you can go a long way with this. Yet although we can't be sure of the significance of the names, neither can we trust

Damon Lindelof all the way when he says, "We just wanted to let the audience know that these philosophers are in our lexicon as storytellers."[2]

John Locke (1632–1704)

Namesake: John Locke, Oceanic Flight 815 Crash Survivor

John Locke was born into a Puritan family in England. He was a gifted student and attended the best schools: Westminster School in London, followed by Christ Church, Oxford, for college. After earning bachelor's and master's degrees and being elected lecturer in Greek at Christ Church, Locke decided to become a physician.

In 1666, Locke met Lord Ashley (formerly, Anthony Ashley Cooper), the First Earl of Shaftesbury, who invited Locke to live with him in London as his personal physician.[3] In 1668, when Ashley had a liver infection, Locke saved his life by supervising the surgical removal of a cyst.

Locke fled England for Holland in 1683 when Ashley lost favor with the king, and there Locke wrote the bulk of his major work *Essay Concerning Human Understanding*. He returned to England after the Glorious Revolution of 1688 and remained there until his death. He never married.

Locke worked outside academia and wrote for the general educated reader. The relative accessibility of his prose is consistent with a strong antiauthoritarian streak that runs through his thinking. One can almost hear him say, "Don't tell me what I can't do." He is considered a founder, respectively, of two individualistic movements: empiricism in epistemology and liberalism in political philosophy.

In *Essay Concerning Human Understanding*, Locke tried to determine the limits of what can be known and to distinguish between knowledge and belief. Arguing against the rationalists of the day, who thought that human beings gain knowledge by reflecting on innate ideas, Locke held that at birth the mind is a *tabula rasa* (or blank slate) on which experiences are recorded. It's because of this idea, that knowledge (with exceptions for math and logic) is dependent on experience, that Locke is known as a founder of empiricism.

Belief for Locke was a matter of thinking something true, whether or not it is supported by experience. So beliefs are uncertain, but they're important, too. Locke thought that we rarely have certainty and must constantly rely on our beliefs in everyday life. We should be sure that our beliefs correspond with experience as much as possible and be tolerant of people who have different beliefs.

Locke's ethical theory is of interest mostly due to its influence on later philosophers, particularly Jeremy Bentham. Both Locke and Bentham thought that everyone was motivated by the desire for personal pleasure or happiness.

Locke was also a man of faith. Some of his later works, including *The Reasonableness of Christianity*, advance the idea that with the assistance of the Scriptures, anyone can find purpose and salvation.

Kate Cooper Austin (1864–1902)

Namesake: Kate Austen, Member of the Oceanic Six

After being raised in the Universalist church, Kate Cooper Austin broke off her affiliation with the religion and became an outspoken feminist and anarchist, writing scores of articles for many radical journals and giving regular lectures near her home in Missouri. In an unpublished essay titled "Woman," Austin wrote,

> Woman and man as well even today are the victims of laws and customs that originated ages ago in brute force among our savage ancestors that lived in caves and fought each other over the possession of a bone or a woman, man the strongest physically but not mentally enslaved the woman and by an exhibition of muscular Power wielded in the shape of clubs over weaker men, enslaved them also.

The "law of might" came and fastened its hold on the Human race and curses Humanity to the present day.[4]

Most of a century later, our survivor, Kate Austen, witnessed repeated abuses of power in her own young life and, like Kate Austin, refuses subservience on behalf of not only herself but of the women in her life as well. It's possible to see Kate's murder of her stepfather as a feminist and anarchic act motivated by a spirit shared with a woman described thusly: "Her devotion to liberty made her an anarchist; her hostility to patriarchy made her a feminist. She was too much the former to join the organized women's movements of her day, and too much the latter to ally with mainline political anarchists—most of them men—whose devotion to liberty often stopped short of women's liberation."[5]

Thomas Carlyle (1795–1881)

Namesake: Boone Carlyle, Oceanic Flight 815 Crash Survivor

Thomas Carlyle was an essayist, a historian, and a satirist associated with Romanticism, a movement that valued passion, vigor, and aesthetic experience over the scientific and rational mind-set of the Enlightenment. Philosophically, he's of most interest for having espoused the glory of heroism, penning a book called *On Heroes, Hero-Worship, and the Heroic in History*.

Carlyle himself lived the unremarkable life of a scholar—and he knew it. His idea of a true hero was the great German poet Goethe, who was known for the fullness of his life, as well as his literary accomplishments. While singing Goethe's praises, Carlyle stopped short of absolute reverence, informing his readers that the hero lives in a world of contradiction and in striving for new and creative ways to live must occasionally fail. There's no shame in this, and to mock the hero is to effectively endorse mediocrity.

Carlyle's relationship with Goethe is in some ways analogous to Boone's relationship with Locke: Boone is the first to see Locke's potential as a hero and sticks with him despite his failures.

Samuel Rutherford (1600–1661)

Namesake: Shannon Rutherford, Oceanic Flight 815
Crash Survivor

Samuel Rutherford was a professor of Latin before being forced to resign due to an inappropriate relationship with a young woman (later to become his first wife). He took up the study of theology and in 1627 became minister of Anwoth until he was banished to Aberdeen for his nonconformity.

In 1638, he was appointed professor of theology at St. Andrews and was allowed to preach every Sunday. Of his several books, *Lex, Rex* (which means "law is king") would cause the most problems for him. Arguing that the monarchy should be limited and beholden to the consent of the people, it would come to influence later political philosophers, such as John Locke.

In 1661, following the restoration of the monarchy, all copies of the book were ordered burned, and Rutherford was charged with treason, for which the penalty was hanging. Yet he was already close to death and said, "Tell them I have got a summons already before a superior judge and judicatory, and I behoove to answer my first summons."

Edward Said (1935–2003)

Namesake: Sayid Jarrah, Member of the Oceanic Six

Edward Said (pronounced just like Sayid) was born in Jerusalem when it was part of the British Mandate of Palestine. He grew up splitting his time between Jerusalem and Cairo, where his father worked. In 1951, his parents sent him to preparatory school in the United States, where he flourished academically. He then attended Princeton as an undergrad and Harvard for graduate school. Said spent his professional career at Columbia University and lectured at many other universities as well. Because of his most well-known book, *Orientalism*, and his public lectures and popular writing, Said was one of the most prominent and controversial intellectuals in America.

In *Orientalism*, Said argued that Western attitudes toward the "Orient"—which term is so broad as to be meaningless (how do we talk about Iraq and Korea as if they are one place?)—have promoted imperial agendas. In the colonial era, the West presented "Orientals" as weak and stupid, thereby justifying their subjugation. In the postcolonial era, the West vilifies Arabs, by deeming them irrational, dangerous, and anti-Western. It surprises exactly no one that on the island, it is Sayid whom Sawyer labels a terrorist after the plane crash.

Said's prescription for response to the otherizing of "Orientals" involves attending to individual narratives, rather than to monolithic groupings. When others are labeled "Others," they are by definition unrelatable and cannot be understood. When they are given a chance to tell their own stories, a chance at self-definition, they can become sympathetic figures to be engaged with on common ground.

One of *Lost*'s recurring tropes was to confound expectations—not only those of the survivors but also those of the audience. After the crash, we, consistent with Said's arguments, expect the island to be inhabited by, frankly, savages—and when the Others begin to appear, we immediately project savagery onto them. That's why the suburban book club scene that opens season 3 is so effective: it reveals to the viewer an assumed Orientalism.

Jean-Jacques Rousseau (1712–1778)

Namesake: Danielle Rousseau, Shipwrecked French Scientist

Jean-Jacques Rousseau was born in Geneva. His mother died from puerperal fever after his birth, and his father abandoned him at age ten, leaving him to be raised by an aunt and an uncle. He left Switzerland at sixteen and wandered his way through Italy and France, working odd jobs until he moved to Paris in 1742. There, he became secretary to the French ambassador to Venice, but he was paid irregularly for his work and developed a lasting resentment toward government. In 1750, he found fame after winning a prize for "Discourse on the Arts and Sciences," an essay arguing that science and the arts corrupt morals.

Rousseau ardently defended the idea that civilization is the root of all evil. "Man is naturally good, and only by institutions is he made bad." Yet he did not condemn all institutions. Rousseau thought that the family structure, for example, made an important contribution to human happiness. The trouble, in his view, started with the development of private property, which led to economic inequality that wasn't present in the state of nature. "The first man, who, after enclosing a piece of ground, took it into his head to say, 'This is mine,' and found people simple enough to believe him, was the true founder of civil society."[6]

It's because of statements like this that many people associate Rousseau with the notion of the "noble savage", but he was not actually a primitivist. His ideal was for individuals to govern themselves without descending to the level of animals—much as Danielle Rousseau was when we first encountered her. In his later years Rousseau withdrew from the public, as he struggled with his mental health, and eventually died of possible suicide.

David Hume (1711–1776)

Namesake: Desmond David Hume, Shipwrecked Scottish Yacht Racer

David Hume was a Scottish philosopher whose empiricism was greatly influenced by John Locke. Hume never held an academic position or had much of a following during his lifetime—his first and most important book, *A Treatise of Human Nature*, which he wrote in his twenties, "fell," in Hume's own words, "dead-born from the press."[7]

Without an academic post, Hume scrounged for a living, working a variety of jobs, including tutor, librarian, and military secretary. Because he had little money, especially as he was beginning his career as a writer and a philosopher, Hume lived almost ascetically, eschewing everything that did not improve his literary ability. Despite never receiving the kind of success he hoped for, Hume was able to remain in good spirits—a disposition he considered a greater fortune than wealth.

While living in Paris as secretary to Lord Hertford, Hume befriended Jean-Jacques Rousseau. Hume even helped Rousseau get established in Great Britain when controversy forced the Frenchman to flee his home country. The relationship ended when Rousseau became paranoid that Hume was plotting against him.

As an empiricist, Hume thought that knowledge comes from experience. Famously, he dared to apply the empirical method to causation and found the notion lacking. His argument goes like this: if we see B follow A enough times, we'll make an inductive leap to thinking B was caused by A. Yet we never observe this thing called *cause*; it exists only in our minds. Hume supported his argument with clever thought experiments like one we have seen more recently. Imagine that if every time you pushed a certain button, the world didn't end. With the right story in your mind, you might begin to think that pushing the button *caused* the world not to end—but all that you have is a repeated experience of two linked events (pushing a button and the world not ending). How do you know there is a connection? Do you keep pushing?

Hume was also skeptical of the notion of the self. The self is something we assume by induction because it's convenient to think that our experiences happen to something. When we look for something constant that is the direct object of experiences, however, there's nothing there: "For my part, when I enter most intimately into what I call *myself*, I always stumble on some particular perception or other, of heat or cold, light or shade, love or hatred, pain or pleasure. I never catch *myself* at any time without a perception, and never can observe anything but the perception."[8] The self, then (to the extent that there is one), is not a continuous entity.

After his death, Hume became recognized as a genius, a man ahead of his time. Einstein credited Hume with giving him the courage to challenge Newtonian physics, and Immanuel Kant credited Hume with interrupting his "dogmatic slumber."

Hugo de Groot (1583–1645)

Namesake: Gerald and Karen de Groot, Cofounders of the Dharma Initiative

Hugo de Groot (also known as Hugo Grotius) was a Dutch scholar who worked in many fields. He entered university at age eleven and published his first book a few years later. Accompanying an embassy to France, de Groot impressed King Henry IV, who called him "the miracle of Holland."

Back in Holland, de Groot started a law practice and was later appointed, first, attorney general of Holland and, second, pensionary of Rotterdam (a high-ranking regional political position). After a coup in 1618, de Groot was sentenced to life in prison. He spent three years in his cell reading and writing. In 1621, he escaped in a trunk full of books and met his family in Paris, where he spent ten years writing, among other things, his very successful book *On the Law of War and Peace*.

After a short return to Holland, de Groot had to flee again, this time to Hamburg, where he became the Swedish ambassador to France. Widely admired, he was soon promoted to a more prestigious position in Stockholm. His ship was wrecked on the way there, but de Groot survived. He returned to Germany a few months later on another rough voyage and died soon after his arrival.

De Groot believed in natural law and thought that God's will accounts for the primary laws of nature, whereas the secondary laws are determined and upheld via reason. Because laws are based on rights, they apply equally to the weak, the powerful, and even the state. Government has no divine authority; its power is dependent on a contract with the people. Not surprisingly, De Groot's writing had an impact on later political philosophers, such as John Locke.

Mikhail Bakunin (1814–1876)

Namesake: Mikhail Bakunin, Member of the Others Stationed at the Flame

After spending most of his teen years in the Russian army, Mikhail Bakunin left the military to study philosophy. His interest in political philosophy led him to become heavily involved with revolutionary movements throughout Europe. Although he was arrested and sentenced to death for his subversive activities, his sentence was commuted and he was sent to Siberia. His ingenuity allowed him to escape and make his way through Japan and the United States back to Europe, where he continued to work for socialist revolution, coauthoring the passionate *Catechism of a Revolutionist.*

Bakunin was a member of the First International, a federation dedicated to overthrowing capitalism and replacing it with a socialist commonwealth, until he was banned for anarchism. Although he was in great agreement with Marx, he denied that state socialism should replace capitalism, thinking that the former would be as oppressive as the latter. In 1873, Bakunin published his most famous work, *Statism and Anarchy*, in which he argued for the abolition of hereditary property, the equality of women, and free education for all children.

Richard Alpert (b. 1931)

Namesake: Richard Alpert, Adviser to Jacob

Richard Alpert taught psychology at Stanford University and the University of California. In 1958, he accepted a position at Harvard University, where he worked in the department of social relations and the Graduate School of Education. There, he met Timothy Leary and helped him conduct the Harvard Psilocybin Project. Although both psilocybin and LSD (which they tested on themselves, as well as on their subjects) were legal at the time, Harvard found reasons to fire both men in 1963. The following year, Alpert and Leary, along with Ralph Metzner, published *The Psychedelic Experience: A Manual Based on the Tibetan Book of the Dead.*

Alpert's interest in altered consciousness led him from drugs to spiritual practice. Later in the sixties, he traveled to India, where he met his guru, Neem Karoli Baba, or Maharajji. Maharajji gave Alpert his new name, Ram Dass, which means "servant of God." Although Ram Dass's spiritual teachings are mostly Hindu-based, he also practices Buddhist meditation and has studied Judaism (his family religion).

After returning to the United States from India, Ram Dass wrote his best-known book, *Remember, Be Here Now*, which was required reading for the counterculture of the seventies and in which he presented a vision of how to expand consciousness by using history's various spiritual traditions instead of drugs. The book emphasizes the importance of remaining in the present moment. Past and future exist only in our minds, and by focusing on them, we cause ourselves to suffer more than we do when our attention is in the present moment.

During the seventies, the eighties, and the nineties, Ram Dass continued to offer his spiritual teachings in lectures, books, and audio recordings. In 1997, while working on a book about aging, Ram Dass suffered a serious stroke. He survived, but the stroke made him reconsider his relationship with his body and the book he was writing. For most of his life, he realized, he'd used his mental and spiritual life as a way of ignoring the body. But now, being in a wheelchair and needing help with daily activities made him aware of the tension between spirituality and embodiment. This new condition did not make him a materialist, however. He still believes in a soul that is permanent and does not change, even as the body and the mind do. "It really helps to understand that we have something—that we *are* something—which is unchangeable, beautiful, completely aware, and continues no matter what."[9] The soul, then, is ageless. It's the same in childhood, adulthood, old age, and even after death.

Edmund Burke (1729–1797)

Namesake: Edmund Burke, Husband of Juliet Burke

Edmund Burke was born in Dublin and served close to thirty years in the British Parliament. Philosophically, he's best known today as a key figure in the foundation of modern conservatism. He wrote a series of pamphlets that articulated skepticism concerning political abstractions and ideologies. No good government, no matter how well intended, Burke thought, ever came from a political theory, because human theories are always flawed.

Revolution and radicalism fail to take into account the limits of human knowledge. The best government is one that draws from history and tradition. For these reasons, Burke was strongly opposed to the French Revolution, which, reflecting the philosophy of Jean-Jacques Rousseau, relied on the abstract ideas of rights and freedom. About Rousseau, Burke once said, "He entertained no principle, either to influence his heart, or guide his understanding, but vanity."[10]

Stephen Hawking (b. 1942)

Namesake: Eloise Hawking, Former Leader of the Others

Stephen Hawking is a theoretical physicist working in the fields of cosmology and quantum gravity. His work with Roger Penrose showed that time and space began with the Big Bang and end in black holes. He also discovered that black holes emit radiation and eventually disappear—this radiation is now known as Hawking radiation.

Because Hawking is a scientist who deals with big pictures and laws of the universe, he's done a fair amount of thinking about philosophical topics such as free will. Hawking has written that if—and this is a big *if*—a theory could perfectly predict behavior, it would disprove free will. Such a theory is virtually impossible, however, because there are too many details for it to account for. Moreover, even if we knew it was true, we could not live by it. Hawking wrote:

> One cannot base one's conduct on the idea that everything is determined, because one does not know what has been determined. Instead, one has to adopt the effective theory that one has free will and that one is responsible for one's actions. This theory is not very good at predicting human behavior, but we adopt it because there is no chance of solving the equations arising from the fundamental laws. There is also a Darwinian reason that we believe in free will: A society in which the individual feels responsible

for his or her actions is more likely to work together and survive to spread its values.[11]

So, according to Stephen Hawking, we make decisions based not on what the universe wants us to do but based on what we think we should do. If the universe course corrects, such course correcting would always be beyond our ken.

Jeremy Bentham (1748–1832)

Namesake: Alias Given to John Locke

Jeremy Bentham was an English philosopher well known for his utilitarian ethics. In Bentham's view, pleasure, or happiness, is the only good and pain the only evil. Living ethically consists, then, in maximizing the total pleasure and minimizing the total pain for all parties who stand to be affected by an action. Although earlier philosophers—most notably, John Locke—had similar ideas about pleasure and pain, Bentham rejected their notion of natural rights, which he called "nonsense upon stilts." Rights, Bentham argued, are created by laws, which are dependent on a state. When the Jacobins—a group strongly influenced by Rousseau's views on the social contract and rights—took power in France in 1792, Bentham was a vocal critic.

The idea that an ethical action is the one that maximizes total pleasure follows, for Bentham, from the premise that we base our actions on what makes us happy. The important step, ethically, is taking into account the happiness of all. Yet when we think about total happiness, we can see an interesting challenge. Suppose an act that greatly increases net pleasure causes the actor great pain. Can someone be morally required to harm or even kill himself for the sake of others?

After Bentham's death, his body was dissected for science. His bones and head were saved, dressed in Bentham's clothes, and put in a box. This auto-icon is now on display, in accordance with Bentham's instructions, at University College London, where at College Council meetings Bentham is listed as "present but not voting."

Hermann Minkowski (1864–1909)

Namesake: George Minkowski, Freighter Communications Officer

Hermann Minkowski was a German mathematician. He discovered that the special theory of relativity—as described by Albert Einstein, who had once been a student of his—works better using four dimensions, rather than three. This four-dimensional space-time is now known as "Minkowski space-time." The space-time continuum was instrumental in Einstein's later theory of general relativity.

One interesting implication of space-time relativity is *time dilation*, in which the passing of time varies inversely with speed. The faster something moves, the slower time moves for it. This phenomenon is illustrated by the twin paradox, which says that if one twin travels the universe in a superfast spaceship, when he returns to Earth, he'll find that he's younger than his twin.

Michael Faraday (1791–1867)

Namesake: Daniel Faraday, Physicist, Son of Eloise Hawking and Charles Widmore

Michael Faraday was an English scientist who made important discoveries about electricity and magnetism. Because he was self-taught and never learned higher math or even basic calculus, his science was largely experimental. He invented the first motor when he discovered that electricity could be created by moving a magnet through a wire coil; an electromagnetic constant is thus named in his honor. The Faraday constant represents the magnitude of electric charge per mole of electrons.

Clive Staples Lewis (1898–1963)

Namesake: Charlotte Staples Lewis, Archeologist/Anthropologist, Born into the Dharma Initiative

C. S. Lewis was born in Belfast, Ireland. His mother died when he was nine, and his father sent him to boarding school. Lewis matriculated at University College, Oxford, and later, after serving in the British army during World War I, he was hired to teach English literature at Oxford. Lewis rejected the Christianity of his youth and was an atheist from his teenage years until 1931, when he converted back to Christianity and became one of the most outspoken Christian apologists of the century.

One of the arguments he implemented in defense of Christianity has come to be called the "Lewis Trilemma." It says that Jesus was not only a moral teacher; he had to be a lunatic, the devil, or the son of God. The argument depends on a literal reading of the four gospels. Although scholars deem the Trilemma a false trichotomy, it remains popular among the devout.

Lewis wrote with a contagious passion and sincerity: "Christianity, if false, is of no importance, and, if true, of infinite importance. The one thing it cannot be is moderately important."[12] Christianity for him was a miracle—the impossible happened. And after years of doubting the miracle, he was able to return to it and, in it, do the work that most mattered to him.

Dogen (1200–1253)

Namesake: Dogen, Leader of the Others Stationed at the Temple

Dogen was born to a wealthy family in Kyoto, Japan, but both of his parents died when he was young. When he was a teenager, he became a Buddhist monk in the Tendai tradition. Yet in Tendai, Dogen found a troublesome contradiction: if everyone is already enlightened, why is it necessary to practice meditation to reach enlightenment? He traveled around Japan visiting monks and asking them this question. Unsatisfied with their responses, Dogen went to China, where after a series of similar disappointments he met Rújìng, a Japanese monk living at Mount Tiāntóng in northeast China. Rújìng's style of Chan (the Chinese and original version of Zen) was different from that of other monks of the time, and Dogen found in him the teacher who would solve his problem.

Dogen returned to Kyoto and the Tendai school and began to teach that zazen (seated meditation) could dissolve the distinction between being enlightened and seeking enlightenment because zazen is itself the very realization of Buddha-nature. Sensing a threat in Dogen, the Tendai school asked him to leave, so he went north and started the Eihei-ji Temple and the Soto sect.

For a monk who put primary emphasis on silent meditation, Dogen was a voluminous writer. His masterpiece, *Kana Shobogenzo*, commonly referred to simply as *Shobogenzo* (*The Eye and Treasury of the True Law*), comprises a mass of challenging essays and commentary, along with the advice not to get attached to thoughts: "To study the Way is to study the self. To study the self is to forget the self. To forget the self is to be enlightened by all things of the universe. To be enlightened by all things of the universe is to cast off the body and mind of the self as well as those of others. Even the traces of enlightenment are wiped out, and life with traceless enlightenment goes on forever and ever."[13]

John Lennon (1940–1980)

Namesake: Lennon, Translator for Dogen

Best known as the leader of the Beatles, John Lennon was instrumental in creating the look and the spirit of the sixties. His shaggy brown hair and circular wire-rimmed glasses are so iconic that the Lennon on *Lost* effectively evokes his namesake before we ever learn his name.

Yet Lennon's interests and creativity went far beyond music and fashion. After smoking marijuana with Bob Dylan in 1964, Lennon continued to use marijuana and LSD to alter his consciousness. He studied *The Psychedelic Experience* by Leary, Alpert, and Metzner and became interested in spiritual practice. In 1967, along with the other Beatles, Lennon went to India, where he stayed at the Maharishi Mahesh Yogi's ashram. Although he later broke off with the Maharishi, he continued to value meditation. Lennon used his rock star status to bring Eastern wisdom to the West.

Besides his interest in consciousness, Lennon was also a committed pacifist, calling for the United States' immediate withdrawal from Vietnam and penning such antiwar anthems as "Give Peace a Chance" and "Imagine." The motivation for his pacifism was his driving love of humanity. After Lennon's murder, Yoko Ono— Lennon's longtime lover, wife, and creative partner—summed up much of his work, saying, "John loved and prayed for the human race."

Søren Kierkegaard (1813–1855)

Author of *Fear* and *Trembling*, Possessed by Rousseau's Team Member, Montand

Søren Kierkegaard was born in Copenhagen and attended prestigious schools as a boy. He later studied philosophy and theology at Copenhagen University, where he was something of an ambivalent student. He finished his dissertation, *The Concept of Irony with Constant Reference to Socrates*, for the sake of his father, a man who valued education, and from whom Kierkegaard inherited his superior intelligence and creativity, as well as his melancholic and guilt-ridden disposition—all of which traits are hallmarks of his writing.

Kierkegaard is considered one of the forerunners of twentieth-century existentialism, because he thought it was an individual's responsibility to determine how he or she should live, based on self-examination. "The thing is to find a truth which is true for me, to find the idea for which I can live and die."[14]

In *Fear and Trembling*, published under the pseudonym Johannes de Silentio (John the Silent), Kierkegaard analyzed the story of Abraham and Isaac. He argued (ironically?) that Abraham's absolute faith in the absurd idea that he should sacrifice his son was somehow justified by a "teleological suspension of the ethical." That is, Abraham put his duty to God in front of his ethical obligations to his son, as Kierkegaard seemed to think he should. Yet knowing whether an ethical suspension is condoned by God (and is therefore virtuous) or not (and is then abhorrent) depends wholly on faith. For Kierkegaard, a man who believes that God wants him to kill his son or that an island has a purpose for him must take a leap of faith and act accordingly.

The End

Of course, there are many other pieces to the puzzle that is *Lost*. An appendix, however, just like a television series, has to end somewhere. Whether these philosophers are red herrings or crucial pieces in the puzzle, knowing a little about them makes for a richer reading of the show.[15]

NOTES

1. Plus, it has to be said, Boone and Shannon are insufferable.

2. "The Men Who Made ABC's 'Lost' Last," *New York Times*, www.nytimes.com/2010/05/16/arts/television/16weblost.html?pagewanted=2.

3. Recall from "Deus Ex Machina" that Locke's con-artist father's real name is Anthony Cooper.

4. Kate Austin, "Woman," http://en.wikisource.org/wiki/Woman_(Kate_Austin).

5. Howard S. Miller, "Kate Austin: A Feminist-Anarchist on the Farmer's Last Frontier," *Nature, Society and Thought* vol. 9, no. 2 (1986): 189–209.

6. Jean-Jacques Rousseau, *A Discourse upon the Origin and the Foundation of the Inequality among Mankind* (Teddington, UK: Echo Library, 2007), p. 38.

7. David Hume, "David Hume: My Own Life," McMaster University Web site, http://socserv.mcmaster.ca/econ/ugcm/3113/hume/humelife.

8. David Hume, *A Treatise of Human Nature* (Mineola, NY: Dover, 2003), p. 180.

9. Ram Dass, *Still Here: Embracing Aging, Changing, and Dying* (New York: Riverhead Books, 2000), p. 6.

10. Bertrand Russell, *A History of Western Philosophy* (London: Routledge, 2004), p. 628.

11. Stephen Hawking, *Black Holes and Baby Universes and Other Essays* (New York: Bantam Books, 1994), p. 134.

12. Clive Staples Lewis and Walter Hooper, *The Collected Letters of C. S. Lewis: Books, Broadcasts, and the War, 1931–1949* (New York: HarperCollins, 2004), p. xi.

13. Hee-Jin Kim, *Dogen Kigen: Mystical Realist* (Tucson: University of Arizona Press, 1987), p. 100.

14. Søren Kierkegaard, *The Soul of Kierkegaard: Selections from His Journal* (Mineola, NY: Dover, 2003), p. 44.

15. For their feedback during the development of this appendix, big thanks to Richard Davis, Shawn Doyle, Bill Irwin, Sharon Kaye, Sandy Newton, and Coach Katie.

CONTRIBUTORS

Jacob's Candidates

Briony Addey is a graduate student in the philosophy department at the University of Bristol. Her research interests are freedom, philosophy of biology and neuroscience, ethics, moral psychology, and philosophy of action. She thinks Vincent is the key to understanding *Lost*, because he had regular, secret animal-cabal meetings with the polar bear, the black horse, and miscellaneous boar, where they plotted to overthrow Jacob and the Man in Black.

Rob Arp is now a working ontologist but still has a hand in the philosophical life. He's looking forward to the series sequel to *Lost . . . Found.*

Michael W. Austin is an associate professor of philosophy at Eastern Kentucky University, where he works in ethics, philosophy of religion, and philosophy of sport. His books include *Running and Philosophy* (Wiley-Blackwell, 2007), *Football and Philosophy* (University Press of Kentucky, 2008), *Wise Stewards* (Kregel, 2009), and *Cycling Philosophy for Everyone* (Wiley-Blackwell, 2010). He loved Hugo before everyone loved Hugo.

Deborah R. Barnbaum is a professor of philosophy at Kent State University. She has published extensively on research ethics and serves on several medical ethics committees. Her most recent book is *The Ethics of Autism: Among Them but Not of Them* (Indiana University Press, 2008). If she weren't a *Lost* fan, she would have had a lot more free time on Tuesday nights.

Jeremy Barris is a professor of philosophy at Marshall University, in Huntington, West Virginia. As a philosopher, he is mainly interested in the relations between reality, thinking, style of expression, humor, and justice. His publications include *Paradox and the Possibility of Knowledge: The Example of Psychoanalysis* (Susquehanna University Press, 2003) and *The Crane's Walk: Plato, Pluralism, and the Inconstancy of Truth* (Fordham University Press, 2009). He lost his bearings years ago and has been wondering ever since.

Shai Biderman is a doctoral candidate in philosophy at Boston University and an instructor in the Bet-Berl College, the Open University, and the College of Management, Israel. His research interests include philosophy of film and literature, philosophy of culture, aesthetics, ethics, existentialism, and Nietzsche. His publications include articles on personal identity, language, determinism, and aesthetics. His most recent publications include articles on the philosophy of Westerns, the philosophy of the Coen brothers, and the philosophy of Steven Soderbergh, all for the University Press of Kentucky. He refrains from boarding airplanes in the Pacific for obvious reasons.

Patricia Brace is a professor of art history at Southwest Minnesota State University, in Marshall, Minnesota. With cowriter Robert Arp, she contributed chapters to the Wiley-Blackwell pop culture and philosophy series books *Lost and Philosophy: The Island Has Its Reasons* (Blackwell, 2007) and *True Blood and Philosophy* (Wiley, 2010). She awaits the *Lost* sequel wherein Hugo and Ben run the island their way, titled *Jacob Who?*

Richard Davies was born in London and read philosophy at Trinity College, Cambridge (PhD, 1992). He now lives in Italy, where he teaches theoretical philosophy and history of philosophy at the University of Bergamo. In terror at finding himself pigeon-holed as some sort of "expert," he has published books and articles on a wide range of philosophical topics. In 2009, he published *Gli oggetti della logica*, a survey of the argumentative tools that philosophers have been developing ever since Aristotle. He thinks that whatever happened, happened.

William J. Devlin is a professor at Bridgewater State College and visiting lecturer at the University of Wyoming. He is interested in Eastern philosophy, philosophy of science, and existentialism and has written articles on Nietzsche, time travel, personal identity, and art. He currently walks through his hometown of Boston waiting for a sign from the city to tell him what to do.

Peter S. Fosl is a professor of philosophy at Transylvania University and a Kentucky colonel (yes, really). Specializing in skepticism, the thought of David Hume, and early modern philosophy, Fosl is coauthor with Julian Baggini of *The Philosopher's Toolkit* (Wiley-Blackwell, 2010) and *The Ethics Toolkit* (Wiley-Blackwell, 2007). He is coeditor with David E. Cooper of *Philosophy: The Classic Readings* (Wiley-Blackwell, 2009). In his spare time, Fosl serves as executive director of the Dharma Project of Kentucky. He is anything but a constant.

Karen Gaffney is an associate professor of English at Raritan Valley Community College in central New Jersey. She teaches classes on composition, gender, race, and popular culture. She is currently working on a book project about the "divide-and-conquer" mentality that tends to pit racial minorities against one another. In her spare time, she wonders whether she is a candidate.

Daniel B. Gallagher has taught philosophy and theology and is the author of numerous articles in metaphysics, aesthetics, and Thomistic philosophy. He has previously contributed to *Basketball and Philosophy: Thinking Outside the Paint* (University Press of Kentucky, 2007) and *Football and Philosophy: Going Deep* (University Press of Kentucky, 2009). A Catholic priest stationed at the Vatican, Father Gallagher can be seen in a rare outtake from the final scene of *Lost* preaching on the importance of remembering your flash-forwards so as to avoid any unpleasant flashbacks as you enjoy the eternal "now."

Dan Kastrul is the founder and executive director of Chez Nous, Inc., a company that has provided residential and training services since 1983 to people considered developmentally disabled. He earned a BA in psychology from the University of Wisconsin, Milwaukee, and an MPH in health education from the University of Minnesota. Dan has been a virtual castaway on *Survivor* MySpace in the Maldive Islands, as well as in the Maruba Jungle of Belize. He also cohosted a *Survivor* MySpace game that was virtually played in the Galapagos Islands. He discovered through past life regression that in a previous incarnation, he was a noted but Oscarless Hollywood movie director. Having found his way through a long hatch into his current lifetime, Dan aspires to bring home that Academy Award. Meanwhile, he can be found on YouTube, playing the piano.

Sharon M. Kaye is a professor of philosophy at John Carroll University in Cleveland. Her most recent books include *Black Market Truth: Volume One of a Dana McCarter Trilogy* (Parmenides, 2008), *Critical Thinking: A Beginner's Guide* (OneWorld, 2009), and *The Onion and Philosophy* (Open Court, 2010). She coulda been a candidate.

Sander Lee is a professor of philosophy at Keene State College in Keene, New Hampshire. He is the author of *Eighteen Woody Allen Films Analyzed: Anguish, God, and Existentialism* (McFarland, 2002), as well as other books and scholarly essays on issues in aesthetics, ethics, social philosophy, and metaphysics. His mom was kind of crazy, too, but she didn't speak Latin (or kill people).

Donavan S. Muir is an MPhil student in Buddhist studies and is working toward a PhD in philosophy at the University of Sydney, where he will study Indian, Chinese, and Japanese Buddhist philosophy, along with contemporary continental philosophy. He is the author of "The Empty Metanarrative: Mādhyamaka Buddhism and Postmodern Science" in *Comparative Philosophy Today and Tomorrow* (Cambridge Scholars Press, 2009). He often daydreams about a life on the lush and mysterious tropical island of *Lost*, where he can enjoy all of the pristine surf spots by himself, never minding the Smoke Monster, Dharma sharks, and Ben Linus.

Scott F. Parker was born and raised in close proximity to Mittelos Bioscience HQ in Portland, Oregon. "Not in Portland" anymore, Parker has published widely on pop culture and philosophy, including essays on golf, football, *Alice in Wonderland*, and the iPod. He is editing of the forthcoming *Coffee and Philosophy* with Mike W. Austin.

Brett Chandler Patterson has long been interested in the intersection of narrative theory and theological reflection. He has studied with religion-and-literature scholars at Furman University, Duke University, and the University of Virginia. He has taught theology and ethics at Meredith College and Anderson University and is currently serving as senior pastor to a rural congregation in South Carolina. He has focused his recent research on the mythopoeic works of MacDonald, Lewis, Tolkien, Card, and Wolfe. He has delighted in "infecting" others with the *Lost* mythology, including his mother (although his father remains a skeptic), his brother and sister, his wife (much to her chagrin), and his children (who seem to know all about John Locke).

Jeremy Pierce is a PhD student at Syracuse University and an instructor at LeMoyne College. His primary philosophical interests are in metaphysics, philosophy of race, and philosophy of religion. He has written chapters on the X-Men and Harry Potter for this series. Jeremy has been pressing a button every 108 minutes ever since meeting a time-traveling John Locke in 1996, convinced that it does matter what he does, even if whatever happens has already happened.

Charles Taliaferro, a professor of Philosophy at St. Olaf College, is the author or editor of twelve books. He thinks he has a special angle on *Lost*, as his father was an airline pilot who survived a plane crash and who moved his family to a mysterious tropical island. The island residents included people named Jack, Kate, and so on. Coincidence? Charles doesn't think so.

Becky Vartabedian is a doctoral student in philosophy at Duquesne University in Pittsburgh, Pennsylvania. Her primary areas of interest include phenomenology (especially Maurice Merleau-Ponty) and the recent work of the French philosopher Alain Badiou. She also serves as affiliate faculty in the philosophy department at the Metropolitan State College of Denver. Becky has spent a good deal of time wandering around Pittsburgh and has come to rely on a knowledgeable group of Others to help her get around the city.

George Wrisley is a visiting professor of philosophy in the history and philosophy department at North Georgia College and State University. His research interests include metaphysics, the philosophy of language, Wittgenstein, and, most recently, the relationship between happiness and a life worth living. After many years of toil sailing on Neurath's ship, he has finally made it back to the island.

INDEX

Oceanic Flight 815 Manifest